CATASTROPHIC MISSIONS

CATASTROPHIC MISSIONS

Christian Evangelization from Alaska to Tierra del Fuego

LEIF G. TERDAL

Order this book online at www.trafford.com
or email orders@trafford.com

Most Trafford titles are also available at major online book retailers.

Printed in the United States of America.

ISBN: 978-1-4669-7470-8 (sc)

Trafford rev. 03/06/2013

 www.trafford.com

North America & international
toll-free: 1 888 232 4444 (USA & Canada)
phone: 250 383 6864 ♦ fax: 812 355 4082

PREFACE

Paul Cartledge in describing how he wrote his book, ***ALEXANDER THE GREAT,*** introduced a caveat. He reminded his readers that Polybius, a major Greek historian of the second century BCE, wrote that a proper history of Alexander the Great couldn't be written except by someone who'd inspected all the scenes of historical action in person. Cartledge stated that if he had tried to visit all the scenes of his battles that he would have had to travel over 20,000 miles. For him those travels were not essential.

For this book my wife and I have travelled extensively in an effort to learn about how Christianity was introduced to the indigenous peoples of the New World from Alaska to Tierra del Fuego. For that purpose we have travelled more than 12,000 nautical miles in British Columbia and Alaska alone. Furthermore, while traveling in Alaska, I was able to repeat the actual journey of John Muir and the missionary S Hall Young who travelled from Wrangell to Glacier Bay (now, the Glacier Bay National Park). Our journey was in essence a retrace of the missionary trail.

Protestant Christianity was introduced to the indigenous peoples of Alaska in 1877, through the efforts of the Presbyterian missionary Sheldon Jackson. The First Nations peoples of Canada were introduced to Christianity in the year 1850, when enrollment of indigenous children in Christian residential schools was mandated by the Canadian government.

We could have travelled to Alaska via a cruise ship. Why did we choose to travel, with less comfort and more expense, in a private boat? The main reason to cruise by private boat was the opportunity to visit the First Nation villages in British Columbia along the way to Alaska, such as Alert Bay, New Bella Bella, Klemtu, the indigenous sites in Prince Rupert, and the historic and now abandoned salmon canneries at Namu and Butedale. As we consider the beautiful waters of British Columbia, keep in mind that the cruise ships don't stop in B.C. at all. They go right past it as most cruise ships make their first stop in Alaskan waters in major ports such as Ketchikan, Juneau or Sitka. (Some cruise ships stop in Victoria, B.C., but all bypass the smaller indigenous villages.)

By traveling independently I could talk one on one with First Nation peoples in British Columbia and members of the Tlingit tribe in Southeast Alaska. I learned that in both Alaska and Canada there were extensive government efforts, supported by mainline Protestant Churches, to suppress indigenous language, culture and religious beliefs and practices. Children were required to speak English (or French in parts of Canada). The use of Native language was suppressed, even outside the classroom. Native religious beliefs and practices were forbidden, and the Christian faith was to be practiced exclusively. Traditional Native hunter-gathering skills were rejected even in areas with abundant fish and game, while poor soil and climate conditions negated the option for agriculture.

Following our study of how Christianity was introduced to natives of Alaska and British Columbia we travelled south to New Mexico and learned about the introduction of Christianity to the Hopi Indians by Spanish missionaries who had accompanied Cortez after he conquered the Aztec Indians of Mexico. We then travelled on to Guatemala, Cuba, Brazil, Peru and Argentina where we completed our journey in Tierra del Fuego.

We learned that Spanish missionaries who accompanied the conquistadors brought with them the zeitgeist of religious intolerance that was the norm in Europe at the time. Jews, who refused to convert to Christianity, were expelled from Spain in 1492. The Moors, who had enriched Spain with their contributions in architecture, literature, medicine and in engineering, had until 1499 to convert to Christianity or face expulsion. The majority chose not to convert and they were expelled.

My focus was on the Introduction of Christianity to Native Americans from Alaska to Tierra del Fuego. I could not possibly investigate how missionaries introduced Christianity in each of the lower 48 States. I chose the first introduction, and that was my focus throughout the book. Whether in Cuba, or Brazil, or New Mexico or Tierra del Fuego of Argentina, what was the story behind the first introduction of Christianity to the indigenous peoples—and how did it go?

CHAPTER 1

Alaska

I have travelled to SE Alaska by private boat each summer for ten-years. My trips have started in Port Townsend, Washington, and followed the Inside Passage through British Columbia to SE Alaska. The Inside Passage is remarkable in terms of outstanding beauty, its history and its suitability for passage by serious boaters. My focus in this chapter is how Christianity was introduced to Natives of Alaska. However, that was not my initial purpose.

In 1994 I planed to retire from the Oregon Health Sciences University. I had worked there for 30 years on the faculty as a Clinical Psychologist. At the Child Development and Rehabilitation Center my responsibilities included evaluating children with a range of developmental disabilities, designing treatment programs, supervising interns and residents and publishing articles and books on behavioral assessment and treatment strategies.

Thinking ahead about my retirement goals, I contacted a company in Portland, named Clipper Craft and signed a contract for them to build by hand a 26 foot wooden boat. The boat was designed and built for cruising to Alaska. It served as a live-aboard for up to two people for cruising in B.C. and Southeast Alaska for up to two months each year. The boat was powered by a four cylinder Volvo Diesel engine with duo-prop. The engine produced 120 HP and burned about 4 gallons of diesel fuel per hour at 16 knots. At seven knots the engine burned a little less than one gallon per hour.

The accommodations included an enclosed stand up head, a large comfortable V-berth (sleeps 2), a dinette table and seating for four. The dinette table and bench seats could fold down and sleep one. Cabin heat was provided by a Dickensen diesel heating stove. As a live-aboard for a two-month period it was equal in comfort to traveling and camping in a 1970 Volkswagen camper. The boat was completed and delivered to me the second week of January 1995. That May my son Paul and I left Port Townsend, Washington and travelled through the Inside Passage to Alaska. I repeated my cruising trips in B.C. and Southeast Alaska for an additional eight years. Before cruising to Alaska in my boat, I had joined Paul in 1993 on his trip to Glacier Bay, Alaska in his 35' Ericksen sail boat.

Purpose of my trips to Southeast Alaska

If I would have said to my wife, Marge, in 1994 that I wanted to buy a boat and take it to Alaska to find out how Christianity was introduced to the Native Peoples of Alaska and British Columbia, there would have been a problem. She would have sat me down and said," We need to talk." If I remained obdurate, the next step would be a family "intervention." My sons would be asked to come over, our minister and perhaps my physician. I would either see the foolishness of my thoughts and be led to at least an elementary level of sanity, or . . .

However, the purpose of my adventure to Alaska was quite sane. I wanted to fish for salmon and halibut. I wanted to experience the wonders of the Alaskan wilderness including the snow capped mountains, the vast Tongass National Forest, the fjords, and the glaciers and icebergs. I wanted to see the abundant wildlife including whales, bears, moose, bald eagles and ravens. I wanted to visit Native villages in British Columbia and Southeast Alaska.

I did learn about how Christianity was introduced to the Native Peoples of Alaska and British Columbia. What I learned about the missionary effort surprised and frankly disturbed me. I was determined to pursue further the history of the missionary effort to indigenous peoples of the Americas. However, I will digress in this chapter to write about the beauties of Southeast Alaska, a few stories of fishing trips, and viewing wildlife. For these diversions, please forgive me.

Wrangell

Wrangell is a historic community about 90 miles north of Ketchikan, situated on the northern end of Wrangell Island. This small SE Alaskan town has the distinction of being the only community in the United States that has had three flags of nationality flown over its domain: Russian, British, and American. It is situated just south of the Stikine River, which drains a significant area of British Columbia, then passes through a mountain range and flows into tide water just north of Wrangell.[1] The Stikine is the fastest moving navigable river in North America. For thousands of years, indigenous peoples from British Columbia and interior areas of Canada travelled the Stikine River and traded with the Tlingit Indians in Wrangell. The tribal chief of the Tlingit tribe in Wrangell had an esteemed position, because he coordinated these trades and knew the tribal histories and chiefs of the Athabaskan tribes in Canada.

Wrangell is also the site of the first American protestant church in Alaska, and the place where the naturalist John Muir teamed up with Reverend S. Hall Young. The two of them travelled extensively in Southeast Alaska, mostly with Tlingit companions in Native canoes.[2] Both were deeply religious. Reverend S. Hall Young was a Presbyterian minister. In contrast, John Muir completely abandoned his father's Christian religion. He worshipped God in "God's own temples." There are vast numbers of God's temples. In the heart and soul of John Muir, Glacier Bay in Southeast Alaska was a magnificent temple of God, where he spent time in spiritual reflection and solitude.

John Muir was quite familiar with the Bible. His father had required that John memorize the New Testament from verse one in the book of Matthew to the last verse in the Book of Revelations. As an adolescent John was physically punished if he made even one mistake in reciting the Bible verbatim. He was very familiar with the Old Testament. One section of the Book of Genesis was especially a problem for him.

Genesis Chapter 1, verses 27 and 28.
God created man in his own image, in the image of God he created him; male and female he created them. God blessed them and said to them, **"Be fruitful and increase in number; fill the earth and subdue it. Rule over the fish of the sea and the birds of the air and over every living creature that moves on the ground."**

In an early journal Muir wrote, "The world we are told was made for man, a presumption that is totally unsupported by facts."[3]

Petroglyphs

The petroglyphs at Wrangell—pictorial carvings in stone—were made in ancient times, perhaps 10,000 years ago. They are open to view on the beach about a mile north of the ferry terminal in Wrangell. Since the Natives who carved the petroglyphs had no written language, assumptions about the meanings remain conjecture. I interviewed some Tlingit elders to hear what their thoughts were about the history of the petroglyphs. The answer was always the same, "no one knows the meaning of the stones."

The Tlingit people had great respect for the power of the oral tradition. A member of the tribe who aspired to be an elder was required to learn a vast amount of stories passed down from the past and be able to retell them perfectly. He, or she, could not retell these stories in ceremonies unless he passed a rigorous oral exam among elders. Much of the Bible also originated in story telling long before the scripture was put down in written form. The Tlingit tradition deserves to be treated with respect and regard. I hoped to have a chance to meet some elders in Wrangell and in other communities in SE Alaska and hear from them stories of the past. I was rewarded richly.

Wilderness trips in Southeast Alaska on the way to Glacier Bay National Park

With Wrangell as a base for travelling to other wilderness areas in Southeast Alaska, I had the opportunity to follow the routes taken by the famous naturalist John Muir and his companion Reverend S. Hall Young. I followed trips they took in 1879 and later years. We start with the Anan Creek area about thirty miles south of what was Fort Wrangell, now Wrangell.

The Anan Creek Bear Observatory

Anan Creek flows into Anan Bay. The area is south of Wrangell Island and on the mainland. The area is noted for absolute abundance of pink salmon. The spawning runs start in mid July and last through much of September. The run historically and to the present day is prolific and serves as a huge magnet for diverse wildlife. The area draws large numbers of bears, both black bears and grisly bears (called brown bears in Alaska). It also draws large numbers of bald eagles and ravens, as well as wolves. It is now designated as the Anan Creek Bear Observatory. The best part of this area is that it is not much different from how it was before white man ever came to Alaska. There are no docks, no restaurants and no roads. There is one observatory (an unprotected wooden deck) where one can stand and view wildlife. There is also one small cabin without running water that can be rented from the US Forest Service.[4] I have travelled the 30 miles from Wrangell on four occasions to visit this area to observe and to photograph the wildlife. I normally stay three to seven days.

I dock my boat about 100 yards from shore and row to shore with a small dingy. I am careful to follow the rules that are clearly reviewed by a biologist stationed at Anan Creek. The first rule is to carry no food when on land. When hungry leave the Anan Creek area, hike back to your dingy, row to your boat, eat a meal, and only then return to hike and view some more.

One difference between coming here now and during the time that John Muir and S Hall Young travelled this area, is the presence of the trained biologist employed by the US Forest Service to instruct people in how to be safe in the wilderness while observing wild animals. In the past Native Americans knew about all this. In fact I asked a biologist of the US Forest Service the question, "How did the Forest Service come to know that it is safe for humans to be this close to wild brown and black bears?" He replied that the practice came exactly from a tradition established by Native peoples, who knew in effect that if there is no history of harm or violence between man and bears, the bears will leave humans alone. The Natives set aside certain areas of their environment to observe wildlife, and other areas to hunt. They may never have hunted the brown bears or black bears in the vicinity of Anan Creek. In fact in all of Southeast Alaska, the Tlingit Natives may never have hunted bears at all during the pre-contact time period. Think about it. If a person is hungry, he is not likely to grab a weapon and look for a bear. If solitude and interest in "where the wild things are," are important to you, Anan Creek then and now is a sacred place.

A Week at the Anan Creek Bear Observatory

Let me share with you what several days to a week is like at Anan Creek. The salmon run starts around mid July, and for the next seven or so weeks the river is literally clogged with hundreds of thousands of returning pink salmon. It is not possible to see the gravel below the clear stream because the salmon fill the river from one side to the other, from top to bottom, and from the mouth of the river where it reaches salt water to the far reaches of the upstream areas. I had with me an underwater camera and I placed it at the edge of Anan Creek and the photo showed salmon stacked one over the other from the bottom of the stream to the surface. Both black bears and brown bears come to feast on these salmon. On a day's outing a typical scene in one section of the river is watching and photographing several black bears for several hours. The black bears had a pattern of when they caught a salmon they would leave the river and climb up on the bank and eat the salmon often behind a rock or a tree. They then returned and "fished" again. Some bears caught salmon by placing their head just above the surface of the stream and ducking their head in the water, with an instant splash, and catching a fish with their jaws; others used their paws. I observed one black bear catch and eat seven salmon in one hour. The pattern changed when brown bears entered the stream. Sometimes a single brown bear would appear, but mostly the brown bears came in small groups. This may seem unusual because brown bears are usually solitary animals with "territorial" domains.

When the brown bears entered the stream the black bears quietly left the stream and disappeared behind trees, well away from the river. Brown bears are absolutely dominant, and black bears do not challenge. On the many islands within the archipelago of Southeast Alaska, no island has both resident black bears and brown bears. Admiralty Island for example has one of the largest numbers of brown bears per square mile in Alaska. It has no black bears. The smaller islands, including Wrangell Island have only black bears. The brown bears are unequivocally the dominant species. Anan Creek is on the mainland within Southeast Alaska, about 28 miles from the border with Yukon Province in Canada. The brown bears and black bears have pretty much worked out their rules of disengagement.

With the vast abundance of salmon in Anan Creek, the bears often take what they want from a salmon and discard the rest. Bald Eagles and ravens feed on the leftovers, which provide very "easy pickings." However, bald eagles are perfectly capable of catching their own salmon and I have observed that many times.

I have observed excellent parenting skills of mother bears while observing them with their cubs along Anan Creek. I have observed mature bears consistently catch a salmon within one second of a strike (usually by the snorkel effort of head down in the water and the take by the jaw), whereas a young bear still under the tutelage of a mother may dash in the river running after a pack of salmon who skirt away in all directions. With this procedure a young bear may work twenty minutes to make a catch. Cubs normally spend about two and a half years with their mother bear. It takes that long before they can be independent. By that time the adolescent bear will be able to feed effectively and learn the other hard stuff of surviving in the wilderness.

During our one week stay at Anan Creek my son Erik Terdal, who has a PhD in environmental science, and I left our boat each morning at 6:00 AM and stayed on the trail along the river until about 6:00 PM (except for a return for a lunch on the boat at about noon). In a week's time we saw about 44 individual black bears, many of them numerous times. We also saw about 20 brown bears, some of them every day. We were able to recognize individual bears by the third day. We saw as many as 40 bald eagles at a time, and numerous ravens.

One night after we settled down in our boat and reviewed our day we were treated to a chorus of wolves. We heard what sounded like a pack of 24 wolves. They howled with enormous intensity and with a range of octaves. The howling could have been heard for many miles away. We were perhaps a quarter of a mile from the wolves, but the decibel level of sound was as if we were sitting in the midst of Mack trucks all with their engines on and horns blasting. Erik told me that wolves project their voices at high intensity levels further than any other mammal with the exception of the howler monkey in Central America. Furthermore, wolves can shift their vocal chords to produce four different octaves simultaneously. Six wolves can present a chorus that sounds like that of 24 wolves. The next morning we spoke with the Biologist stationed at Anan Creek. He heard the wolves and stated that either the Alpha male was rejected as the Alpha male, or another wolf was rejected by the pack and driven off. Either way the howling signified to one wolf, "*You are permanently rejected from our pack. You will not get a second chance! Off with you!*" The biologist agreed with my son Erik that the pack was of six wolves. Wolves are social animals and live and hunt in hierarchical packs. They don't kill a fellow wolf who has failed in some way, but they banish by ostracism. For a wolf banishment from a pack is often a lethal punishment.

During our week at Anan Creek about 50 persons a day came to observe the bears, salmon, eagles and other wildlife. Our boat was the only private boat the whole week. The others came for day trips via charter boats from Wrangell or by float planes from Ketchikan.

Anan Creek has another special meaning to our family. Our son Paul and his wife Tatiana spent their honeymoon in 1999 at Anan Creek.

I have often pondered about how this sacred place would change if the heavily timbered area of Anan Creek was open to road building and logging. I hope that never happens.

Chief Shakes Community House:
An unexpected visit with a granddaughter of Chief Shakes

Shakes Island is a park on a small island within the Wrangell boat harbor. The park has several totem poles as well as the Chief Shakes Community House. That house is a replica of ones that existed throughout SE Alaska before Protestant missionaries exerted their influence. The long houses, as they were called, accommodated many families including the chief and his family. In the past Tlingit Indians did not live in individual houses that only contained a nuclear family i.e., a married couple and their children. Instead, the long houses may have accommodated 100 people. On my fourth year of traveling by boat to Alaska from the Pacific Northwest, I had an opportunity to speak with Nellie Torgemson, who is the granddaughter of the last chief of the Tlingit Indians in Wrangell. With her was Nora Rhinehart, a member of an Athabaskin tribe in the interior of Northern Canada. Ms. Rhinehart is employed by cruise ship companies to give talks on Native Alaskan history and to comment on pre-historic customs, art work, food gathering and to answer questions. Her ancestors may well have travelled the Stikine River to trade with the Tlingit Indians at Wrangell. Both Ms Torgemson and Ms. Rhinehart agreed that I could interview them (and tape record) about their understanding of the history of Wrangell before the Russian period and before the sale of Alaska to the US in 1867.

I asked Ms. Torgemson, "I am honored to have a chance to talk with you. Please tell me about your grandfather and his role as chief of the Tlingit Indians in Wrangell." She answered, "I know very little about him, and I have almost no personal recollection of him." I replied, "How could that be?" She told me she was taken from Wrangell as a young child in 1937 and sent to a residential school in Haines for Alaskan Natives.

Without interruption from me, she spoke in a quiet and measured voice:

"We learned nothing about Indians at the school."

She re-asserted the word, *"Nothing!"*

She paused to reflect, and then she continued:

The Presbyterians made it a rule that Tlingit elders couldn't teach Native language, culture or the old ways. Up the road from our boarding house in Haines there was an Indian village, and once they invited us to a potlatch. But we could not go, because a potlatch ceremony was thought to be pagan. There were about 50 Native children at the Haines House when I lived there. Native children were not used to experiencing physical punishment, because it is not how Natives discipline their children. But at the Haines house, we were physically punished, and I remember being beaten with a stick. Speaking our Native language was one of the things that would bring on punishment. Once and then again, a child would run away. But there were people who earned money—so much a head—to recapture a runaway child and return the child to the boarding school."

She continued: *"I believe they* (the staff at the boarding school) *figured it was best for us to forget about our culture and become like white people. That is why they did not teach us any history of our own people. The world would be a better place if the civilized world would have learned from Natives. Indians knew which roots and herbs had medicinal value, and they knew how to survive. But the attitude was that if the Indians knew something it wasn't any good."*

She paused in her story and I was without words to ask her another question. I pondered during a break in our conversation to reflect on the meaning of what she had already said.

It was clear to me that this Native Alaskan, born to a family of elders including chiefs of the Tlingit tribe in the Wrangell area, had lost her first language by the time she became a teenager. Her grandfather died shortly after she returned to Wrangell from the boarding school in Haines, which explained her lack of personal memories of him.

I had intended to ask her about the petroglyphs on the north edge of Wrangell, but it slipped my mind as I focused on her story, one of personal tragedy. I considered what her removal from her community and her placement in an English language only boarding school in SE Alaska cost her.

Aside from her loss, she knew that her people were losing their language.

Let us put the loss of language in perspective. John O'Donohue writing about ancient Irish Celtic Wisdom states,

The Attempt to destroy Gaelic was one of the most destructive acts of violence of the colonization of Ireland by England. Gaelic is such a poetic and powerful language, it carries the Irish memory. When you steal a people's language, you leave their soul bewildered.[5]

She lost the opportunity as a young child to learn about her family, the larger Tlingit culture and its practices and beliefs.

She lost the opportunity in her youth to acquire a sense of spirituality that had been developed by her people over countless centuries.

In her adult years she recognized that aside from her personal loss, Native cultures throughout Alaska suffered irretrievable brokenness that cannot be put back together again in a sense of wholeness. I was determined to find out more about the Christian missionary effort in Alaska.

I then asked her how I could learn more about the early missionary effort in Alaska and how it was practiced. She told me that much of the practices of Protestant missionaries from the United States had been established by a very powerful man, the Rev. Sheldon Jackson. He established an Institute in Sitka and personally selected large numbers of Missionaries and positioned them in Alaska. He was dictatorial and had no personal interest in Native Alaskan culture, their beliefs or ways of living. He wanted Native Alaskans to be like white folks. In Wrangell two significant missionaries who had great impact were S. Hall Young and a woman Mrs. McFarland. She added that prior to the coming to Alaska of Protestant missionaries from America, there had been a large number of Russian Orthodox missionaries who came during the long period when Russians hunted for sea otters and had established a major port in Sitka and also one in Wrangell as well as a number of settlements along the Aleutian Islands. The Russian Orthodox Church, she stated, was lenient in its approach to conversion of Alaskan Natives.

I pondered her comments about her experience with missionaries and the Christian residential school as I continued my travels in Alaska.

Small Boat Cruising to Glacier Bay

Visiting Glacier Bay National Park was one of my reasons for taking my own boat to Alaska. I did not want to limit my stay in this Park for just the brief hours that occur on cruise ship travels, because Glacier Bay National Park is the world's largest wilderness preserve. The first Euro-Americans to visit the area during the glacial retreat were John Muir and Reverend S. Hall Young. They travelled from Wrangell to Glacier Bay with many stops. Their guides were Tlingit companions who paddled a 35 foot hand carved Tlingit canoe. One of the Tlingit men was fluent in English. Muir was interested in everything about Alaska. Certainly the glaciers were a strong interest, but he was also enthralled by the forests, the wildlife, the storms and the Alaskan Natives. In contrast S. Hall Young was focused on spreading the Christian message to Alaskan Natives. His strategy was to meet first with Indian chiefs in the different villages to explain the Christian message. If the chief could be "converted" the task of converting the rest of the clan was facilitated.[6] I happened to have on my boat many books including the works of John Muir as well as the booklet, *Alaska Days with John Muir*, by Samuel Hall Young. It was very interesting for me to read their accounts of their voyages in Alaska, particularly after talking with the granddaughter of Chief Shakes.

S. Hall Young specifically states that Chief Shakes had been converted and was a member of the Presbyterian Church in Wrangell. On January 7, 1909 the *Wrangell Sentinel* included a news account of Chief Shakes which supports the comment by Rev. Young about the missionary strategy of first converting Chiefs and other native leaders:

Jan. 7. 1909: *Chief George Shakes of the Tlingit tribe of Indians last week came to the conclusion that the town was becoming too dull and in order to enliven things a little he organized a company of about thirty of his braves and proceeded to give an old fashioned native dance for the entertainment of the "Boston men" and women of Wrangell. The dance was given at Red Men's Hall Saturday evening. A spectacular street parade took place before the performance. Upon returning to the hall the chief made a short speech setting forth his "tum-tum" to the white people. Chief Shakes talk at the dance was along the lines of an expression of gratitude and appreciation for the benefits derived by the natives from the white man's laws, education and religious teaching and that the Indians desired to depart from their old customs and live in a civilized manner and at peace with their white neighbors.* (January 8, 2009 **Wrangell Sentinel** "The Way We Were 100 Years Ago.)

Petersburg

Petersburg is about 40 miles from Wrangell. From Wrangell I proceeded west about 20 miles along Sumner Strait. I then entered Wrangell Narrows at Point Alexander on Mitkof Island, and proceeded up 21 miles of waterway to Petersburg. I was able to cover the first 20 miles with my diesel powered craft in about one hour and fifteen minutes. John Muir and S. Hall Young probably covered that distance by hand powered canoe in about seven hours. I covered the 21 miles up the Wrangell Narrows in about three hours, probably the same time required by the Tlingit powered canoe back in 1879. Tidal currents are strong in the narrows and traveling north one should begin passage on the last part of the flood tide. By proceeding at the last part of the flood tide, the strong tidal flow pushes you along until you reach an area called Green Point at slack high tide. Then with the ebbing tide you again have a favorable current all the way to Petersburg. There are now 66 navigational markers from Point Alexander to Petersburg. There were, of course, none for Muir and Young and their Tlingit companions. Also Petersburg did not exist as a community at the time of their travel, as the Tlingits did not establish permanent long houses in the area. Wrangell was a chosen location for Native Alaskans because of its proximity to the great Stikine River.

Petersburg was founded by Peter Buschman, who arrived in the area in 1897 from Norway and found that the location had a suitable area for a harbor and excellent fishing for halibut and salmon. What added to his interest were the large amounts of ice from the Le Conte Tidewater Glacier that flows to the area. The ice enabled him to ship large amounts of salmon and halibut to Seattle in refrigerated form rather than salted which brought a substantial increase in value and price. Petersburg remains a prosperous small town. It is the most important center for commercial fishing in Southeast Alaska. Currently the fishermen from Petersburg, many with Norwegian heritage, have modern boats and travel extensively to many areas of Alaska. During the summer months the cold storage plants work 24 hours a day unloading salmon, halibut, shrimp and crab and cleaning and packaging. The economy has been hit, however, with the increase in fuel costs and the vast quantities of pen reared salmon that now glut the world market.

Frederick Sound and Stephens Passage: Petersburg to Juneau

The distance between Petersburg and Juneau is only 108 miles; however, the scenic wonders along the way are so outstanding that rushing through them to get from one place to another is not recommended. A mountain range starting from the Stikine River (25 miles below Petersburg) continues north about 100 miles; many of its peaks range from 7200 to 10,000 feet in altitude. This range has enormous ice fields and active glaciers which come into view when one leaves Petersburg and enters Frederick Sound. The Le Conte Glacier (about 20 miles south of Petersburg) is the southernmost tidewater glacier in North America. Just north of Petersburg is Thomas Bay with Baird Glacier providing very scenic views.

About 35 miles north of Petersburg in Frederick Sound is the prominent Cape Fanshaw where one enters Stephens Passage. This whole area is a major passage way for salmon and halibut and also for humpback whales. While trolling for Chinook salmon with a friend of mine Russ Jackson, I was absorbed watching humpback whales surface; sometimes a whole pod of whales surfaced simultaneously as they were feeding on massive schools of herring. Russ then blurted out, "There is a Chinook!" I looked over the waters and said "where?" He said: "On your line!" I grabbed my rod from the pole holder and brought in a nice 18 pound Chinook. I had been so completely distracted by the wonders around me that I had forgotten that I was fishing.

About 45 miles north of Cape Fanshaw is Holkham Bay. There is safe anchorage within Holkham Bay in Williams Cove. A major attraction is *Tracy Arm*, a 22-mile-long fjord which leads to both North Sawyer Glacier and South Sawyer Glacier. These tide water glaciers are very active and lots of huge icebergs break off these glaciers daily. A boater must be careful and not get too close, because large icebergs breaking off these glaciers have sent powerful waves causing damage and injuries to boats and boaters. From a safe distance the action is beautiful. As is true in any part of Southeast Alaska, you will see bald eagles and perhaps some seals while exploring Tracy Arm. I have often spoken to boaters about Tracy Arm. A number of boaters coming from the lower 48 States have said to me, "I did not want to go in there because my sailboat only travels at the speed of five knots, and it would have taken me a whole day to go in an out." I tell them it always takes a full day to travel the 22 miles into Tracy Arm to see the glaciers and return. Furthermore, even if a boater doesn't make it to the glaciers they would experience the beauty of the steep-walled granite cliffs and remarkable waterfalls. There is so much floating ice and large icebergs that it is difficult (actually not possible) to average more than four knots. My speed on my trips through Tracy Arm was probably the same as experienced by John Muir and S. Hall Young with their Tlingit companions.

After spending a day in Tracy Arm in 1998, my wife Marge and I upon our return to Stephens Passage travelled 20 miles north to Taku Harbor. This area provides good anchorage and a state float (no charge). A couple who anchored along side us was having a major celebration. They had just returned on their 42 foot sailboat from a five year cruise around the world. They had taken a five year leave from their home in Juneau, and considered Taku Harbor as "close enough" to call home after their event-full journey.

Juneau is about 25 miles north of Taku Harbor. During our 1998 trip we left Stephens Passage by turning north at Point Arden on Admiralty Island and entered Gastineau Channel, and proceeded the additional nine miles to Juneau.

Juneau

Juneau, the state capital, was founded during the gold rush in 1890 and named after Joe Juneau, who discovered gold in the area. For a long time the main industry was fishing, boat maintenance and repair, gold mining and timber harvest. The resource base is still very strong in Alaska; however, about one half of the work force in Juneau is currently involved with government work, including federal, state and local government operations. The population of Juneau is about 30,000—nearly one-half of the population of Southeast Alaska. Set against Mount Juneau to the east and Gastineau Channel to the west, Juneau is a beautiful city in a remarkable setting. Historic buildings include the St. Nicholas Russian Orthodox Church built in 1894. The Alaskan State Museum is excellent and provides interesting information about Native cultures in Alaska, the Russian period, the gold strike and gold mining, and wildlife and habitat in Alaska.

As is true in all of southeast Alaska one can not drive to Juneau. (One cannot drive from one city to another in Southeast Alaska). Travel to Juneau is by boat or airplane. Juneau, as is true in all of southeast Alaska, has excellent harbor facilities for transient boaters. The cost for me to moor my boat at the harbor was about $7.00 per day. When travelling by private boat it is recommended that one avoid Gastineau Channel and instead travel around Douglas Island and obtain moorage at Auke Bay. Auke Bay provides moorage exclusively for transient boaters, and there is good public transportation from Auke Bay to downtown Juneau and also to Mendenhall Glacier.

Juneau is the headquarters for the SeaAlaska Corporation, a successful Native Alaskan corporation with operations in the timber industry, fishing, and tourism.

In his book, *Travels in Alaska*, John Muir devotes one brief paragraph to Juneau:

June 21. We arrived at Douglas Island at five in the afternoon and went sight-seeing through the mill. Six hundred tons of low-grade quarts are crushed per day. Juneau, on the mainland opposite the Douglas Island mills, is quite a village, well supplied with stores, churches, etc. A dance-house in which Indians are supposed to show native dances of all sorts is perhaps the best-patronized of all the places of amusement. A Mr. Brooks, who prints a paper here, gave us some information on Mt. St. Elias, Mt. Wrangell, and the Cook Inlet and Prince William Sound region. He told Russell that he would never reach the summit of St. Elias, that it was inaccessible. He saw no glaciers that discharged bergs into the sea at Cook Inlet, but many on Prince William Sound.[7]

What is of interest is that one half of the brief paragraph on Juneau is information that John Muir received from a chance encounter with a Mr. Brooks about mountains and glaciers far removed from Southeast Alaska. Another point is his reference to Juneau as "quite a village, well supplied with stores, churches, etc." There is one important church that did not exist during the visit by John Muir. The St. Nicholas Russian Orthodox Church was built in 1894. I attended this church on two occasions and spoke with the priest about the history of this historic building.

The St. Nicholas Russian Orthodox Church

I asked the priest, Fr. Thamas Mowatt, "How was it that this Russian Orthodox Church was built 27 years after Russia sold Alaska to the United States?"

He told me that a number of Tlingit elders asked some Russians who remained in Alaska after 1867 for a Russian Orthodox Church to be built in Juneau like the ones in Sitka and in other places in Alaska. The Russians initially said "no" and explained that they had no money to build a church, and that Alaska was now a territory of the United States. Undeterred, the Tlingit elders offered to pay for the materials, and to provide labor to help build the church. With this promise, which the Tlingit's fulfilled, the Russians agreed to supply the church with religious icons and to provide clergy to operate the church as a place to worship God.

I asked the Russian Orthodox Priest why the Native Alaskans specifically asked for a Russian Orthodox Church. The Priest answered that the Russian Orthodox missionaries conducted their effort to convert Native Alaskans to Christianity in a very different way than the Protestant missionaries who came later. First of all the Russian missionaries preached to Native Alaskans in their vernacular. The missionaries hired Tlingit elders to teach the Russians the Tlingit language. Furthermore, the Russian Orthodox missionaries did not disparage or try to suppress Tlingit ceremonies, especially the potlatch which was so important to them. The Russian Orthodox missionaries never had a policy of conversion via coercion. The Tlingit Natives were always free to reject the religion of Christianity or to blend their Native beliefs with their understanding of Christianity.

The priest suggested that for further information about the Russian Orthodox missionary effort in Alaska that I obtain the book written by Sergei Kan. The book is entitled, ***Memory Eternal:* Tlingit Culture and Russian Orthodox Christianity through Two Centuries.**

After returning to my boat I reflected on the few words that Nellie Torgemson had shared with me about the "Russians being more lenient and understanding of the Native cultures than Sheldon Jackson and S. Hall Young." I also focused on positive aspects of Native spirituality, which John Muir also clearly appreciated. While John Muir and S. Hall Young were companions on many trips throughout Southeast Alaska, Muir clearly had a more positive view of Tlingit spirituality than did S. Hall Young. Author Richard Nelson, in his introduction to John Muir's book, *Travels in Alaska,* wrote:

"Muir found much to admire in the Tlingit Indians' traditional religious beliefs. In his Alaska journal, he penciled: *"To the Indian mind all nature was instinct with deity. A spirit was embodied in every mountain, stream, and waterfall."* He recorded a fascinating interchange in which the Tlingit chief Kadachan asked Reverend Young if the wolves have souls. The Indians believe they do, said Kadachan, because wolves hunt so cleverly and know better than to kill off the animals they depend on for food. Muir explained that the Tlingit considered it *"wrong and unlucky to even speak disrespectfully of the fishes or any of the animals that supplied them with food."*[8]

Hoonah

Hoonah is about 70 miles from Juneau and only 20 miles from Glacier Bay. It is located on the northeast shore of Chichagof Island. The harbor at Hoonah is excellent, perhaps the best in Southeast Alaska. Many boaters who are waiting to enter Glacier Bay National Park wait at Hoonah should they arrive earlier than the date specified on their permit. Hoonah, population 900, has the largest settlement of Tlingit Indians in S.E. Alaska. The Natives settled here about 250 years ago when the glaciers advanced in Glacier Bay and forced them to move. (Hoonah is the Native community whose members helped guide John Muir and S. Hall Young on their first trip to Glacier Bay in 1879.) The economy of Hoonah, like much of S.E. Alaska is based on natural resources, commercial fishing, primarily salmon and halibut, and the timber industry. As in many other places in Alaska, residents make substantial use of subsistence hunting and fishing.

The community of Hoonah suffered a devastating fire in 1942 that destroyed many residences and priceless historic Tlingit cultural artifacts, including totem poles, ceremonial masks and other works of

Native art. The Hoonah Cultural Center is well worth visiting, but the collection of artifacts is not as comprehensive as it would have been had the destructive fire not occurred.

Glacier Bay National Park

Glacier Bay National Park is pristine wilderness and the world's largest wildlife preserve. Twelve glaciers reach tidewater within the park, bringing with them huge amounts of ice formed by substantial precipitation falling as snow on very high mountains within the park, including Mount Fairweather at 15,300 feet in elevation. Once within the park a boat operator must radio the office at Bartlett Cove and give the approximate time of arrival at the park headquarters. Checking in at the park headquarters for an orientation is required.

The park ranger will review the rules of the Park concerning boat speed within the park, how to handle your boat so as not to disturb the whales and other marine mammals, and which areas are off-limits when seals and sea lions have their pups or when birds are nesting. The park ranger will also give information about best places to anchor and to view wildlife. The whole park is excellent for viewing humpback whales, but if you are interested in seeing bears and mountain goats, the park ranger will give you current information. The quality of the information during the orientation is superb. The park employees are knowledgeable and view Glacier Bay as sacred ground and worthy of its designation as a World Heritage Site.

We checked in at Bartlett Cove and headed out for our first-night's anchorage at Berg Bay; we saw two whales outside of Glacier Bay Lodge as we left. Our first anchorage was at Berg Bay. We left the next morning early and stopped briefly at Blue Mouse Cove, a protective cove, and then headed into the west arm of Glacier Bay. We began to see large ice chunks and larger icebergs. We arrived at Reid Inlet that afternoon and anchored on the west side. We dropped our dinghy, rowed to shore, and hiked along a glacial moraine up close to the face of the glacier. We saw many signs of bear, as well as a fascinating bird—the oyster catcher. This bird has a bright red beak and engages in dramatic antics, apparently to distract potentially harmful folk away from her offspring. We returned by dinghy back to our boat, and as nightfall came, I spent much time in the cockpit at the back of the boat looking for signs of wildlife. A large brown bear appeared that evening and walked along the glacial moraine.

The next morning we left Reid Glacier and very slowly moved through that section of Glacier Bay into Blue Mouse Cove and anchored. We hiked along the shore primarily to stretch our legs and get off our boat. We saw moose droppings and talked to a biology research team studying intertidal areas. As we returned to our boat, we met two biologists who were housed at a small park service houseboat at Blue Mouse cove. They had been to Reid Glacier the night before—as we had been—and talked about the large brown bear that appeared along the glacial moraine.

We left Blue Mouse Cove at 1 p.m. and arrived at Sandy Cove east of Puffin Island at 2:30 p.m. Two other boats were moored there. We ate lunch and then paddled our small dinghy to shore. We came upon an area where bears sleep-the indentations in the grasses were about 12 feet by 5 feet. We had no interests in challenging a bear and left shortly after and rowed back to our boat. We watched from the back of our boat and spotted a total of nine bears strolling along the shore.

The next morning we left Sandy Cove. As we approached South Marble Island on our way back to Bartlett Cove, we saw many sea lions, humpback whales, and lots of bird life. We anchored at Bartlett Cove, paddled ashore, hiked, revisited the lodge, and ate dinner at the lodge. Our entire stay at Glacier Bay was graced with sunny and warm weather-unusual, but we enjoyed it. As we left the next day to return to Juneau, we reflected on our visit to this remarkable place-Glacier Bay National Park. What is special about Glacier Bay National Park is not just the mountains, fjords, glaciers, whales and other wildlife, but the knowledge that Glacier Bay is the most active place in the world for glacial retreat and advance and for plant-life recovery after glacial retreat. Just two hundred years earlier the bay was a thick sheet of ice that covered not only the present bay and inlets but also the entire land mass that is now at different stages of becoming reforested. The knowledge that Glacier Bay is the most reactive area in the world to glacial advance and retreat adds tremendous interest to this beautiful place. The concept of "succession"—where vegetation forms in stages after glacial retreat from lichen and moss to grasses and alder and cottonwood to "climax" forests of spruce and hemlock—is also remarkable to witness as it unfolds.

Haines and Skagway

After leaving Glacier Bay National Park on one of our trips, we (my wife Marge, our son Erik and I) turned north at the junction of Icy Strait and Chatham Strait and followed Lynn Canal the 85 miles to Haines. Lynn Canal is deep and varies in width from 3 to 6 miles. Glaciers and high mountain peaks line both sides. Davidson Glacier is especially impressive, and is within full view while in Lynn Canal at Seduction Pt.

Nearing Haines and Skagway we were treated to a spectacular display of humpback whales. We first noted one blow, so we slowed down and got out our cameras. I opened the hatch above the helm and photographed one humpback whale to the starboard side. Then a very large humpback whale surfaced just in front of our boat. The whale had swum under our boat and traveling in our direction he surfaced just in front of our bow, displaying his tail which was wider than my boat. In the excitement I managed just one photo.

As we arrived in Haines we pulled into the harbor, and the harbormaster assigned us a berth. We very much enjoyed attending a performance of the Chilcat Dancers and viewing Native art that is on display in Haines. The Chilcat Dancers had been dormant for over 40 years as a direct consequence of the suppression of Native art and culture in Alaska. The performances were re-established in 1956. The Sheldon Museum and Cultural Center in Haines is excellent and provides informative pamphlets and displays on topics such as Tlingit History, Tlingit carving, Potlatches, Fishing, the Gold Rush and the Chilkat Bald Eagle Preserve. A pamphlet at the museum in Haines provided a succinct overview of Tlingit culture and History:

Tlingit History

The origin of the Tlingit people is not certain. It is possible the people came from the coast of Asia and Japan migrating north and east across the Aleutians and Gulf of Alaska into Southeast Alaska. Art forms and physical features of the Tlingit are similar to some Pacific groups.

Southeast Alaska provided an idyllic setting for the villages and contained abundant local resources. The forests supplied shelter, game and wild berries while the ocean was a storehouse of fish and sea mammals. In contrast to interior peoples of North America, the Tlingit spent relatively little time surviving (gathering food) so were able to become traders and craftsmen.

The ocean provided not only food, but also a transportation corridor. Highly skilled navigators with seaworthy canoes, the Tlingit thought nothing of paddling for days in any direction. The Chilkats and Chilkoots also had overland trade routes to the interior. A great trade empire was established from interior Alaska/Canada south to northern California. In the Americas, this trade empire was rivaled in size only by the Incas.

The Chilkat Valley and Lynn Canal inhabitants—Chilkats and Chilkoots—had trade access with the Athabascan Indians over the Chilkat, Chilkoot and White Pass routes. These trade routes were jealously guarded, especially with the coming of the Russian and Hudson Bay Co. fur traders in the 1700's. Highly skilled traders, the Chilkats and Chilkoots would meet the Russian and English ships towards the end of the Chilkat Peninsula to trade far away from the overland trade routes. They would then take the goods over their trails to trade with interior Indians.

In 1879, the Tlingits asked Dr. Sheldon Jackson to establish a mission. A site for the mission was chosen at Dei shu ("The end of the trail.") In 1881 Presbyterian missionaries, Rev. and Mrs. Eugene Willard, first brought the Word of God to Chilkat country. Canneries were started nearby and with the advent of the Gold Rush many people came into this area. The town of Haines was established around the mission site and Ft. Seward was built nearby.[9]

I was mindful of the trip by S. Hall Young and John Muir to this area in 1879. While John Muir had respect for the Tlingit people, the Missionary unfortunately did not. Rev. Young records this trip as follows:

The climax of the trip, so far as the missionary interests were concerned, was our visit to the Chilcat and Chilcoot natives on Lynn Canal, the most northern tribes of the Alexandrian Archipelago. Here reigned the proudest and worst old savage of Alaska, Chief Shathitch. His wealth was very great in Indian t reassures, and he was reputed to have cached away in different places several houses full of blankets, guns, boxes of beads, ancient carved pipes, spears, knives and other valued heirlooms. He was said to have stored away over one hundred of the elegant Chilcat blankets woven by hand from the hair of the mountain goat. His tribe was rich and unscrupulous. Its members were the middle-men between the whites and the Indians of the Interior.

About the first of November we came in sight of the long, low-built village of Yin-des-tuk-ki. As we paddled up the winding channel of the Chilcat River we saw great excitement in the town. We had hoisted the American flag, as was our custom, and had put on our best apparel for the occasion. When we got within long musket—shot of the village we saw the native men come rushing from their houses with their guns in their hands and mass in front of the largest house upon the beach. Then we were greeted by what seemed rather too warm a reception—a shower of bullets falling unpleasantly around us. Instinctively Muir and I ceased to paddle, but Towa-att commanded, "Ut-ha, ut-ha—pull, pull!" and slowly, amid the dropping bullets, we zigzagged our way up the channel towards the village. As we drew near the shore line of runners extended down the beach to us, keeping within shouting distance of each other. Then came the questions like bullets—"Gusuwa-eh?—Who are you? Whence do you come? What is your business here?" And Stickeen John shouted back the reply: "a great preacher-chief and a great ice-chief have come to bring you a good message." [10]

Rev. S. Hall Young describes a great feast provided by chief Don-na-wuk. Chiefs of other villages were contacted and invited as well as numerous natives from the area. Rev. young began to preach in the morning and with the many questions asked by the natives, the service lasted until midnight. Young could not have been more pleased with the outcome. He wrote later in his autobiography:

I offered them a missionary and teachers and had told them of my attention of building a new Christian town. I asked them to name a place where we could build this new town. They selected this harbor, and I formally took possession of it.[11]

The Beginnings of the Presbyterian Church in Chilkat Valley

It is interesting that the Tlingits asked Dr. Sheldon Jackson to establish a mission. Here the indigenous peoples were explicitly open to hearing and learning about the Christian religion. The Tlingits also wanted basic education so their people could learn to read and write. However, there were big problems:

The Tlingit Indians did not ask the missionaries to remove their children and place them in residential boarding schools.

The Tlingit Indians did not ask the missionaries to suppress their rich and expressive dances, songs and ceremonies.

The Tlingit Indians did not ask the Presbyterian missionaries to suppress their language.

These unasked for stipulations or requirements appalled and angered the Tlingit peoples, putting the missionary effort in Haines on an early track for failure.

While in Haines I stopped to visit the beautiful Presbyterian Church and met with Rev. Shirl Butler. I asked him for permission to record a conversation with him about the history of the Presbyterian Church in the Chilkat Valley. He kindly agreed and stated that Sheldon Jackson had been denied funds from the Mission Board for the Chilkat venture. However, Jackson then bypassed the Mission Board. He contacted Mrs. F.E. Haines, a wealthy Presbyterian, who donated money generously and was helpful in raising additional monies. Sheldon Jackson named the town after her. With substantial funding from Mrs. Haines, the mission was established in 1881 with the arrival of Rev. Eugene Willard and his wife Caroline and their young daughter. Jackson built a boarding school for Tlingit children in 1884. The natives resisted the missionary efforts, and threatened the Willard's who withdrew in 1890.

The boarding school was destroyed by fire in 1896. During the next sixty years a total of thirteen missionaries served the Chilkat Valley mission. The average term was just under five years.

Rev. Shirl Butler shared with me a pamphlet entitled *The Beginnings of the Presbyterian Church in the Chilkat Valley:* **To Bring a Good Message.** The pamphlet provides a concise review of the history of the Presbyterian Church in Chilkat Valley. It has photos of Rev. Sheldon Jackson, Rev. S. Hall Young, and Rev. Eugene Willard and his wife Caroline, and a photo of Mrs. R.E. Haines. The pamphlet includes a brief paragraph of the Haines House:

In 1921, a second building was added, and Haines House, familiar to a generation of Presbyterians as a children's home, was founded. It was discontinued in 1960. On the site of the now-dismantled buildings, a new church was built and dedicated on Thanksgiving Day in 1969. Early Palm Sunday morning in 1973, the whole interior and roof of the building was destroyed by an arsonist's fire. The church building was rebuilt, much of it with volunteer labor, and was in use again by the fall of that year. [12]

As Rev. Butler and I continued our conversation, I shared with him my interview with Nellie Torgemson and her continuing life struggle and anger over suppression of Native language and Native culture that she experienced during her childhood at the *Haines House.* He agreed with me that the history was unfortunate, and that the Church thought it was helping by speeding up the process of "assimilation" of Natives to be "American."

Rev. Butler stated that he tried very hard, i.e., "We think we have taken every possible step (to reconcile), but the Natives are not interested." He added the focus on "English only" was a priority of the B.I.A.

The Reverend Sheldon Jackson

In his biography of Sheldon Jackson, author J. Arthur Lazell writes that "Jackson understood no law beyond that of his conscience." [13] This was true for both government law as well as for orders from the

Presbyterian Board of Missions. If he disagreed with the Board of Missions, Sheldon Jackson went his own way.

Reverend Sheldon Jackson was not authorized by the Presbyterian Board of Missions to go as a missionary to Alaska.

When the golden spike was driven into place at Promontory, Utah in May 1869, Sheldon Jackson recognized the opportunity to expand missionary work to the Western territories. Anticipating that great event, Jackson made a presentation in April 1869 to the Mission Board urging them to expand missionary work to the rapidly developing west. The Board then enthusiastically appointed Jackson as missionary superintendent for the Iowa, Nebraska, Dakota, Idaho, Montana, Wyoming, and Utah to establish churches and missions and to recruit clergy to serve the parishes. Later, in 1869, Colorado and New Mexico and then Arizona were added to his responsibility. In addition to church support, he sought and obtained federal funding and approval from the U.S. Board of Indian Commissioners to establish schools for Indian children. [14]

The Presbyterian Board of Missions recognized there were serious constraints and difficulties in providing missionary work in the rapidly developing western territories. The first was the ruinous state of the economy of the United States and devastated morale following our catastrophic civil war. Furthermore, as settlers poured into the western territories, they did so without effective law enforcement, and without hospitals or medical clinics or emergency services.

Alaska was purchased from Russia in 1867 and then essentially abandoned by the US government.[15] The Board of Missions recognized the opportunities for Christian Missionary work in Alaska; however, they felt constrained to wait until the mission work in the newly developing Western States and territories was firmly established and the US government had the time to establish governmental legal infrastructure including law enforcement and protective services in Alaska.

Without completing objectives assigned to him by the Board of Missions in the western territories, Sheldon Jackson was set on traveling to Alaska to establish missionary schools to educate and convert Alaskan natives. Jackson travelled to Portland, Oregon and met an old friend,

Mrs. Amanda McFarland. She was interested in doing missionary work and agreed to travel with Sheldon Jackson to Alaska.

Lazell writes: *He explained to her that she would have to be prepared to risk the uncertainties of life in a strange land among a primitive people; in addition she would have to work without official recognition, for Jackson had no authority to organize mission work in Alaska.* [16]

After hearing of Jackson's plan to travel to Alaska without authorization, Henry Kendal, the senior secretary of the Presbyterian Board of Home Missions, issued a rebuke to Sheldon Jackson stating: *We think you have never done any thorough work in Montana. You have dashed in and out again. The Church has come to demand something better.*

Alaskan Governor recommends that Missionaries not be placed in charge of schools

Early in 1885 John H. Kinkead, the Alaskan governor, made a series of recommendations to Washington about public education in Alaska. He recommended that there be separate schools for Indian children and "white" children (Euro-American). He asserted that schools should be secular and not placed in the hands of missionaries.[17] His advice came late. Sheldon Jackson, then a Presbyterian missionary, had already started in 1877 a vigorous campaign to establish mission schools in Alaska. He travelled extensively in the States and made over 900 speeches to church groups and secular organizations to gain support and to raise funds to establish a public school system for Alaska. As a result of the intensive efforts of Sheldon Jackson and his reputation as an expert on the needs of Alaska, John Eaton, Commissioner for Education in Washington D.C. ignored the advice of Kinkead and appointed Sheldon Jackson as general agent for education for all of Alaska in 1885.[18]

The arrest and internment of Reverend Sheldon Jackson

According to Lazell, Sheldon Jackson had been very disturbed with Haskett because Haskett wanted sescular educational programs in Alaska and specified that he did not want school programs run by missionaries.[21] Jackson wrote to President Cleveland a strongly worded diatribe about E.W. Haskett, the first United States attorney assigned to Alaska, stating: *he was uneducated, spending much of his time in saloons, a gambler and rowdyish in his manner, vulgar and obscene in his conversation, low in tastes, a confirmed drunkard, with but little knowledge of the law.*

Sheldon Jackson corresponded with a fellow missionary, a brother to President Grover Cleveland, and stated that Governor John H. Kinkead was a *broken-down politician of no intellectual force . . . treacherous behind your back.* In the same letter he described United States Marshall M.C. Hillyer as a "gambler." [22]

Lazell adds that a source to Sheldon Jackson provided the following opinion of Federal Judge Ward McAllister, Jr.: *destitute of almost every attribute which would entitle him to the supreme control of the judicial, legal, and executive offices of a great, half-civilized territory.*[23]

As a result of these communications, President Grover Cleveland dismissed all four of these men. The replacements were in route to Sitka during the legal problems faced by Jackson. With the removal of these four top Alaskan officials, the charges against Sheldon Jackson were dropped. Lazell writes: *It was said too that Jackson's church affiliation kept him out of jail. True enough, the Church was an influential factor in the life of the territory, and Presidents Harrison and Cleveland were Presbyterians, as were many of their cabinet officers. Under such circumstances, lit was not difficult to argue that a guilty Jackson had been shielded from his just fate.* [24]

The Charges alleged by the Granddaughter of Chief Shakes Regarding the Purpose of the Mission Schools

Nellie Torgemson, the granddaughter of Chief Shakes stated to me, "I believe they (the staff at the boarding school) figured it was best for us to forget about our culture and become like white people."

There is direct confirmation that Nellie Torgemson was correct. The goal of the Protestant effort in Southeast Alaska was to Americanize the Natives, and to destroy the cultural and economic base of their society (subsistence hunting and gathering performed at the communal level) and substituting individualism and a trade based economy. For example, Rev. Sheldon Jackson addressed members of the House and Senate and outlined a mission statement for a school system for Alaskan Natives. *To provide an education in the common branches of an English education, the principles of a republican government, and such industrial pursuits as may seem best adapted to their circumstances.*[25] Lazell states that Sheldon Jackson warned that without this education the Alaskan Natives would *remain a burden to the white man.* [26]

S. Hall Young in his book, *Alaska Days with John Muir,* wrote about his (Young's) vision and purpose in his work in Alaska, "to do what I could towards establishing the white man's civilization among the Tlingit Indians." [27]

Forced Attendance at the Christian Boarding Schools

The granddaughter alleges, "Once and then again a child would run away, but there were people who would be paid, so much a head, to find these children and force them back."

Lazell states, *A small but important incident occurred when Jackson reached Dutch Harbor to inspect the school located there. A few days before his arrival a native woman had taken her child from the school. As soon as he knew of the woman's action, Jackson asked the United States Commissioner to effect the child's return. When the woman barricaded her home, he had the door knocked in and the child removed. The affair served notice on everyone that Jackson would not tolerate interference with the operation of the schools nor allow anyone to obstruct their prime purpose, namely, to train native children to live in a world that was changing rapidly.* [28]

The Suppression of Native Language

The granddaughter of Chief Shakes stated, "Speaking our Native language was one of the things that would bring on physical punishment."

Once again the charge made by the Native Alaskan is borne out by the words of the missionaries. For example, S. Hall Young stated that the Tlingit language was "inadequate to express Christian thought" and stated he would rather see "the old tongues with their superstitions and sin die—the sooner the better—and replace these languages with that of Christian civilization." [29]. Sheldon Jackson agreed stating that there "was no benefit, only retardation of progress in the use of the vernacular." [30]

The Issue of Physical Punishment

The granddaughter of Chief Shakes stated, "We were physically beaten (at the Christian boarding school) that is not the way that Tlingit parents raise their children."

In his book, *Alaskan Apostle*, Lazell makes only one reference to physical punishment. Lazell stated, "He (Sheldon Jackson) disliked having to whip the boys in order to maintain discipline." [31]

John Brady, a former Presbyterian Minister serves as Governor of Alaska

Rev. John Brady was recruited by Sheldon Jackson in 1878 and briefly served as a missionary in Sitka. He remained in Alaska as a business and a government official. He became governor of Alaska in 1897. Lazell writes that Governor Brady was not popular with business people in Alaska who felt that he was not progressive enough. Many of them wanted the capital moved from Sitka to Juneau, but Brady opposed the proposal. When his term came up for reappointment in 1904, Sheldon Jackson wrote a letter to influential friends asking them to support John Brady:

> *The appointment of the Reverend John G. Brady, Governor of Alaska, terminates on the sixth of June. In the whole history of Alaska it has had but two good governors, James Sheakley a Democratic appointee by Mr. Cleveland on*

his second term, and Brady appointed by Mr. McKinley just previous to his death.

The friends of good order and the substantial property holders of Alaska are in favor of Governor Brady's reappointment. His opponents are men who stand for measures which we deem pernicious and which he had persistently fought.

If you are willing to help us in Alaska to good government, will you not write President Roosevelt and ask that Mr. Brady be continued as governor because of the good, faithful, honest, and efficient services he has already rendered in that position. Please do not use my name in writing to him.

Very truly yours,
Sheldon Jackson
General Agent of Education in Alaska [32]

The Investigation of Gov. Brady and his removal, ordered by President Roosevelt

Although very unpopular throughout Alaska, Brady was reappointed in 1904. Lazell states that the "continued control of Alaska policy by the powerful Presbyterian Board of Home Missions which was so powerful that the party leaders were unwilling to oppose it."[33] However, by 1905 President Teddy Roosevelt did authorize a formal review of grievances. He appointed Frank C. Churchill to go to Alaska and to report on the "condition of educational and school service and the management of reindeer service."

Churchill travelled to Alaska in the summer of 1905 and added supplements in the following year. His report was critical. He was especially critical of the practice of placing reindeer herds at mission stations and that Jackson received funds from the Presbyterian Board of Missions in addition to his salary as a government official. This laid open the perception that Jackson was influenced to favor the church. There was also pressure to stop the practice of government subsidy of mission schools. One outcome of the Churchill report was that governor Brady was removed from office by President Roosevelt.[34] What became clear was that the Presbyterian Church had exercised a powerful influence in Alaska, and both political support and government funds supported the effort of the Presbyterian Church in Alaska along the lines pursued by Rev. Sheldon Jackson.

The Russian Orthodox Church in Alaska

Beginning in the 1760's Christianity had been introduced to Alaskan Natives along the Aleutians and in Southeast Alaska by Russian Orthodox missionaries. While the Russian Orthodox missionary effort had been quite successful in converting Aleut Natives to Christianity, the Orthodox missionaries experienced little success among the Tlingit Indians. The Russian presence in Southeast Alaska, however, was significant. By 1804 Sitka was the largest seaport on the west coast of North America, and with a strong outpost in Wrangell, the Russians had established control of the fur harvest and engaged in significant trading activities with Tlingit natives.[35]

While Russian Orthodox missionaries were not highly successful in their efforts to convert Tlingit peoples prior to 1867, large numbers of Natives expressed a strong interest in Russian Orthodox beliefs after they were exposed to the Protestant missionaries. The approach of the Russian missionaries had been vastly different. They learned the language of the Alaskan Natives, and had hired Natives to translate and interpret for them. This was in marked contrast from the perspective taken by the American missionaries i.e., the belief that the Tlingit language was inferior, and not suitable to communicate with God. The Russian missionaries never attempted to remove children from their parents and Native villages, and raise them totally apart from their culture. The Russian missionaries did not prohibit (or attempt to outlaw) Native ceremonies, such as the potlatch.

A dramatic illustration of the draw of the Russian Orthodox is that by the year 1890 a large number of Tlingit Indians asked for the construction of Orthodox churches in the following villages, Juneau, Killisnoo (near Angoon), Yakutut, Kake and Wrangell.[36] As stated above the St. Nicholas Church in Juneau was built and dedicated on June 12, 1894. The initial membership consisted of 25 Russians, 7 Greeks, and 123 Tlingit. The church remains a historic landmark. A Russian Orthodox Church, St. Andrews Chapel, was also built in Killisnoo and completed in 1889). However, the Orthodox Mission did not have the resources to construct churches and serve the communities of Yakutut, Kake or Wrangell.

It is worth considering the written guidelines for missionary work in "Russian America" by the remarkable Russian Orthodox priest, Ioann Veniaminov. In 1844 Vieniaminov wrote some guidelines as to how missionaries were to conduct themselves in working with Alaskan Natives. [37]

Clause 271: Natives who do not profess the Christian faith shall be permitted to carry on their devotions according to their own rites.

Clause 272: Russian clergy in making converts among the Natives shall use conciliatory and persuasive measures, in no case resorting to coercion.

Clause 274: Natives professing the Christian faith who, through ignorance, transgress ecclesiastical regulation shall not be subject to fines and punishment: instruction land persuasion being the only proper remedies in such cases.

The Veniaminov Bicentennial Year

Tony Knowles, Governor of Alaska, declared 1997 to be the Veniaminov Bicentennial Year. In his Executive Proclamation Tony Knowles wrote the following:

1997 marks the bicentennial of the birth of Ioann (John) Veniaminov, the distinguished Russian Orthodox missionary, teacher, administrator, linguist, ethnographer, and architect. John Veniaminov served as the first priest at Unalaska, the first Orthodox bishop in Alaska, and head of the Orthodox Church of Russia. In 1997 he was canonized a saint, St. Innocent, Apostle to North America and Siberia.

John Veniaminov (Bishop Innocent) is honored by Alaskan Natives for his dedication to preserving Native languages, for his development of a Tlingit Alphabet. He is also honored as a teacher, founder of the first school at Unalaska and of the first Orthodox school, seminary, and orphanage at Sitka.

The Village of Kake "Burns" its Traditions

About 20 years after the request by villagers in Kake for an Orthodox Church was denied, a significant number of villagers came to accept the new ideology and Christianity as introduced by American Protestant missionaries. Conversion to Christianity meant rejecting the "old ways." With encouragement from Protestant missionaries, some members of the village burned all of the mortuary and memorial totem poles in Kake in January 1912.[38] For decades no memorial potlatches or other traditional ceremonies were celebrated in Kake. This act of destruction of Native traditions by Tlingit members who had converted to Christianity is a prime example of the dissention among Natives brought on to a culture when another and more powerful group demands compliance to a total change of values. Large numbers of Natives in Alaska were deeply troubled by the action taken in Kake. Imagine the stress experienced and the sense of loss by Native Americans who deeply valued their culture to find that these cultural traditions can be destroyed with impunity. Or, imagine the sense of dismay for parents whose children are taken away, and when returned can not speak the Native language and disparage their own culture and traditions.

Continued Growth in Membership of the
Russian Orthodox Church

Sergei Kan (1999) in his review of Christian Missionary work in Southeast Alaska refers to documentation that at the eve of the 1917 revolution in Russia the number of Russian Orthodox among the Tlingit in Sitka outnumbered the Presbyterians by two to one. Although the Russian Orthodox Mission to Alaska was completely cut off from Russia at the start of the 1917 Revolution, the Russian Orthodox Church continued to grow. Elizabeth Brady, wife of ex-governor John Brady, estimated that in the early 1920's four of five

Natives in Sitka were Russian Orthodox.[39] She speculated that the Orthodox clergy did not require Natives to give up old customs, and that the Orthodox priests did house to house visiting, which was not done by the Presbyterians.

Native Culture Resolution of the Alaska Presbytery

After travelling eight summers throughout Southeast Alaska and becoming increasingly aware and informed about the early history of the Protestant missionary practices, I spoke with Rev. Ralph Miller about the early history of his church, the first American Protestant Church in Alaska, and abuses against Native cultures. I specifically asked if the church has formally apologized to Alaskan Natives. Rev. Miller impressed me by his awareness of the history. He told me that he would ask a Native Alaskan, who is a member of the First Presbyterian Church to send me a copy of the formal apology. A short time later I received a very thoughtful letter by Ms. Teddy Williams and a complete copy of an apology by the Presbyterian Church. A portion of that apology in the form of a resolution is as follows:

The Presbytery of Alaska

Lew Rooker
Stated Clerk
Box 20186, Juneau, Alaska 99802
October 21, 1991

Dear Friends:

At it recent meeting in Auke Bay the Presbytery of Alaska passed the following Resolution, and instructed me to inform you of our action. If you have any questions or comments concerning the resolution feel free to contact me.

Sincerely,
Lew Rooker
Stated Clerk

NATIVE CULTURE RESOLUTION OF THE
ALASKA PRESBYTERY

WHEREAS, some Presbyterian missionaries, with best intentions in bringing the Gospel to Alaska, were among those who misunderstood the nature and purpose of native culture, art and artifacts, (for example mistakenly teaching that totem poles were idols), and

WHEREAS, this misconception still exists among some Christians in Southeast Alaska, and native culture is still held in suspicion by some native and immigrant Christians as a result of these teachings, and

WHEREAS, both the early destruction of native art, the continuing denigration of native cultures, and the desecration and pillage of native gravesites did not, and do not, promote the Kingdom of God, but rather represent a kind of violence against some of God's children and a loss for us all,

We disavow those teachings which led people to believe that abandoning native culture was a prerequisite for being Christian. We deeply regret the church's part in the destruction of native artifacts and the church's part in the loss of native languages. We further call upon all members of our churches to pray and work for reconciliation between the peoples and cultures of our region and to bring to an end the misunderstandings, especially of native cultures mentioned above.

May God grant us grace to value all cultures and all peoples, and courage to transcend cultures and cultural differences as together we seek to be obedient to God's will.[40]

WW II, Statehood, Prudhoe Bay Oil, and ANCSA

After the 1867 purchase of Alaska from Russia, the development of Alaska proceeded very slowly. Once the fabled gold rush of the 1890's died off, Alaska was seen as too remote and too wild to develop. The first real push to develop Alaska followed the Japanese attack of Alaska in 1942. Although the attack was diversionary, that fact was not immediately clear. The Japanese attack was the singular event that prompted the US government to build the Alcan Highway. To the credit of engineers, construction crews and the strong cooperation between Canada and the US, the vast Alcan Highway was completed in less than twelve months. The war effort provided the stimulus to build ports, housing, airports and other requirements to assist in military operations.

The end of the war brought on an even stronger surge in the economic development of Alaska. By the time Japan surrendered, 65 of its cities were devastated, as well as its rail lines and bridges. Japan did not have the timber resources to rebuild, but the US agreed to help Japan reconstruct itself by opening up for the first time on a large scale the vast timber resources of the Tongass National Forest. In the 1950's, the US Forest Service issued long-term (500-year)) timber contracts to two large corporations. One went to a Japanese company, Alaska Pulp Company, who proceeded to build a very large pulp mill in Sitka and a large lumber mill in Wrangell. The second contract went to the Louisiana Pacific Company, who built a large pulp mill in Ketchikan. These two companies for a number of decades provided the largest year-round employment in Alaska. Many Native Alaskans worked in these operations. Both of these lumber operations are now shut down.

Alaska achieved statehood in 1959. With a very small population and minimal tax receipts, the first governor of the state of Alaska, Bill Egan, faced a seemingly impossible job. He had little revenue to cover the tremendous needs of Alaskans for schools, water and sewer lines, roads, electricity and health care. Then huge deposits of oil were discovered at Prudhoe Bay in the northernmost part of the state in 1968. President Nixon had the foresight to postpone oil development until some unresolved issues were addressed.

Nixon persuaded the then Alaskan governor Walter J. Hickle to step down as governor to be Secretary of the Interior to solve two problems, 1. to resolve Alaska Native land claims and, 2. to establish guidelines for the construction of the Trans-Alaska Pipeline from Prudhoe Bay to Valdez.

The Alaska Native Claims Settlement Act of 1971 (ANCSA)

Several years of negotiations between representatives of the state of Alaska, Alaskan Natives and the federal government resulted in the Alaska Native Claims Settlement Act of 1971. As a result, Alaskan Natives received 44 million acres of land and $962 million in compensation for the settlement of Aboriginal claims. The state of Alaska negotiated terms to collect, in future years, billions of dollars in royalties, rents and taxes from the development of the North Slope oil fields. The oil companies obtained the rights to develop the North Slope oil fields and to build the oil pipeline from the oil fields to the seaport at Valdez. [41] The Trans-Alaska Pipeline was constructed by the oil companies for $8 billion, and oil began to flow in 1977 with up to two million barrels of oil a day. In 2008 the flow had slowed to about 700,000 barrels a day. The flow is expected to decline at the rate of about six percent a year.

The Alaska National Interest Lands Conservation Act

Major conservation groups, both in Alaska and throughout the rest of the United States, campaigned to enact laws to protect vast lands in Alaska. During Stewart Udall's tenure as Secretary of the Interior, from 1961 to 1969, he laid the groundwork for a national consciousness of protecting wilderness settings by helping to establish national trails and the wild-and-scenic river system. His brother, Morris Udall, senator from Arizona and chairman of the powerful Interior Committee, helped push through the Alaska Lands Act. Finally, President Carter convinced Congress to pass the Alaska National Interest Lands Conservation Act of 1980. This protected 104 million acres in Alaska, the single largest conservation act in US history. If Alaska would have been developed and populated within the same time frame as Washington, Oregon and California, these environmental safeguards would not have been considered.

I will reserve my evaluative comments about the Christian missionary effort in Alaska, and for the early Christian missionary efforts in British Columbia, the Pueblo Indians of New Mexico, Cuba, Guatemala, Peru, and Tierra del Fuego for the chapter entitled 'Tis a Pity.

End notes Chapter 1

1. Newman, Peter C. (1985). *COMPANY OF ADVENTURERS: The Story Of The Hudson's Bay Company.* Viking. Ontario, Canada.

2. Muir, John. (1996). ***John Muir:*** *His Life and Letters and Other Writings.* Edited and introduced by Terry Gifford. The Mountaineers. Seattle.

3. Muir, John. (First published in the United States by Houghton Mifflin Company, 1915). Republished with an introduction by Richard Nelson, 1993. *Travels in Alaska.* Penguin Books, New York. p. XII.

4. Note: The U.S. Forest Service has prepared a pamphlet describing a number of Recreation Cabins within the Stikine Area Tongass National Forest, including the one at the Anan Creek Bear Observatory. The pamphlet can be obtained from: Wrangell Chamber/ Box 49/ Wrangell, AK 99929.

5. O'Donohue, John. (1997). *ANAM CARA: A Book of Celtic Wisdom.* HarperCollins, New York.

6. Muir, John. (1996) with introduction by Terry Gifford. Op.cit., page 641.

7. Muir, John.(1915) with introduction by Richard Nelson. Op.cit., page. p. 208.

8. Ibid. page XIII

9. Pamphlet entitled, **TLINGIT HISTORY,** is available from the Sheldon Museum and Cultural Center, P.O. Box 269 Haines, Alaska 99827. I quote from this pamphlet to contrast the portrayal of the Chilkats and Chilkoots in this document from the much more negative portrayal by S. Hall Young in his writing. (next endnote)

10. Young, S. Hall. (1915) *Alaska Days with John Muir.* In edited book with introduction by Terry Gifford. Op.cit., p. 643.

11. Ibid. p. 645.

12. Note: This is a church pamphlet available from the Haines United Presbyterian Church, Haines, Alaska.

13. Lazell, J. Arthur. (1960). *ALASKAN APOSTLE: The Story of SHELDON JACKSON.* Harper & Brothers, Publishers. New York. p. 18.

14. Ibid., pp. 31-34.

15. Moore, Denton Ricky. (1994). *Alaska's Lost Frontier: Life in the days of homesteads, dog teams and sailboat fisheries.* Prospector Press. Moore Haven, Florida.

16. Lazell, op.cit., p. 55.

17. Ibid. p. 71.

18. Ibid. p. 71.

19. Ibid. p. 18.

20. Ibid. p. 19.

21. Ibid. p. 20

22. Ibid. p. 21.

23. Ibid. p. 21.

24. Ibid. p. 21.

25. Ibid. p. 202.

26. Ibid. p. 64.

27. Young, op.cit.,

28. Lazell. op.cit., pps. 92-93.

29. Kan, Sergei. (1999). *Memory Eternal: Tlingit Culture and Russian Orthodox Christianity Thought Through Two Centuries.* Seattle, University of Washington Press. p. 222. Sergei Kan also refers to the ideas of Reverend Livingstone Jones, who served as a Presbyterian minister is several Tlingit communities. Kan writes, *In his 1908 article published in the Training School Newspaper (Thlinget, vol. 1, no. 5) and his book-length **A study of the Thlingets of Alaska** he argued that the missionary should not learn Tlingit, since that "dialect" had only limited distribution and was doomed to "speedy decay and extinction." Like other Presbyterian missionaries, Jones correctly identified Tlingit as both a major mechanism of perpetuating traditional (pre-Christian) beliefs and a marker of a distinct identity. In his black-and-white view, those who spoke Tlingit supported the "old customs" and those who preferred English were getting away from them.*

30. Lazell. op.cit., p. 25.

31. Ibid., p. 189.

32. Ibid., p. 190.

33. Ibid., pp. 192-202.

34. Ibid., p. 200.

35. Chevigny, Hector. (1965). *Russian America: The Great Alaskan Venture 1741-1867.*Binford and Mort, Portland, Oregon.

36. Kan, Sergei. op.cit., pp. 256-266.

37. Chevigny, Hector. Op.cit, p. 208. Note: Sergei Kan states that during the reign of the last Russian Emperor (Nicholas II) that some Russian Orthodox Priests advocated harsh measures regarding indigenous customs and beliefs and were skeptical of liberal missionaries' efforts to translate Orthodox texts and liturgical materials into local languages. He specifically identified the following Russian Orthodox missionaries, working in "Russian America," who advocated harsh treatment against "old customs:" Kamenski, Dashkevich, Iaroshesvich, and Orlov. P. 349.

38. Kan, Sergei. op. cit., p. 461.

39. Ibid., p 461.

40. Ibid., p. 470-471.

41. A copy of the complete resolution can be obtained from many Presbyterian churches in Alaska. It can also be obtained from, Presbytery of Alaska/ Box 20186, Juneau, Alaska 99802. It is my understanding that the resolution was given to Native Alaskans in one on one contact with dialogue.

42. Halliday, Jan. (1998). *Native Peoples of Alaska.* Sasquatch Books, Seattle. Pps. 266-268.

CHAPTER 2

The introduction of Christianity to British Columbia

Pros and Cons of Cruise Ship Travel versus Independent Boat Travel

Follow me along as we travel the Inside Passage through Beautiful British Columbia. About a million people a year travel via cruise ships to Alaska and go past British Columbia. There are vast differences in the experiences of travelers who go by cruise ship versus private boat to Alaska. This has been pointed out to me in numerous conversations with those who have returned from cruise ship travel. While most speak highly of the trip and their enjoyment of wondrous scenery and remarkable chances to view wildlife, their memory for places is quite different from that of independent boaters. Those operating their own vessels must review navigational charts, plot a course, measure its distance, estimate running time, and keep a log. They also must keep in mind options to change plans when the conditions warrant. This mental activity not only adds enjoyment and risk appraisal, but also reinforces memory of places and scenic wonders encountered along the way. As an example, all boaters who navigate Seymour Narrows must be aware of its potential hazard and know how to plan for a safe passage.

I have not met one cruise ship passenger who had any memory of this dramatic place or any appreciation of its significance. The same is true for other places along the Canadian Inside Passage, such as historic- and now abandoned—canneries, Namu and Butedale, or the Native villages of Alert Bay, New Bella Bella and Klemtu.

Other differences between traveling by private boat versus cruise ship involve time and money. Most recreational boaters traveling the Inside Passage from the Puget Sound area to Alaska plan on a two-month trip, whereas cruise ship travel typically lasts one week. The time difference is not due to the speed of the vessels, but the itinerary, as cruise ships travel 24 hours a day on certain legs of the trip. Recreational boaters don't do that, but will allow time to explore remote places and small anchorages in coves and other places inaccessible via cruise ships. Cost is another difference. Traveling by private boat is more expensive than by cruise ship because of costs associated with vessel ownership, including depreciation, operating and maintenance expenses and insurance. There are also special costs for navigating the Inside Passage. Navigational charts to cover the distance cost about $1,500 (assuming about 90 charts). Dinghies are necessary because anchoring and rowing to shore are common in remote sections of Alaskan waters where there are no docks. Fuel costs are a major consideration. For example, fuel costs for a round trip from Port Townsend, Washington, to Glacier Bay National Park in Alaska will equal the price of about 500 to 600 gallons of diesel for a single engine boat. A cruiser with twin gasoline engines may require four times that amount of fuel. Regarding costs, keep in mind that the most expensive boat is the one you *own and don't use.* If you own a suitable boat and have the experience, a trip to Alaska may be very affordable.

As we consider the beautiful waters of British Columbia, keep in mind that the cruise ships don't stop in First Nation villages in B.C. at all. Some stop for a visit to Victoria on Vancouver Island, but most make their first stop in Alaskan waters in major ports such as Ketchikan, or Juneau or Sitka.

The Historic Inside Passage Route taken by
Indigenous Peoples for eons of time

In this chapter we will travel through First Nation villages; we will encounter tidal currents that might trouble your sleep (it has troubled mine). We will encounter whales, bald eagles and we will pass over salmon spawning grounds. This passage has been travelled by expert sea faring peoples for thousands of years. The First Nation peoples who lived in places like Alert Bay, Bella Bella and Klemtu were not sit-at-home stationary people. They travelled these waters and they did so in canoes. Furthermore, the Tlingit people of Alaska were neighbors and regularly travelled through this great passage and many went on down into areas now known as the States of Washington, Oregon and California. We will be travelling through this sacred passage to sacred lands.

Visits to Native Villages in Alert Bay,
New Bella Bella and Klemtu

The starting point for our trip to visit these three First Nation villages in British Columbia is Port Townsend, Washington, about 260 miles south of Alert Bay. The first leg of the trip is from Port Townsend, to Campbell River, British Columbia, a distance of 160 miles. The route I have taken to reach Campbell River is to follow the west side of Georgia Strait. I check in at Canadian customs at South Pender Harbor. With everything in order my visit at Canadian customs usually takes about five minutes. I then follow the protected route of Trincomali Channel to Gabriola Passage to enter the Strait of Georgia and proceed through this often rough and choppy body of water to the town of Campbell River. Once, when sea conditions were unusually calm, I covered the 160 nautical miles in 10 hours. On more normal days with the tide moving in one direction and the wind from another direction (causing rough seas), I make the passage in about 20 hours of running time (with an overnight stop at French Creek). From Campbell River I proceed up a long, beautiful and hazardous journey passing through

Seymour Narrows. I then follow Johnstone Strait to the northern end of Vancouver Island and reach Port Hardy.

Campbell River is right at latitude 50. This places the community south of Mt. Waddington, with an elevation of 13,177 feet, the second highest mountain in British Columbia. A range of very high mountains continues on for another 120 miles to the north. These high mountains are not visible from a boat because the much smaller coastal ranges on the mainland block the view from sea level. It is interesting to remember and appreciate the dramatic fashion in which these very high mountains have left their imprints on the land and on the inlets. The mountains still have massive snowfields and glaciers. During the ice ages they carved the fjords and inlets that are so pronounced. Some of the fjords go back 50 miles from the inside passage, and the dramatic cascading waterfalls are reminders of the work of massive and deep glaciers. Campbell River is a designation point for sport fishermen. I have caught nice salmon and ling cod in these waters, but that is another story.

Discovery Passage and Seymour Narrows

Seymour Narrows is just eight miles north of Campbell River. That short distance makes Campbell River a convenient starting point to proceed north, because it is essential to cross Seymour Narrows at slack tide. The Narrows during the midst of a bull or ebb tide has dangerous rips, whirlpools and large waves. The waters are comparable to the swift, swirling and dangerous waters called *Maelstrom* near the Lofoten Islands off the northwestern coast of Norway. I was there as well during a cod fishing trip with my relatives who own a farm in the Lofoten Islands. Passage is safe at slack high or slack low tides and lethal otherwise. Allen Edgar Poe accurately described the severity of the waters in his poem, *The Maelstrom.* If you make a mistake in these waters the mistake can be lethal.

In 1995, my son Paul and I wanted to see the action that develops at Seymour Narrows when the tidal current is strong. After crossing safely at slack high tide, I anchored the boat in a cove north of the Narrows. Paul then lowered our dinghy, rowed to shore and hiked to the edge of the bluff on Maud Island. From this overlook he was able to view the strong whirlpools and steep waves that develop every day when the tide is "right" i.e. running strong. Dangerous currents develop every day, but are predictable. Tidal currents, not wind, are the cause of rough conditions at Seymour Narrows. Paul and I wondered about the tremendous skill of the Aboriginal people who navigated this dangerous area without clocks to measure time and without tide charts. They were able to determine when to make passage when the "safe" time was limited to as little as 20 to 30 minutes during a tide change of six hour duration. How did they do that?

Ripple Rock: An Infamous Navigational Hazard

Prior to 1958, Seymour Narrows was a vastly more dangerous navigational hazard than it is now and had claimed over one hundred ships. In the early 1950s, several unsuccessful efforts were made to destroy Ripple Rock by positioning a drilling barge over the rock and drilling into it to set off an explosion. On the last effort with that strategy, the cables that had secured the barge broke and all nine men aboard were drowned. Engineering plans were then made to drill a tunnel from Maud Island straight down and then, at a 90 degree angle, through the bedrock to a position under Ripple Rock. The effort to dynamite and "dig" through the bedrock creating the tunnel took two and a half years. In the spring of 1958, engineers detonated 1,300 tons of TNT that had been placed at the end of the tunnel under Ripple Rock. The explosion blew rock and water ten thousand feet in the air. To this day the explosion at Ripple Rock remains the largest non-nuclear explosion ever. The success of this complex and dangerous engineering project neutralized the severe navigational hazard. Prior to 1958, this area was dangerous even within minutes of slack tide and catastrophic during strong tidal flows.

The best option going north is to cross Seymour Narrows at slack high tide because, as the current begins to ebb, the tidal current will flow in the direction of the boater as he proceeds north up the remainder of Discovery Passage and into Johnstone Strait. This is especially important if the boat has a cruising speed of less than eight knots. The same principle holds on a return trip from an upstream anchorage, such as Kelsey Bay. It would be good to leave there at low tide and travel with the incoming tidal flow and plan to arrive at Seymour Narrows at slack high tide for a safe crossing.

Chatham Point and the Entrance to Johnstone Strait and Point Hardy.

Chatham Point is at the northern end of Discovery Passage (off Vancouver Island) and has several lighthouse keepers' houses; the light is an important navigational marker and is placed on Beaver Rock. This is about 12 miles from Seymour Narrows and connects with Johnstone Strait; it is about 88 miles from Point Hardy. A good refuge point on the way to Port Hardy is Kelsey Bay. I always break up the long stretch to Port Hardy with an overnight stay at Kelsey Bay.

Kelsey Bay

Kelsey Bay is at the mouth of the Salmon River, an operation center for a very large-scale lumber operation. The shallow delta of the river has five large sunken freighters that form a breakwater. I have enjoyed walking the road from the bay to the small town about two miles in land. The town, which supports the rural timber operation, has a good grocery story and a small park. It's a great place to stretch the legs.

Robson Bight and Orca Whales

About 20 miles west of Kelsey Bay, in Johnstone Strait, is an area called Robson Bight. It is a protected area for a pod of Orca, or killer, whales. While it is against the law throughout the world to hunt Orca whales, the rules in this area are even more restricted. A boater is not allowed to go out of his way to follow them. Also, in the Robson Bight area, one is not allowed to beach his boat or launch a dinghy to approach the Orca whales or to go on shore. We have consistently seen and photographed Orca whales within Robson Bight, but we have also seen them at other points from the Juan de Fuca Strait up into Alaska.

Orca whales seem to be more prevalent in the Robson Bight area of Vancouver Island than in other places.

A memorable experience for my wife and me on one of our trips occurred on a July day. We decided on a hot lunch, so I slowed the boat down to idle and kept it in gear to maintain steering and vessel control. While enjoying our lunch we watched four sea kayaks in the area. Suddenly three Orca whales came into view and swam toward our slowly moving boat. One swam underneath our boat and surfaced within 30 feet of a kayaker, who himself was only about 60 feet from us. The whale remained motionless for a while on the surface, perhaps watching us, and then continued on its way. We took some nice photos. Whale watching doesn't get much better than that!

Alert Bay, Cormorant Island

Alert Bay is located on a small island, Cormorant Island, 21 miles west of Robson Bight. At the center of the bay is a good breakwater and behind it are docks and floats for fishing vessels and small craft. The town is the location of the Nimpish Indian Village. I have enjoyed visiting the totem poles and the U'Mista Cultural Center about one half mile northwest of the dock.

The U'Mista Cultural Center was incorporated in 1980. It tells a powerful story of the history of struggles and conflicts between First Nation Peoples and the Canadian Government. Even before contact with European-Americans ("dominant white culture"), this area was a focal point or center for creative Native art and culture. With the coming of European settlers, who took control of the land and its resources, the situation changed drastically. The Canadian government enacted laws that prohibited First Nation peoples from performing traditional ceremonies. For example the potlatch was an important ceremony used to mark important occasions such as the naming of children, marriage, mourning the dead, and transferring rights and privileges. The practice was banned by law in 1884 in an effort to "civilize" Natives.[1],[2].

In 1886, Franz Boas, a German with a PhD in physics, boarded a steamer in Victoria, Canada, and headed to the northern coast of

Vancouver Island. His goal was not engineering which would have been consistent with his doctorate, but anthropology i.e., to study the languages and culture of Indian villages in the area. He reached the Indian village of Newhitty on the northern coast of Vancouver Island. He came not as a tourist, but to live with the Indians and learn from them. At first he was treated with suspicion. The Indians thought he had been sent by the government to force them to give up their culture. The young researcher convinced the Indians that he did not disapprove of their culture, but would be interested in learning from them. The people of Newhitty invited Boas to a special ceremony during which Boas listened to speeches and songs and enjoyed a feast of fresh halibut along with the tribal members. The hosts also distributed gifts and blankets to Boas and other guests.

Boas spent the next 50 years studying the Kwakiutl, and agonized at the increasing signs that the Canadian government, with the aid of missionaries, in fact wanted to force assimilation and to bring to an end the languages and cultural practices of the Native peoples of Canada. That ominous threat forced a change in Boas' plans. He was determined to record as accurately as possible all aspects of the Kwakiutl culture, including the ceremonies, rituals, beliefs and language. He did not want to change any of it. Note: The name *Kwakiutl* refers to the Native villages along the northern and eastern coasts of Vancouver Island and the adjacent mainland of British Columbia. This covers a distance of about 170 miles from Cape Mudge on Quadra Island to Rivers Inlet (east of Calvert Island). At the time Boas worked this area there were about 30 large Native villages; together they were the Kwakiuitl.[3].

As Boas was doing his work to record (thus help preserve) as much as possible of Native culture in Canada, the Canadian government implemented draconian measures against their own people. These threats included removing children from their parents and raising them in boarding schools (run by various Christian denominations), prohibiting the use of Native languages, banning the practice of Native Ceremonies and confiscating traditional ceremonial artifacts.

One major example of outright persecution occurred in Alert Bay in December 1921. A Kwakwaka'wakw man named Dan Cranmer held a major potlatch ceremony. The ceremony was interrupted by a large number of Canadian policemen, led by William Halliday who represented the Canadian government. Twenty three Natives were sent to prison for extended periods. They were charged and convicted of crimes such as dancing, making speeches and giving gifts. In addition twenty two others had their sentences suspended, but only after their entire tribe handed over all of the Native ceremonial masks, costumes and other regalia used in the Potlatch ceremony. In addition they had to promise never to participate in a potlatch again. A vast number of Native artifacts were confiscated, and these artifacts were presented to museums who accepted them without challenging the fact that the valuable items were confiscated (stolen) by government officials in a raid. [4].

The U'Mista Cultural Centre presents outstanding art work created by First Nation peoples. Some treasures on display are the artifacts that had been confiscated during the devastating raid by Canadian police officers back in December 1921. The first curator of U'Mista Cultural Centre was Gloria Cranmer Webster, who is the granddaughter of George Hunt. Hunt was the Native, fluent in English, who collaborated over a number of years with the anthropologist Franz Boas and taught him the Kwak'wala language, for which Boas then created a written language. Hunt and Boas then carefully recorded traditional customs and ceremonies so that all were in a written language form before government laws in the early part of the twentieth century prohibited their practice.

The U'Mista Cultural Centre opened in 1980, and successfully carries out the following aims:

1. To collect, preserve and exhibit Native artifacts of cultural, artistic and historic value to the Kwagu't People.
2. To promote and foster carving, dancing, ceremonials and other cultural and artistic activities engaged in by the Kwagu't People.
3. To collect, record and make available information and records relating to the language and history of the Kwagu't people for the use of the Kwagu't people.

4. To promote, build and maintain facilities for carrying out the above aims and objects.

5. To recover from other institutions and individuals artifacts and records of cultural, artistic and historical value to the Kwagu't people.

Note: Not all of the confiscated items from the 1921 raid have been returned. The British Museum in London has refused to return an artifact the Kwakwaka'wakw people assert is central to their culture. All other museums that had booty from the raid in 1921 have returned the valuable artifacts that had been in their possession: The Royal Ontario Museum in Toronto, the Canadian Museum of Civilization in Ottawa, and the National Museum of the American Indian, now associated with the Smithsonian Institution. Only the British Museum, holder of a single transformation mask, a crest that opens up to reveal a human head, has refused. The museum director, Dr. Robert Anderson, is reported to have said, "My job is to arrange for the presentation of world cultures to the five million people a year who come here. I would in fact be breaking British law (if I returned it)." Andrea Sanborn of U'Mista Centre is persisting in efforts to have the valuable item returned.[5] I support her efforts.

The efforts by the Canadian government to restrict aboriginal people by laws prohibiting cultural practices, as described above, was followed by a massive program incorporated into the Canadian Indian Residential School System to rid Canada of aboriginal ways. They took the children away.

Canadian Indian Residential School System

Founded in the 19th century, the Canadian Indian Residential School System was designed to force the assimilation of Canadian Aboriginal peoples into European-Canadian society. The program has been aptly described as "killing the Indian in the child."[6] Enrollment in the residential program was mandatory by law starting in 1850. Although the program was fiercely opposed by aboriginal leaders, parents faced imprisonment if they failed to cooperate when their children reached the age of six through age fifteen, when attendance in the residential programs was required.

Although funded by the Canadian government, the residential programs were run by Christian churches of various denominations. Roman Catholics ran 60% of the residential programs; the Anglican Church of Canada and the United Church of Canada ran 30%; and the remaining 10% of the residential schools were run by Presbyterian, Congregational and Methodist churches.[7]

The educational goals of the residential schools, in working towards assimilation, included the following:

The students were required to speak either English or French. The use of Native language was suppressed. More specifically the prohibition of speaking Aboriginal languages extended even outside the classroom. Students were subject to corporal punishment for even lapses of speaking in their own language.

The Christian faith was taught and any practice of Native religious beliefs was suppressed and students who violated this policy were subject to corporal punishment.

Agricultural skills were taught and traditional Native hunter-gatherer skills were rejected as primitive.

If a student were "successful," that is "sufficiently advanced in the elementary branches of education" he would qualify to be given land and enfranchised, which would remove any tribal affiliation or treaty rights. (The Gradual Civilization Act of 1857).

Native children who were forced to attend residential schools faced severe and inevitable losses. They faced the loss of their Native language, loss of companionship and support of their families of origin, and they were confronted with the knowledge that their society and culture were in the process of extinction. Unfortunately, many Native children who attended Church run residential schools were also physically and sexually assaulted by their caretakers. Who would believe reports given by Native children living in a Christian residential school that they were physically or sexually abused? Apparently not many people believed these reports. Reports began to appear as early as 1900, but those initial written reports were suppressed and not made public until the 1960's, when large numbers of reports were made public and Canadians paid attention.

In the late 20th century widespread recognition over sexual abuse in residential schools finally led religious denominations to issue apologies to the Aboriginal peoples of Canada. The United Church of Canada and the Anglican Church issued an apology in 1986. The Canadian Conference of Catholic Bishops held a three-day meeting in Saskatoon in March 1991 and issued an apology for "the pain, suffering and alienation that so many experienced" in residential schools. The Presbyterian Church issued an apology in the fall of 1994. Miller, in his comprehensive review of physical and sexual abuse of Native children in residential schools, states that "none of the missionary bodies apologized for the failure to deal with the problems earlier, even where the existence of abuse and the identity of the perpetrator had been known."[8]

Gathering strength: Building a Better Relationship between Aboriginal And non-Aboriginal Canadians

In January 1998, Jane Stewart, Minister of Indian Affairs and Northern development, initiated what many hoped would form a new era in the relationship between Aboriginal and non Aboriginal Canadians. She announced the creation of *Gathering Strength—Canada's Aboriginal Action Plan*, which calls for 1) recognizing past mistakes and injustices, 2) commencing reconciliation, and 3) rebuilding on strengths and successes.

Reconciliation and expression of regret

Coinciding with the announcement of Gathering Strength, the Government of Canada in 1998 offered a Statement of Reconciliation to aboriginal people in Canada. A lengthy portion of this Statement of Reconciliation says:

> As Aboriginal and non-Aboriginal Canadians seek to move forward together in a process of renewal, it is essential that we deal with the legacies of the past affecting the Aboriginal peoples of Canada, including the First Nations, Inuit and Metis. Our purpose is not to rewrite history, but, rather to learn from our past and to find ways to deal with the negative impacts that certain historical decisions continue to have in our society today.
>
> The ancestors of First Nations, Inuit and Metis peoples lived on this continent long before explorers from other continents first came to North America. For thousands of years before this country was founded, they enjoyed their own forms of governments. Diverse, vibrant Aboriginal Nations had ways of life rooted in fundamental values concerning their relationships to the Creator, the environment and each other, in the role of elders as the living memory of their ancestors. And in their responsibilities as custodians of the lands, waters and resources of their homelands.
>
> The assistance and spiritual values of the Aboriginal peoples who welcomed the newcomers to this continent too often have been forgotten. The contributions made by all Aboriginal peoples to Canada's development, and the contributions they continue to make to our society today, have not been properly acknowledged. The Government of Canada today, on behalf of all Canadians, acknowledges those contributions.
>
> Sadly, our history with respect to the treatment of Aboriginal people is not something in which we can take pride. As a country, we are burdened by past actions that resulted in weakening the identity of Aboriginal people, suppressing their language and cultures, and outlawing spiritual practices. The government of Canada today formally expresses to all Aboriginal people in Canada our profound regret for past actions of the federal government which have contributed

to these difficult pages in the history of our relationship together.[10]

In addition, the 1998 *Statement of Reconciliation* specifically included a statement of apology to those people who had been sexually or physically traumatized while attending residential schools. The government established the Aboriginal Healing Foundation, which was funded to establish community-based healing projects to attempt to heal the "innumerable events and countless injuries to First Nations individuals and communities."

In that context Justice Minister Irwin Cotler called the decision to place First Nation children in church-run residential schools "the single most harmful, disgraceful and racist act in our history." The point raised by Cotler is that, aside from the serious issues of sexual and physical abuse suffered by a large percentage of Native Canadians in residential care, the whole practice of mandatory residential confinement of Native children represented wrongful confinement. [11].

The people of Canada have moved forward by acknowledging their contribution to the tragedy and their willingness to make extensive and costly amends. On November 23, 2005, the Canadian government announced a $1.9 billion compensation package to help thousands of survivors of abuse suffered at native residential schools. National Chief Phil Fontaine of the Assembly of First Nations has stated that the package covers "decades in time, innumerable events, and countless injuries to First Nations individuals and communities." Fountaine is among those who suffered abuse while in custody in residential placement. Among other uses of the monies, all First Nation persons who were enrolled in a residential school are eligible for financial compensation that takes into account their years of confinement. The Catholic Church has paid an additional $79 million, according to the Canadian bishops' conference. [12]

Chief Fontaine meets with Pope Benedict XVI

On April 29, 2009, Chief Fontaine, and other First Nation leaders, met with Pope Benedict XVI and reviewed the history of abuse suffered by First Nation citizens in Church—run residential programs. Following the meeting, the Vatican released an apology:

> *His Holiness recalled that since the earliest days of her presence in Canada, the Church, particularly through her missionary personnel, has closely accompanied the indigenous peoples. Given the sufferings that some indigenous children experienced in the Canadian Residential School system, the Holy Father expressed his sorrow at the anguish caused by the deplorable conduct of some members of the Church and he offered his sympathy and prayerful solidarity. His Holiness emphasized that acts of abuse cannot be tolerated in society. He prayed that all those affected would experience healing, and he encouraged First Nation People to continue to move forward with renewed hope.*[13]

Of 29 First Nation members of the delegation who went to Rome for a hoped for meeting with Pope Benedict XVI, five had a private meeting with the Pope. Phil Fontaine stated afterwards, "What we wanted the Pope to say to us was that he was sorry and . . . that he deeply felt for us. We heard that very clearly today."[14].

In addition to the five Indians who met with the Pope, five church representatives also were present. Archbishop of Winnipeg James Weisgerber, who is head of Canada's bishop conference, stated that "the coming to Rome was a high point on the road to reconciliation."

As stated above the United Church of Canada, Presbyterian and Anglican churches had previously apologized for their roles in the abuse of First Nation peoples.

In summary the forced attendance of aboriginals into Canadian schools was an effort by church personnel and government officials to assimilate Native children by the extinction of their language, their Native religious beliefs, their ceremonies and all aspects of their culture. In the process a very large number of these children were sexually and physically abused. Pope Benedict XVI apologized only for the sexual and physical abuse, not the overall tragedy of the Church-run residential schools that sought to extinguish the Native Indian way of life. I view the apology by the Pope as only a start. If it is not followed up by a more comprehensive and thoughtful apology with amends, the apology is woefully inadequate. I have hope that my fellow Christians will come to see the larger picture, which includes a dark side of the Christian church in how it carried its message to Aboriginal peoples.

Port Hardy

As I left Alert Bay for the short 20 mile run to Port Hardy, I shifted my focus. I put away my notes from what I learned and experienced at the museum and the interesting visit along the grounds viewing the totem poles and outstanding Native carvings. My focus was on preparation for the crossing of Queen Charlotte Sound.

Port Hardy, located near the northern end of Vancouver Island, is the last place to obtain fuel and provisions before crossing the open waters of Queen Charlotte Sound and then continuing north on the Inside Passage. It is a pleasant town geared for boaters, both major commercial fishing boats as well as private cruising boats. The harbor master is consistently accommodating. I fueled up at the Chevron station, and used the on shore shower facilities. I then stocked up on groceries. Aside from two small Native villages (New Bella Bella and Klemtu), there are no towns, villages or communities to obtain fuel or provisions until Prince Rupert, a distance of 270 nautical miles.

I gathered information about weather, including expected winds, wave conditions, and prospects for fog or rain. I reviewed tide charts to plan for optimal times and a range of satisfactory times to leave port. Marine weather forecasts in this area are outstanding. I reviewed my navigational charts that cover the route from Port Hardy to Safety Cove on Calvert Island and on up to Fitz Hugh Sound. I established way points in latitude and longitude from Port Hardy to Safety Cove, an area beyond the open-ocean crossing. I prepared myself to wait if conditions are too marginal. I have made this open-ocean crossing in fog three times. However, I have not started this trip when in addition to fog there were also bad seas or a combination of moderate seas and an ebbing tide. The global positioning system (GPS) and navigational charts make it possible to follow an appropriate route under conditions of poor visibility.

Crossing Queen Charlotte Sound (approximate distance 75 miles): Port Hardy to Safety Cove

This portion of the Inside passage is not "protected" but is open to large swells and the potential for storm force winds coming in from the ocean. Tidal currents and fog are additional concerns. These may combine. For example, during an ebb tide strong currents will pour out of the large inlets, such as Rivers Inlet. If these tidal currents are met with wind and waves from the opposite direction (the open ocean), the seas will be very rough. Fog is another concern.

A word about fog. Fog at sea used to bother me a lot. However, based on experience I now reduce my anxiety about boating in the fog by establishing course lines, taking compass readings and measuring distances between way points before leaving the dock. While underway I keep track of boat speed and time when way points are reached, and I make regular entries in my log. I use a GPS to continuously monitor position in latitude and longitude. I have made this crossing under conditions of heavy fog, but I have not had an unpleasant crossing. With these very standard precautions I have been able to make the crossing under conditions of fog in a reasonable time for my vessel. Averaging about 15 knots, it takes between four and five hours to go from Port Hardy to Safety Cove, an area sheltered within Calvert Island. Under more difficult conditions, I have made the trip safely in ten hours. At other times I have remained at Port Hardy a day or two until conditions settled down.

Pruth Bay on Calvert Island

About seven miles north of Safety Cove is Kwakshua Channel, which lies between Calvert Island and Hecate Island. About five miles into Kwakshua Channel is Pruth Bay and an excellent anchorage. My wife and I took that side trip in 1995, and anchored about one-quarter mile from the west end of the bay. We launched our dinghy, rowed to shore, and walked around the grounds and buildings of the Hakai Beach Resort. The resort offers lodging, meals, boats and guides who take guests on fishing trips in nearby waters for salmon and halibut. What we especially enjoyed was the short hike from the beach at Pruth Bay to the beach facing the ocean on the west side of Calvert Island. The beach is strewn with logs beached from heavy winter storms. The Pacific Ocean west of Calvert Island is at the same latitude as Siberia.

Namu

In early June 1997, Dick Ecklund, a retired engineer from North Carolina, and I were making this trip and had just come across the sound from Port Hardy in the fog. As we approached Calvert Island, we left the fog behind us and enjoyed sunny skies and mild temperatures. Moving north through Fitz Hugh Sound, we came across several Dall porpoises. They swam right up to us and made multiple leaps along the waves created by the bow of our boat. They turned at will, jumping freely and at tremendous speed, which I estimated at about 25 to 30 knots. They must have thought our speed (about 16 knots) was slow indeed. Dall porpoises are the only mammals in the whale group that actively play with a boat and surf the waves coming off either the bow or the stern. Good numbers of them are seen along the Canadian portion of the Inside Passage.

As we continued on our way we decided to go to Namu and explore the ghost town. Namu is about 20 miles north of Safety Cove, just off the eastern shore of Fitz Hugh Sound. It is situated so close to the main route of the Inside Passage that it is not out of the way should one stop there. As Dick and I slowly approached this town we were struck by how pretty it looked from a distance. We could see a large building (the cannery) on the northwest section of "town" and attractive white-painted houses dotting the hillside. We saw what looked like a dormitory and a number of other large buildings.

We tied up our boat to a float east of the cannery building and met a man at the company dock. He introduced himself as Jack Cabena, the caretaker and the sole resident of Namu. He welcomed us and said we were free to walk around, take pictures and ask questions.

Dick and I walked up the ramp and looked through a window of the company store, still stocked with canned food although it had not been open for decades. We visited a warehouse that housed seven large diesel-powered generators that once supplied electricity for the town and the substantial power needs of the cannery. While we were there, Jack Cabena activated one engine for maintenance purposes. All the generators were in operating condition, he said. We hiked to a large lake one mile southeast of the town and admired the large diameter pipes, constructed of wood, that supplied the substantial water needs of the cannery and people who once lived and worked at Namu.

Two First Nation men recall a past and vibrant Namu

As we hiked back from the lake to town, we noticed two men approaching in an outboard-powered, open aluminum skiff. They ran their boat almost to shore in front of the large building that looked like a dorm. They stopped only 30 feet from where Dick and I were standing. I knew they likely did not come from Port Hardy in their type of boat, and the only town nearby was the town of New Bella Bella about 15 miles northwest of Namu.

I asked if they were fishing.

"No," said the boat operator, "Just looking."

I asked if they could tell me about Namu. Neither said a word.

"Are you familiar with the name Boas?" I asked.

"Do you mean Franz Boas, the anthropologist?" One replied. I said "Yes." That broke the ice. Both men said they had read three books written by Boas and told me they appreciated his work. They were very knowledgeable about the work of Boas, who struggled to preserve the language(s) and cultural practices of First Nation peoples of British Columbia.

The man operating the boat went on to say that he and his friend had worked at Namu for about 15 years, from the 1960's and up until the cannery closed in about 1976. He told us there were three kinds of workers and they were separated by wages, work assignments and where they lived. He pointed to several large buildings and said, "Natives from New Bella Bella and surrounding areas lived in those buildings." He added, "Chinese laborers worked at the canneries after their work was completed on the Canadian Railway system. They lived in that large building in front of us. They were paid "Chinese wages," he said, with a subdued chuckle.

"Some of us Natives fished with company boats and delivered the fish to the cannery. We were paid 30 cents a fish, regardless of the size. Others of us worked in the cannery, including a lot of Native women. Chinese workers also worked in the cannery."

The man paused and then said: "Then this cannery shut down; in fact, the only canneries still operating are at Prince Rupert or Vancouver. All the canneries in central BC are shut down. That is too bad for us. At one time about 39 percent of the commercial catch in BC was made by Natives; now it is down to about 2 percent. Many Natives worked in canneries like this one, but all of those workers lost their jobs and many are now on welfare."

I asked him why the cannery had been shut down and why the Natives were now almost completely out of the business of salmon fishing and fish processing. He paused for a while and must have remembered how our conversation had started. I had asked him about the anthropologist Franz Boaz and he had already done his homework. Now, when I asked about Native fishing, their work at the canneries, and the end of it all, it was my time to do some reading and homework. He said,

When you get to Prince Rupert look it up. They have an excellent library. Learn about the decisions of the company and the laws enacted by the government that resulted in these changes. And then, if you have any questions give me a call." He then gave me his name, phone number and fax number.

New Bella Bella

From Namu we proceeded north into Fisher Channel, and just past Fog Rocks we turned to the west at Kaiete Point and into Lama Passage to the First Nation town of New Bella Bella. Fuel is available and the public docks offer moorage for transient vessels at no charge.

Greenpeace is frequently present in New Bella Bella. I spoke with Catherine Stewart of Greenpeace in Canada. She explained that Greenpeace is attempting to alert Canadians to the destructive clear cutting logging practices that have essentially removed all old-growth timber in British Columbia, with little regard for providing buffers near streams and rivers or on steep slopes. These destructive practices have seriously damaged the habitat for salmon and are one factor that has contributed to reduced wild salmon runs in British Columbia.

I then spoke with five members of Greenpeace who had just returned to New Bella Bella after having chained themselves to a yarder to halt logging in a nearby timber harvest area. A motto of Greenpeace is that when industrial practices are destructive to the environment, they will not occur without witness or protest. The group of five—three women and two men—had spent five days and nights in the outdoors to make their protest.

Klemtu

Klemtu is another Native village, about 40 miles north of New Bella Bella. Two miles north of New Bella Bella a lighthouse marks the entrance to Seaforth Channel. Thirteen miles along that channel, we arrived at Ivory Island and the entrance to Milbanke Sound. Milbanke Sound is open to swells from the north Pacific; when the conditions are hazardous, it is wise to avoid it and follow the more protected route of Reid Channel, which leads to Jackson Passage and cuts west to Finlayson Channel. Klemtu is situated on Swindle Island, just west of Finlayson Channel. The small harbor is extremely well protected, with Cone Island only 200 yards to the east, separated from Swindle Island by a narrow but deep channel. Klemtu once had a cannery, but it closed in 1969, as did all the others along the many miles of the Inside passage in British Columbia.

The Anglican Church at Klemtu

In July of 1996, I pulled into Klemtu on a Sunday afternoon, fueled up and decided to stay there overnight. I parked the boat within the inner harbor and walked through the small town. I noticed an Anglican Church about two blocks from the south part of the harbor. A sign indicated the evening service would begin at 7 p.m. I returned to my boat, fixed a dinner, and around 6:30 p.m. I heard church music broadcasting from large speakers attached to the outside of the church. I walked to the church and arrived in front of the open doors just before the scheduled starting time. I looked inside and saw that the church was empty except for the minister who stood in front by the pulpit, and a woman, probably his wife, who stood beside him. I cancelled my church plans and walked away from the entrance and back towards the center of town. I came across two elderly Native men sitting on a bench along the boardwalk along the west side of the bay. I stopped and asked if local Natives attend the church. The church music was still playing in the background, but I saw that no one had entered the church.

"No!" said one of the men. The other man looked at me and shook his head in agreement indicating no. One of the men than said the following,

> We elders believe it is very important for the young people to learn about our history, our language and our customs. If you want to see something, go over to the dock on the other side of this bay. There you will see a canoe, about 40 feet long, that was built by a master canoe-builder with the help of seven young men from our Native village (Klemtu). The master canoe-builder is from Kitimat; his father was a master canoe-builder, as was his grandfather. He learned the art of canoe-building from them and he is passing on his knowledge and expert craftsmanship to some of our young men. This is very important to us and we are very proud. Next year some tribal leaders will paddle that sea-going canoe through the Inside Passage to Victoria and then to Neah Bay on the coast of Washington. In the past, this was a very traditional voyage for our people, and we want to repeat this trip at least once every four years.

I walked over to look at the canoe. I was stunned by the high quality of the workmanship. It was made out of one very large cedar log, with slats of hewn boards set as seats to provide for a crew of twelve or more. I photographed the canoe, returned to the two men, and expressed my admiration for the workmanship. They told me the project took one full year to complete This was a reminder to me of a renewal in British Columbia, as well as in Alaska, of Native culture as evidenced by a resurgence of interest in art, woodwork, carving, Native language usage and ceremonies.

I interpret the absence of church attendance in Klemtu as a statement of rejection of those who had for hundreds of years coerced indigenous peoples to abandon Native ways and adopt an exclusive adherence to European-American language, customs and religious beliefs.

The small Native community of Klemtu is the last inhabited village along the Canadian Inside Passage until one arrives in Prince Rupert, about 140 miles away. The passage from this point is a continuation of a natural marine water passage that is narrow and deep and protected by steep, heavily forested coastal mountains on the mainland side and steep forested hills on the large islands that separate the passage from the Pacific. Waterfalls are evident on both sides of the Inside Passage. The deepest part of the entire Alaskan-Canadian Inside Passage is in Finlayson Channel, just east of Klemtu. The depth reaches an astonishing 418 fathoms (2508 feet).

Princess Royal Island: Home of elusive white bears and an abandoned company town

Forty miles north of Klemtu, tucked into a small bay on the east side of Princess Royal Island, is the abandoned cannery town of Butedale, once operated by the Canadian Fishing Company. The plant closed in 1969 as part of the massive restructuring of the commercial salmon industry in B.C. following the enactment of the Davis Plan. My son Paul and I spent two days at Butedale in June of 1995; we hiked to a large lake about a half mile from Butedale and walked through the rain forest. The large lake has an outlet creating a fast moving stream that cascades down the steep hillside into the salt water bay at

Butedale. The Cannery owners had built a large hydropower plant to create the very substantial power needed for the cannery operation and the housing facilities for the hundreds of workers. When the cannery was shut down, no one turned off the lights and the town of Butedale remained lit for two years before the system broke down.

As we hiked through the thick undergrowth and forest by the lake we looked for clearing spots in hopes of spotting some white bears. Though rare, they are more prevalent on Princess Royal Island than anywhere else. These white bears are in fact black bears with white fur. The name is Ursus Americanus Kermodei, which was designated by the naturalist William Hornaday in 1904. There is speculation that these bears have white fur due to adaptation during the Ice Age and that the trait continues. In Canada, these bears are protected by law. Paul and I did not have the luck of seeing any of these bears, although we did see some deer. We very much enjoyed the hike and appreciated even the chance to see such a bear in the wild. Later on our journey we saw bears and other wildlife.

Bishop Bay Hot Springs

About 12 miles north of Butedale is the end of Princess Royal Island and the beginning of McKay Reach, which begins the last stretch of the passage to Prince Rupert. However, just eight miles north of the entrance to McKay Reach is Bishop Bay and its famous hot springs. Local people from Kitimat have built an enclosed and covered pool, which is fed by a continuous flow of hot spring water. The area is user-maintained and is well worth a stop and a lengthy, refreshing hot bath. A 70-foot float provides moorage at no charge.

Grenville Channel to Prince Rupert

From Bishop Bay one must backtrack to McKay Reach, cross Wright Sound and enter Grenville Channel. This channel is the narrowest and straightest part of the Inside Passage. The channel is 45 miles long, and on the mainland side there are several excellent inlets providing good anchorage, including Lowe Inlet, Klewnuggit Inlet,

Baker Inlet, and West Inlet. Grenville Channel ends at the mouth or delta of the Skeena River, which is second to the Fraser River in terms of its importance to the commercial salmon industry in B.C.

Prince Rupert, the "gateway to Alaska" city, was established in 1905 as the terminus of Canada's second transcontinental railroad—the Canadian National Railroad. The city is situated on Kaien Island and was founded by a U.S. citizen, Charles Hayes, who recognized its potential to be a world-class port and transportation center. Prince Rupert has the second deepest harbor in the world and is a major transportation center for shipping fish and timber. The northern B.C. fishing fleet is centered in Prince Rupert. The Skeena River, south of Prince Rupert, and the Nass River, north of Prince Rupert, continue to be major salmon producers. As stated above, fishermen, with fast and modern fishing fleets, now bring boatloads of fish from distant fishing grounds as well as from the local area.

The city received its name in 1906 as a result of a contest sponsored by the Grand Trunk Pacific Railway. The company offered a prize of $250 for the best name for the city. Eleanor MacDonald won the prize with the suggestion of Prince Rupert, named after the first governor of the Hudson Bay Company. The railroad was completed in 1914 at a cost comparable to the construction cost of the Panama Canal. With a population of about 18,000, Prince Rupert is the second largest city on the B.C. mainland coast. The only other city on the north B.C. mainland coast is Kitimat, with a population of about 12,000. The Native villages, such as New Bella Bella and Klemtu, are much smaller in population and are situated on islands, separated from the mainland by the Inside Passage. This is a very pleasant and modern small city with excellent restaurants and ample moorage facilities for transient boaters. Ketchikan, Alaska, is just 90 miles away—and the border to Alaska is part way across the Dixon Entrance.

One of the pleasures of cruising is meeting people. I once met a young man in Hoonah, Alaska, who sailed solo from Japan to Glacier Bay. I have met sailors from Western Europe who crossed the Atlantic and went through the Panama Canal to reach their goal of Glacier Bay, Alaska. I have met sailors from New Zealand and Australia while cruising in Alaskan waters. All of them arrived in Alaska on their own boats. In 1996 when I pulled into a marina at Prince Rupert, I moored next to a 36' sailboat. I may have banged the dock a bit as I pulled in. A man appeared out of the cabin of his sailboat, smiled and said, "Hello, my name is Jonathan. Where are you headed?" We chatted a bit, he at the back of his boat and me on the back of my boat. I talked about my previous trips to Alaska and some of the highlights. He invited me aboard his sailboat. For a while we chatted about this and that, for example, the scenery, the mountains and glaciers, and the wildlife including bears, eagles, wolves and whales. Then our conversation shifted to a discussion of First Nations people in B.C. and the Tlingit Indians in Southeast Alaska. Jonathan made comments like the following,

Of all the tribal groups in North America, the Indians of the Inside Passage had left the richest body of ceremonial and domestic art, and the most voluminous oral literature. Their culture was the most nearly intact because it had been invaded late in the New World Discovery.[15] Then he said the following,

The systematic extermination of Indian languages, customs, and beliefs, carried out by zealous Christian ministers and government agents, had been so shockingly successful that no present-day Indian could possibly know what his great-great-great-grandparents had really believed. So it was now easy to attribute to the ancestors almost any belief that was thought desirable for them to have possessed.[16]

I absolutely share his concern, but things have changed a bit since we shared our thoughts and perspective on July 12th, 1996. I have witnessed a remarkable effort and commitment by First Nation people to find their way back to the essence of their culture and sacred values. This includes not only the outstanding U'Mista Cultural Centre but also the efforts such as the master carver from Kitimat who was willing to donate a year of his time to teach young men in Klemtu the art and skill of building a traditional Native canoe. Furthermore, the Canadian government and all their church denominations have made some level of apology to the Aboriginal people of Canada, and the government is committed to substantial financial amends. In part this reflects on the ability of aboriginal people in Canada to present their case. They have done so.

I asked Jonathan about his career. He said, "I am a writer. I left London about six years ago to come to Seattle. I marvel at the library at the University of Washington. It is better than the libraries in London. As for writing, I write about the sea." He gave me a copy of a book he had compiled, *The Oxford Book of the Sea,* and he signed it for me.

He asked about me. I said, "I am a retired clinical psychologist, and served on the faculty at the Oregon Health Sciences University. (I paused, then said) I too was in London, but it was back in December 1941, during my family's escape from Nazi-occupied Norway. I was four at the time." I told him I also write, and I gave him a copy of *Fishing Beyond the Buoys.* The book relates to my experiences as a commercial salmon troller off the coasts of Oregon and Washington. The "Jonathan" I spoke with is the author Jonathan Raban. In 1999, he published his best selling book, *Passage To Juneau: A Sea and Its Meanings.*

North Pacific Cannery Village Museum: Port Edward, British Columbia

The North Pacific Cannery was built in 1889 at Inverness Passage near the mouth of the Skeena River. It closed in 1972 but was declared a National Historic Site on its 100th birthday in 1989, and is open to the public as a historic museum. The location of the museum at Port Edward is only a few miles south of Prince Rupert. Information about the North Pacific Village Museum is available at the Museum of Northern B.C. in Prince Rupert.

British Columbia is a resource-rich Province, with timber and fish (particularly salmon) being of critical importance to the economy. For thousands of years the ancestors of current First Nation Peoples developed effective means of catching and preserving salmon.

Between the years 1864 and 1966, 250 canneries were built in British Columbia. The number of fish processing plants is now reduced to six, and those six are very large and modern plants in either Prince Rupert or Vancouver. They now work 12 months a year and often 24 hours a day. They handle many kinds of fish in addition to salmon, as well as shrimp and crab. Most of the fish are now processed and shipped either fresh or frozen. Canning is much less important than previously.

The North Pacific Cannery is the oldest intact cannery on the B.C. coast. Many of the abandoned canneries in the middle section of the Inside Passage in B.C. were built on pilings, and the structures are rotting and falling into the sea. Many small Native communities that supported these canneries are also abandoned and covered over by the heavy growth, casualties of the temperate rain forest environment. That makes it all the more important that British Columbia decided to keep this cannery intact and open to the public to create a better understanding and appreciation of the past.

David Boyce reviews the British Columbia Salmon Cannery Industry

I met David Boyce at the Port Edward Cannery Village Museum in 1997. Mr. Boyce has studied extensively the history of the salmon cannery industry and has written research reports on Salmon Cannery lifestyle for both the Museum Industry in Seattle and the Canadian Museum of Civilization in Hull. I was particularly interested in obtaining answers to comments and issues raised by the two Natives I had met at the abandoned cannery at Namu the year earlier.

The Role of Chinese Workers in the Cannery Industry.

I repeated to Mr. Boyce what I had heard from the two Natives at Namu. The Natives had told me, "Chinese laborers worked at the canneries after their work was done on the Canadian Railway system. The Chinese workers lived in this dorm (pointing to a large building) and we lived over here. The Chinese were paid Chinese wages." Their comment implied clear cut segregation of workers by race.

Boyce stated that the separation of workers by color in fact represented the ethnocentric mindset of the cannery owners; *If the different racial groups do not have the opportunity to interact on a social or work time basis then each group will be ignorant of what is being paid out in wages to the other groups.* (This assures that) *no form of organization can take place and the management can continue to dictate the terms of the employment.*[17]

Boyce continued to focus on Chinese workers at the canneries. He stated that many Chinese men were brought to British Columbia each May from cities like San Francisco, Seattle, and Victoria and were sent back when the canning operations ended sometime in September. The Chinese workers had specific tasks such as can maker, fish cleaner, retort man, labeler and box maker:

Can Maker: This involved cutting the shapes from the tin and soldering them together with lead. They worked in poor lighting conditions, and of course worked continuously with hot soldering irons. Thirty men could make 7000 cans in a day. Other Chinese men made wooden crate boxes for the cans.

Retort Man: These men were in charge of the steam driven Retort ovens for cooking the fish in the cans. They also loaded and unloaded cans. These men worked in the presence of high heat and steam; the work was dangerous because the cans sometimes exploded.

Box Maker and labeler: Using locally milled wood, these workers manufactured cases to hold 48 one-pound cans of salmon. The labelers required good hand-to-eye coordination and tolerance for fumes from the glues.

Pay for Chinese Workers: The cannery operators did not pay the Chinese workers directly. Instead, a man identified as the "China Boss" negotiated his own contract with the cannery. He then hired Chinese workers from as far away as San Francisco and Seattle and worked out the terms of employment. He was also in charge of working conditions and safety of the Chinese workers. If he paid the Chinese workers little, the "China Boss" could make a substantial profit. The Chinese workers sent most of their earnings back to their families in China. Chinese women comprised only 1.2 percent of the Chinese population, a ratio of one Chinese woman to 82 Chinese men. Then Boyce referred to the infamous exclusion law of 1923.

The Chinese Immigration Act and Head Tax, 1885: The Chinese Exclusion Act of 1923

Institutionalized racism in the late 19th century and much of the 20th century fostered the belief that immigrants, such as those from China and Japan, were a burden on white society. Chinese immigrants (males only) were accepted during the construction of the Canadian Pacific Railway (CPR) from 1880 to 1885, when the government needed cheap and expert labor to carve the railroad by dynamiting a huge path through the Canadian Rockies in British Columbia. During the construction, observers reported seeing numerous bodies floating down the Frazer River resulting from accidents during the construction of the railroad. [18]

Between 1880 and 1885 about 15,000 Chinese laborers were brought into Canada for this work. How dangerous was the work performed by the Chinese? In the first year (1880) 5,000 Chinese workers came to work on the Canadian railroad in British Columbia. Three thousand five hundred of them were killed in accidents that first year. The Chinese workers had hoped that their work would help them escape from the crushing poverty they experienced in China.[19]. That was not to be. In 1885, with the railroad finished, the Chinese workers who survived did not have enough money to return to China.

The Canadian government wanted no more Chinese workers and instituted the Chinese Immigration Act and Head Tax in 1885, which required a tax of $50 for a Chinese person to come to Canada. This was increased to $500 in 1903. In that year the tax would have been equal to two years wages for a Chinese worker in Canada. The Chinese Exclusion Act of 1923 went further than the "Head Tax" and simply prohibited any Chinese person coming from China to Canada. This Act was repealed in 1947.

Boyce reports that up until 1923, about 24% of the workforce at the canneries were of Chinese origin. After the exclusion law of 1923, the numbers dropped and the percentage of workers from the mid

1930's to the year 1945 was about 8%. The much reduced numbers represent those who had come prior to the Exclusion Act and remained in Canada.[20]

The history of the Chinese story in Canada from 1880 until 1947 reminds me of a statement made by a friend of mine who survived the Holocaust. Alter Wiener has said, "All Jews suffered in the Holocaust, but not all who suffered were Jews." The suffering of the Chinese people who worked so hard during that period is a tragedy that we should not forget.[21] I chose to include this very brief account of the Chinese life in Canada during this period, while my main focus is on Native Americans, because the treatment experienced by the Chinese also reflects the institutionalized racist mindset so prevalent among us Caucasians.

First Nation Workers

The two Native men I met at Namu stated that Native fishermen caught about 38 percent of the salmon, prior to the shut down of the canneries in the central reaches of the Inside Passage. In fact, David Boyce presented figures that show the significant contribution of Native Canadians to the commercial fishing effort. He cited numbers that between the years 1906-1928 40% of the fishing fleet were Native, 32 % were White fishermen and 28% were Japanese fishermen. (These figures pertain to fishermen and not workers in the cannery.) During WW II the Japanese were prohibited from participation in the industry and many White men were drafted, so the percent of Native fishermen increased. Boyce reported that in 1949 59% percent of the work force was First Nations staff.

The roles of male Natives were fishing and boat building; and they were paid by the management. Native women and older Native children made up almost 40% of the Native workforce. They worked either in net making or fish cleaning, working along side Chinese workers. They also were paid by the "China Boss," and not by the management per se.[22].

Native Fishing Restrictions

In 1904, cannery operators convinced government officials in Ottawa that if the Natives on the Skeena River did not stop their salmon fishing, the canning industry on the Skeena would be destroyed. Hans Helgesen, a fisheries overseer, was sent by the Canadian government to inform the chief of the Babine Indians that their fish traps on the Skeena River were illegal and must be removed. He also told the chief that it was illegal for Indians to sell fish independent of the canneries, and that they must have a permit to catch fish for food, known as subsistence fishing. Natives could fish only out of company-owned boats and deliver their catch to the canneries, and they could work in the canneries. Other fishing done by Natives was viewed as poaching, unless they had a permit for subsistence fishing. These policies severely restricted Native fishing even for their own use; however, Native fishermen continued to supply a large percentage of salmon delivered to the canneries.[23].

Not until 1942 were Natives in B.C. given the right to purchase and own commercial fishing vessels; Sames Sewid, a Kwakiutl seine fisherman, was the first Native in B.C. to own his own boat as an independent fisherman. He sold his catch to canneries. Eventually many Natives were able to build or purchase a vessel for commercial fishing, but they could not independently sell fish. Nor could they rise to the point of ownership or management of a cannery or a fish processing plant.[24].

The Davis Plan

On September 8, 1968, Jack Davis, the Canadian fisheries minister, announced a plan to limit licenses of commercial fishing vessels. Under the assertion that there were too many boats and fishermen chasing too few fish, he announced a plan that significantly changed commercial salmon fishing in B.C. He announced a two-tier vessel license program. Highly productive fishermen—those who had landed 10,000 pounds of salmon or more in the years 1967 or 1968—were given "A" licenses. Those who had caught less than 10,000 pounds were given a "B" license. The "B" licenses were set to expire in ten years. Companies that owned a large number of small fishing boats leased to fishermen could trade in the "B" permits, canceling out their smaller vessels, and obtain additional "A" permits. They then built new, large and fast commercial fishing boats. These new and modern boats had effective refrigeration systems which enabled the fishermen to stay on the fishing grounds for days at a time until they were at capacity with fish. With a full load of fish they travelled either to Vancouver or Prince Rupert to unload their large catches to modern fish processing plants. This caused all the commercial processing plants along the Inside Passage to close abruptly.[25]

By 1969, more than a thousand shore workers—mostly Natives—lost their jobs. More job losses followed. The great majority of Natives who had acquired their own commercial boats had "B" licenses, which expired in 1979.

David Boyce stated that many of the barriers have since been removed, and that Natives are gradually assuming more important roles in the Salmon fishing industry. Beyond the role of independent fishermen, they are now able to move into roles of plant managers and owners of canneries and fish processing plants. This still leaves First Nation towns like New Bella Bella and Klemtu, far removed in space and time from the two centers of action.[26].

Museum of Northern British Columbia

The Museum of Northern B.C. has long been present in Prince Rupert. In 1997 the museum was moved to a new and more spacious location. The Museum's architecture is based on Native longhouse design, which adds to the experience of art. The museum represents a major public investment in urban renewal. More importantly, it provides a statement that the major art forms it displays are local to the area and are of exceptional quality. The museum reviews the history of Euro-Canadian settlement in Northern B.C. and provides information about the commercial fishing industry. It houses a significant display of Native art, including art from Haida Indians of the Queen Charlotte

Islands and from Klingit and Tsimshian peoples who live along the coast and inland in B.C.

While visiting the museum in its new facility in June 1998, I met two Native artists in residence at the museum. Mr. Lee-Am-Lachoo was busy creating a ceremonial robe to be presented and worn at an upcoming Native festival. He told me that natives in British Columbia regard Prince Rupert as a center for the most productive and highest quality Native art. Also present at the museum was Mr. Moral Russ, who is a master sculptor of a rare stone obtained from Slate Chuck Mountain on the Queen Charlotte Islands. His work is also of museum quality and many of his creations are displayed in Canada and in other countries. A point to remember is that the opportunity to talk in person with Native artists greatly enhances the appreciation of viewing the art in this museum.

'Ksan Historical Village, Hazelton, British Columbia

The 'Ksan Historical Village is located at the Junction of the Skeena and Bulkley Rivers. For thousands of years, this area was the home of Gitksan and Wet' suewe' ten Indian peoples. They share a common linguistic root with the Tsimshian people from the mouth of the Skeena. The 'Ksan Historical Village is not along the Inside Passage; it is 180 miles east of Prince Rupert (288 kilometers). Rail and bus service is available from Prince Rupert, or one can drive along Highway 16. Each option follows the scenic Skeena River.

The 'Ksan Historical Village contains totem poles and seven reconstructed longhouses, each with a capacity to house a clan or a group of many families who are descended from a common ancestor. Longhouses are magnificent structures, built of planks from large cedar trees and with a central area for a fire pit and one hole in the roof for the smoke to exit. This village shows how First Nation peoples lived prior to first contact—and after. One longhouse (The Frog House of the Distant Past) is furnished in the manner prior to white contact. Another is furnished as if in preparation for a potlatch. Three longhouses are used as a museum, a gift shop with a book store, and a carving school. Over the centuries First Nation peoples spent considerable time as artists crafting ceremonial masks, totem poles, wall panels and jewelry. This tradition continues at 'Ksan and visitors can view artists creating works at the House of Wood Carving. Young Native artists are taught these skills to ensure the preservation of artifacts and ancient ways and to breathe new life into a tradition of First Nation creativity so their art will continue to develop and not remain static.

Crossing the Dixon Entrance: Prince Rupert to Ketchikan

The distance from Prince Rupert to Ketchikan, Alaska, is about 90 miles, and it includes an open ocean crossing—the Dixon Entrance—of about 30 miles. I made the crossing under good weather conditions in six hours. In Ketchikan I met two friends of mine, Bob and Joanne.

I asked, "How did you get here." Bob answered, "We took a cruise on the Sky Princess." I asked Bob if the cruise ship went through the Inside passage or if it went on the outside and travelled north along the west side of Vancouver Island. Bob said, "I have no idea." "What was your first stop?" I asked. "Our first stop was right here in Ketchikan." "Do you know how long it took you to go from Vancouver, B.C. to Ketchikan?" "Well," he answered, "I have the itinerary for Princes Cruises right with me." He showed it to me.

The information about the cruise mentioned that the trip to Ketchikan from Vancouver would cover 565.5 nautical miles and the nonstop trip to Ketchikan would take 36 hours traveling at the cruising speed of 16 knots. I checked my log and told Bob and Joanne that my trip took me 45 hours and my trip from Port Townsend, Washington, to Ketchikan covered 635 nautical miles.

"Did you leave just two days ago?" Joanne asked? "No" I said. "I left two weeks ago but I made a number of stops along the way. The 45 hours represent running time."

Moments later, Joanne said, "Oops, it is getting late. We gotta get back to the ship. See ya!"

End notes Chapter 2, British Columbia

1. Cole, Douglas, and Ira Chaikin. (1990) *An Iron Hand upon the People: The Law Against The Potlatch on the Northwest Coast.* Vancouver, B.C., and Seattle: Douglas and McIntyre and University of Washington Press.

2. Beck, Mary G. (1993) *Potlatch: Native Ceremony and Myth on the Northwest Coast.* Alaska Northwest Books, Anchorage, Seattle, Portland.

3. Walens, Stanley. Frank W. Porter III, General Editor. (1992). *The Kwakiutl.* Chelsea House Publishers, New York

4. Walens, Stanley. Op.cit., Note: Walens provides a further elaboration of the raid on Alert Bay in Dec. 1921.

   "In late December 1921, a large potlatch, attended by more than 300 guests from virtually every Kwakiutl village, was held at Village Island near Alert Bay. Afterward, several Indian and non-Indian informants pressured Halliday to establish his authority and prosecute some of the participants. He responded by having 80 high ranked Indians from all the tribes of the Kwakiutl Nation arrested. The quick trial was a travesty, if only because its proceedings were conducted in English and could not be understood by many of the Kwakwala-speaking defendants. Thirty were sentenced to prison for periods ranging from two months to a year, and while there they were physically and emotionally degraded. The 50 other defendants received suspended sentences, but only after they surrendered the potlatch regalia—and promised never to potlatch again. The confiscated potlatch paraphernalia, a total of about 600 pieces, was sent to the Royal Ontario Museum and the National Museums in Ottawa. Part of it was later sold to George Heye, founder of the Museum of the American Indian in New York City. The arrest and imprisonment of so many Kwakliutl chiefs and the confiscation of so much important and valuable Native ceremonial material would foment resentment and anger for the next half century. (p. 89)

5. Jack Knox. (Monday, July 08, 2002. Times Colonist (Victoria), "Hand it over, say Island Aboriginals, but British Museum is unmoved."

6. Symington, Fraser (1969). *The Canadian Indian: The illustrated History of the Great Tribes of Canada.* Toronto: McClelland & Stewart. Symington cites a letter from a public servant (a teacher or a government agent) to the Deputy Minister of Education of Ontario, 1 December 1918, quoting,

"These children require to have the 'Indian' educated out of them, which only a white teacher can help to do." (p. 228)

7. Miller, J.R. (1996). *Shingwauk's Vision: A History of Native Residential Schools.* University of Toronto Press. Note: The author lists on maps each residential school by denomination for each of the ten Provinces of Canada.

8. Miller, J.R. Ibid., This book provides a comprehensive analysis of the problems faced by Aboriginal students in residential schools.

9. Haig-Brown, Celia. (1988). *Resistance and Renewal: Surviving the Indian Residential School.* Published by Tillacum Library, Vancouver, B.C. This book contains personal accounts by Aboriginal Canadians who "survived" the Indian Residential schools. One section is entitled, THE SCHOOL DAY,

In the morning, we had to get up at six o'clock, perfect silence. We all took turns going into the bathroom: We'd wash, take that basin, empty it, clean it out, put it back, fix our bed, get dressed and as soon as you've finished—you only had half an hour to do all this—brush your teeth, get in a line and stand it line in perfect silence. If you're caught ever speaking one word, you got cuffed around.

And then we marched from there down to the chapel and we spent over an hour in the chapel every morning, every blessed morning. And there they interrogated us on what it was all about being an Indian. He would just get so carried away; he was punching away at the old altar rail to hammer it into our heads that we were not to think or act or speak like an Indian. And that we would go to hell and burn for eternity if we did not listen to their way of teaching. (Sophie) (p. 54)

10. The address given by the Honourable Jane Stewart, Minister of Indian Affairs and Northern Development, occurred January 7, 1998 in Ottawa, Ontario. The complete copy of the report and updates since 1998 can be obtained from the Minister of Indian Affairs ands Northern Development/ Ottawa, Canada.

11. Government Compensation Package. According to Wikipedia: on 2005, Nov. 23.

12. Ibid.

13. "Canadian Indian residential School System." Wikipedia, 2009-March, 15. @http://en.wikipedia.org/

14. The Catholic Register—Chief Fontaine Leaves a Legacy. www.catholicregister.org/content/view/3175/849/

15. Rabin, Jonathan. (1999). *Passage to Juneau: A Sea and Its Meanings.* Vintage Books. A Division of Random House, Inc. New York. p. 29.

16. Ibid. p. 348.

17. Boyce, David J.C. (1997). *Red Yellow, White: Colours of the Salmon Canning Industry. An Over View of the Salmon Canning Industry on Inverness Passage and How Racial Roles Have Changed From 1876-1996.* Prepared for the Canadian Museum of Civilization on behalf of North Pacific Cannery Village Museum. Questing archival research & creative developments. P. 6.

18. Meggs, Geoff. (1991).*Salmon: The Decline of the B.C. Fishery.* Douglas & McIntyre, Vancouver/Toronto. (Chapter 9. pages 90-100).

19. The Chinese Exclusion Act of 1923. www.canadiana.org/citm/specifique/asian-e.html

20. Boyce. op.cit., "Roles of the Chinese People" pages 35-38.

21. Wiener, Alter. (2007) *From a Name to a Number.* AuthorHouse publisher.
   Note: Alter Wiener was rescued from Auschwitz at the end of the war. He lost 123 relatives in the Holocaust. In a conversation with me he said when WW II ended he realized the extent to which other people also suffered, including people who resisted the Nazi racist ideology in occupied countries and were executed because they opposed Hitler. In the context of British Columbia during the long period of time of forced assimilation of First Nation people. It is clear that the Chinese workers also experienced great suffering and untenable working conditions in both their work on the Canadian railroad and in the salmon cannery operations.

22. Boyce. op.cit.,*The First Nations Traditional Fishery: The traditional roles of men and women in then fishery and a brief overview of methods used by the Tsimpshean peoples. pages 15-28.*

23. Meggs. op.cit. pages 76-80.

24. Ibid. pages 191-195.

25. Ibid. page 194.

26. Boyce. Op.cit., page 25.

CHAPTER 3

Catastrophic Mission to the Hopi Indians

The first Indigenous peoples, within the present boundaries of the United States, to be introduced to Christianity were the Hopi Indians of the Southwest; this vast area included wide portions of present day New Mexico, Arizona and Texas. The Native population of the Hopi Indians in the early 16th century was estimated to be about 80,000. They lived in about 110 Pueblos. While they lived peacefully among themselves, the Indians of these Pueblos were not united. Details of their religious beliefs, cultural practices and even language varied from one pueblo to another. They had no central government and no army. Hopi Indians never imposed their religious views on neighboring groups. The word "Hopi" means "Peace." The Spanish word "Pueblo" means "town."

In April 1540, Francisco Vazquez de Coronado left Mexico and travelled north with a large army in search of vast riches in gold. His army consisted of 350 Spaniards, about 1,300 Indian allies from Mexico and four Franciscan friars.[1] He found instead villages with houses made of stones and mud mortar. As the winter of 1540-1541 approached, Coronado needed food, blankets and winter quarters for his troops. The Hopi Indians refused to help and the Spanish attacked with a strong show of military force. In the conflict many Hopi Indians were killed; others were forced out of their homes, which were then taken over by the Spanish. Other villages were burned to the ground. The Spaniards also confiscated their food.[2] The Hopis struggled during the winter months under harsh Spanish rule and occupation.

One Hopi Indian devised a plot to rid the area of the Spanish. He told Coronado that far to the east he would find the gold and the silver that he wanted. This Indian agreed to serve as a guide. In April 1541 Coronado set out with his force of 1700 men (including Puebloans enslaved the previous winter) to explore the area east of what is now New Mexico in his search for fabulous wealth. The Spanish nicknamed the Hopi Indian "Turk." His identity is otherwise not known.[3] Coronado and his troops travelled as far east as Oklahoma and Kansas. To this present day, highway markers commemorate the travels of Coronado.

For example, as I drove along Interstate 40 to retrace a portion of the route of Francisco Vasquez de Coronado, I came across this sign:

KANSAS
HISTORICAL MARKER
THE SMOKY HILLS REGION

This area of Kansas contains the Smoky Hills, an area of rolling hills with occasional mesas and buttes. Pawnee Rock, Coronado Heights, and Rock City are notable elements of the landscape, as are the rock "toadstools" in this park. More of these unique forms, sculpted by erosion, may be seen at Mushroom Rocks State Park near Carneiro, east of Ellsworth.

For centuries, Native Americans lived in this area. European claims began with the Spanish explorer Francisco Vasquez de Coronado, who came here in 1541. A French explorer, Etienne de Bourgmont, passed near here in 1724. The area became a U.S. territory in 1803 with the Louisiana Purchase. The first American expedition to come here, in 1806, was led by Zebulon Pike. From here he traveled on to the Rockies and the peak that now bears his name.

The costly and time consuming expedition of Coronado, traveling east through the area that is now Kansas and Oklahoma, produced no gold. Greatly frustrated the Spanish tortured and then executed the Hopi Indian they had named "Turk."[4] Coronado then returned to the land that was sacred to the Hopis. The Hopis endured the winter of 1541-42 with the large and unwelcomed Spanish force still within their midst. Disgusted and angry with his failure to find wealth, Coronado led his army back to Mexico in April 1542. For the next forty years the Hopi people lived without the constraints imposed by the Spanish; but they expected, and dreaded, the day of their return.

In 1582 the King of Spain decreed that it was time to settle and Christianize Nuevo Mexico

A Spanish general named Don Juan de Onate y Salazar left the outpost of Santa Barbara in January 1598 and arrived in Nuevo Mexico (approximately in the area of what is now El Paso, Texas) on April 30, 1598. He made a formal proclamation of his possession of Nuevo Mexico for King Philip II.[5] He faced no immediate opposition. He had come with a significant force of 560 armed men plus large numbers of women and children. Along with the pilgrims were some 7,000 cattle, sheep, goats, oxen and horses. His settlers were prepared to develop homesteads and farms, for with them were plowshares, tools such as hammers, saws, bolts and nails. For defensive purposes they brought along eighteen barrels of gunpowder, and weapons including cannons. Eight Franciscan friars accompanied the vast group; they came to spread the Christian faith to the pagan Indians of the New World.[6]

At Santo Domingo Onate made pronouncements to chieftains of thirty-three different pueblos. The message was translated by a pair of Mexican Indians who probably did not know any of the languages of the Hopi.[7] Nevertheless, Spanish documents record the following:

Onate told them the following: *He had been sent by the most powerful king and ruler in the world, Dear Philip, king of Spain, who desired especially to serve God our Lord and to bring about the salvation of their souls. If they were baptized and became good Christians they would go to heaven to enjoy an eternal life of great bliss in the presence of God. If they did not become Christians, they would go to hell to suffer cruel and everlasting torment.*[8]

Onate, the Spanish leader, built his capital of Nuevo Mexico within the boundaries of a Hopi pueblo. He named his capital San Gabriel. Then he built his first church (the first Christian church built in what is now the United States) in his new headquarters. The church was built on top of a pueblo site called Yunge Oweenge. Onate then traveled and explored the vast area of the new Spanish dominion. He travelled north to Taos, east to Pecos, south into the Galisteo Basin, and far west into Jemez country. In these travels he searched for rich ore deposits, but found none. He visited the ancient Hopi village of Acoma built on a mesa or "table top" surrounded on all sides by 400-foot cliffs.

Marge and I have visited this area many times during the past forty years. We have camped in public as well as private campgrounds during these trips and have hiked through the canyons and walked around pueblos and admired Indian art. Our son Erik joined the faculty at Northeastern State University of Oklahoma, after obtaining his Ph.D in Environmental Science. This has encouraged us to make even more regular trips by car to explore the Southwest areas of the US on the way to visit our son, his wife and our two grandchildren. Our appreciation and knowledge of Native American history and culture has been enhanced by taking part in three different Elderhostel experiences, or "Adventures in Lifelong Learning." One of these programs was Elderhostel Santa Fe's **"Native American Arts and Crafts"** program held in March 2007. During these sessions we visited Acoma, a remarkable and beautiful place. The Pueblo of Acoma is the site of the oldest continuously inhabited community within the boundaries of the United States. Small adobe dwellings are perched at the top of the 365-foot-high outcropping rising from the plains of central New Mexico. Currently about 20 to 25 individuals live permanently on the mesa, but about 55,000 day trip tourists visit this site annually. Some of the walls of the adobe buildings still bear the scars of cannon fire from the attack led by the Spanish conquistador Juan de Onate in 1599.

In December 1598 some Acoma Indians learned that one of the conquistadors, Juan de Onate, planned to colonize the region. In response to that threat the Acoma Indians killed eleven Spaniards and two Mexican "servants."[9] In January 1599 Onate asked the Franciscan Friars whether the Acoma attack on his men were grounds for a "just war." The priests agreed and Onate ordered his army to avenge the Spanish losses.[10] The Spanish attacked on January 22 and the slaughter lasted two days. Spanish accounts of the battle state that between 600 and 800 Hopi were killed and over 500 women and children were taken in captivity and made to serve as slaves. Men over 25 years of age who survived were sentenced to the loss of their right foot. The pueblo of Acoma was utterly destroyed and for thirty years no survivors or their descendents were allowed to return to rebuild their pueblo on top of the butte.[11] The Spanish did not lose a single soldier in the massacre.

The fears of the tribe were realized. Onate introduced two Spanish practices, the *encomienda* and the *repartimiento,* as forms of heavy taxation and slavery on natives. Encomienda, as a policy, gave Spanish settlers the right to collect regular tribute, in the form of food or blankets, from Puebloans. Repartimiento, as a policy, required tribute in the form of forced labor. Forced labor included obeying orders to destroy their own sacred kivas and then to construct a Christian church in their place.[12]

Famine Strikes the Spanish Occupied land of the Hopis

A severe drought developed during the early 1600s causing Spanish colonists and Indians alike to suffer food shortages. Thousands of Indians perished. A number of Spanish deserted Onate and returned to Mexico City. They reported that conditions in Nuevo Mexico were terrible, that starvation was widespread, that Onate was cruel to the Indians, and no riches were found. Onate was ordered back from the colony to face trial in Mexico City. He was exiled in Mexico City for four years. With Onate discredited and in custody, the Spanish population of New Mexico dwindled to about 200.

The Spanish consider the option of abandoning New Mexico

Chronic shortage of food and the threat of mass starvation, the mistreatment of Indians, and the failure to find vast riches led to a consideration by the Spanish to abandon Nuevo Mexico. A committee, the Council of the Indies, considered the problems and costs of the new colony, and on September 13, 1608, formally recommended that Nuevo Mexico be abandoned.[13] The proposed abandonment might have taken place, except that a Catholic priest, Fray Lazaro Ximenez, reported that large numbers of Indians had already been converted to the Christian Catholic faith. It was not an option for the Spanish government to abandon their Christianized Indians. Roberts summarizes the dilemma of the Catholic priests as follows:

Fray Lazaro Ximenez, who had already recommended giving up the colony, returned in December from a second trip to New Mexico with the glorious but problematic news that by now, no fewer than 7,000 Indians had been converted and baptized. In the logic of Catholic thinking, it was unconscionable to abandon Christianized natives. Once baptized, an Indian risked far greater spiritual ruin in the temptation to return to old, discredited gods than did a "heathen" who had never been converted in the first place.[14]

To start anew, and with the main focus to convert natives to the Christian faith, Pedro de Peralta, the new governor, arrived in New Mexico in the winter of 1609-10. Two years later a Catholic priest, Fray Isidro Ordonez came to Nuevo Mexico and ran into conflict with Governor Pedro de Peralta. Ordonez announced to Spanish colonists and Natives alike that, "I can arrest, cast into irons, and punish as seems fitting to me any person without exception who is not obedient to the commandments of the Church and mine."[15] He arrested Governor Pedro de Peralta and assumed totalitarian leadership over the colony. He was also severe in his treatment of Puebloans.

With the renewed thrust to introduce Catholic orthodoxy to Nuevo Mexico, the Holy Office of the Inquisition was formally introduced in 1626. Fray Alonso de Benavides was appointed to become the commissary of the Inquisition in 1626. Under his leadership Churches were built all across Nuevo Mexico. They were usually built on top of existing kivas to demonstrate the superiority of the Christian faith over the "primitive" kachina religion. From time to time Hopi Indians were confronted with tragedy. One year a smallpox epidemic killed thousands of Indians. Some Puebloans interpreted crop failures and the severe onset of lethal diseases (never encountered before) as evidence that the native gods were angry. In desperation many Puebloans returned to their native kachina religion and performed dances and sacred ceremonies openly. In return Spanish friars led an assault against the Puebloans. Roberts states that, "At the most extreme, some of the punishments carried out by friars against Puebloans bespeak a cruelty, guided by religious bigotry, whose horror still reverberates more than three centuries later."[16]

In 1629, 30 years after the destruction of Acoma, the Spanish erected a large Catholic Church, and named the church San Estevan del Rey. Actually, the Spanish did not build the church. The church was built by Hopi Indians, under duress. When my wife and I visited Acoma and the church, San Estevan del Rey, in 2007, a Hopi guide walked us through this ancient pueblo, and let us walk into the beautiful church. My wife and I were part of an Elderhostel study group of about 35 people. We were not allowed to take any photos of the church or the community of Acoma.

After his introductory presentation, the knowledgeable and informed Hopi guide asked the members of our group: "Do you have any questions?"

I knew from my readings how the church was built, and that the church is still referred to as the "slave church." However, I wanted our Hopi guide to tell the story to our group. So I asked: "Can you tell us how this church was built; and, has the Catholic Church apologized to the Hopi people?"

Our Hopi guide paused, perhaps to reflect on the hundreds of times he had heard the story of San Estevan del Rey and the painful memories still very much alive almost four hundred years later. He looked directly at me and spoke in a clear, loud voice. All 35 members of our group could hear his answer.

Let me tell you about this Church. It was built over our sacred Kiva. The Spanish demanded that we, the Hopi people, destroy our sacred Kiva. Under duress of armed Spanish soldiers, we had to do that. When our Kiva was utterly destroyed we were then required to build the Christian church.

But, there were no trees nearby. As you can see this pueblo is in the midst of a desert. Our men had to climb down this high mesa and walk about forty miles to the nearest forest and then begin the task of cutting down the large trees. The Spanish had horses and wagons, but our men were not allowed to haul the huge logs on their wagons. We had to carry them the forty miles and then carry them up the 400 foot cliffs leading to the top of this mesa. We did all this before we could actually start building the church.

He paused; then answered the second part of my question, i.e., "Has the Catholic Church apologized to the Hopi people?" He answered: *No! The Catholic Church has not apologized to our people!*

I then asked how often Christian services are held in the church and how many Hopi attend. He answered: *Our people permit the Catholic priest to come to Acoma for a few hours on Wednesday afternoons to conduct services at this church. No Hopi attend.*

There were two other problems that were endured during the introduction of Christianity to the Hopi people. They are described in a book derived from extensive interviews with thirty elders of the Hopi Indian tribe in Northern Arizona. The elders reported that in the 17th century if a Hopi were caught practicing his Native religious beliefs he faced brutal punishment and possible execution. For example,

It is recorded that at Oraibi in 1655, when Friar Salvador de Guerra caught a Hopi in "an act of idolatry," he thrashed the Hopi in the presence of the whole village till he was bathed in blood, and then poured over him hot turpentine.[17]

In addition the elders also reported that sexual misconduct by the clergy was common in every Hopi village that had a Christian church and a priest. Numbers of illegitimate children, fathered by Catholic priests, were born to Indian women.[18]

By the 1670's the Puebloans Face Extinction under Spanish Oppression

In 1670 another smallpox outbreak brought disease and death among the Hopi people in the Spanish controlled lands of our

Southwest. In addition, a severe drought brought on crop failure, and famine spread over the land. In despair many Hopi secretly conducted their midsummer ceremony, the Niman Kachina, among the cliffs. Some rains then came and many Hopi believed that the Christian religion was not good for them. Death from disease, from executions by the Spanish and from famine had reduced the population of the Hopi people from 80,000 to less than 20,000 in the period of the one hundred and thirty years of Spanish rule.[19]

In 1675 Governor Juan Francisco Trevino was angered by indications that Puebloans were being led back to pagan practices by Hopi "sorcerers." He ordered forty-seven shaman to be arrested; most were from Tewa pueblos. Public hangings were held at three pueblos, Nambe, San o Felipe, and Jemez, to serve as a "lesson" to the others. Others were brutally flogged and imprisoned.[20]

A large number of Hopi Indians marched to Santa Fe. They met with the governor and demanded that the beaten and flogged shaman be released. The level of protest was unusual for the Hopi people, and the governor broke from his normal pattern of brutal aggressiveness and freed the surviving prisoners. One of the freed men was Pope, a forty-five year old shaman from San Juan Pueblo.

Pope moved to Taos. In a kiva he beseeched the kachinas (the spirits of the invisible forces of life) and the gods and pondered the question of how to drive the hated Castillas (Spanish) out. He met with shamans and other leaders from all the pueblos. He developed a plan that changed the course of his people forever. He planned and then led the Pueblo revolt of 1680.[21]

Note: There is no official written document by the Hopi people about the 1680 revolt. From oral history all Hopi people are aware of the Pueblo Revolt; however, not enough time has passed for the Hopi people, or for the Catholic Church, to reconcile or come to grips with the events that led up to this dark period. The following brief account was prepared with the consultation and approval of thirty elders of the Hopi Indian tribe in Northern Arizona.

The Pueblo Revolt of 1680

The time was ripe. Throughout all New Mexico every tribe and village was planning to rebel against its ruthless subjugation. The leader of this vast, concerted uprising was Pope, a Tewa Indian of San Juan Pueblo on the Rio Grande, who made as his headquarters the always obdurate pueblo of Taos. Knotted cords were sent to each village indicating August 13, 1680, as the day to strike. The secret leaked out, and Pope struck at once—on August 10. Every pueblo revolted; the Indians killed nearly five hundred Spaniards, including twenty-one missionaries at their alters, tore down churches, destroyed government and church records, sacked Santa Fe, and drove the surviving Spaniards back to Mexico.

The Spanish return to the Hopi in 1692

The Spanish returned in 1692. How did it go? A large number of Hopi people fled as soon as the Spanish arrived, and, as refugees, traveled as far away as they could. The whereabouts and the question of survival for that group are not known. Those who stayed encountered many obstacles, but they persevered. Author David Roberts states that:

. . . *the Puebloans never lost their languages, their dances, their tales that conjure up their history. No Native American peoples anywhere in the United States have kept their cultures more intact than the twenty pueblos in New Mexico and Arizona.*[22]

Time Frame: How Long Ago Was 1540?

The Spanish first arrived in the land of the Hopi in 1540, but it was 1582 when the King of Spain decreed that it was time to Christianize the Hopi people. How long ago was that? That was yesterday, because the trauma remains. Yesterday? How could that be? The pain of that catastrophic period was like it happened yesterday. Remember the Hopi people shared information about their sacred beliefs and traditions. David Roberts summarizes the tragedy of the missionary effort and the Puebloan response:

Of all the traits that stamp Puebloan culture, secrecy is the hallmark. And no wonder: in the seventeenth century, when Spaniards hanged and whipped shamans for practicing "sorcery," burned their kivas and kachina masks, preached to them daily about the eternal flames of hell they must endure unless they embraced Catholicism, the Puebloans learned to hide the religion that had sustained their ancestors—as in the secret, ordinary rooms at Gran Quivira where twentieth-century excavators found all the paraphernalia normally stored in the kivas. In the view of many accomplished scholars, including France Scholes and Elsie Clews Parsons, the Puebloans developed secrecy as a defense against Spanish oppression.[23]

What happened to the Hopi people starting in 1540 is like it happened yesterday. The impact remains today. The ancient sacred beliefs remain, but they are not shared with outside groups.

History Changed again and again for the Hopi Indians.

Spain suffered a devastating defeat in the famous battle of Trafalgar led by Lord Nelson on October 21, 1805. In that battle Lord Nelson surprised the enemy by having his ships cut through the powerful French and Spanish war ships. Without losing a single ship, the British fleet destroyed or captured more than half of the French and Spanish fleet. This ended the plan of Napoleon Bonaparte to invade England. For Spain the defeat meant the beginning of the end of their vast colonial empire. The Spanish no longer had a navy sufficient to protect their interests in the New World.

The indigenous peoples of what is now New Mexico, Arizona, Utah, Nevada and California lived under Mexican rule, without the influence of Spain. This provided the potential for change to undo or correct the oppressions brought on by the three hundred years Mexico had been dominated by both the Spanish crown and the Roman Catholic Church. Supplies and funds for the colonists, including the Roman Catholic priests, were cut off. The missions run by the Catholic Church were secularized. However, the Republic of Mexico would have no time and no opportunity to develop a plan for the indigenous peoples such as the Hopi.

The United States invades Mexico

In 1846 the United States, under the presidency of James K. Polk, invaded Mexico and defeated the Mexican army and occupied their capital city of Mexico City. With the Spanish military out of the picture, the recently independent Mexico was totally unable to defend itself against the U.S. forces. Mexican forces were quickly defeated and their capital city of Mexico City was soon occupied by U.S. forces. With no option left but to endure more losses, Mexico surrendered in 1848. By the treaty of Guadalupe Hidalgo, the United States acquired from Mexico the territory that now comprises the states of California, Nevada, and Utah, as well as parts of New Mexico, Arizona, Colorado and Wyoming.

The Hopi Indians under U.S. Rule. The United States forges ahead to develop a direction for Native American policy without a compass

Racism and the issue of slavery

President Polk favored spreading slavery into these new lands. Unfortunately, strong elements within the Christian church also advocated slavery and claimed the Bible provided support for the institution of slavery. So the Hopi Indians, as well as all Native peoples living in the U.S., were living in a country that supported slavery. Who among the Christians supported the institution of slavery? Among them were prominent Christian leaders. My focus is on two:

James Henley Thornwell

James Henley Thornwell was a Presbyterian minister and from 1855 until his death in 1862 a professor of theology at Columbia Theological Seminary. In 1845 he was a delegate to the Presbyterian

General Assembly where the issue of slavery was a major focus. He stated his position as, "I have no doubts but that the Assembly, by a large majority, will declare slavery not to be sinful, will assert that it is sanctioned by the word of God, that it is purely a civil relation with which the Church, as such, has no right to interfere, and that abolitionism is essentially wicked, disorganizing, and ruinous."[24]

When Presbyterians split over slavery in 1861, Thornwell wrote a manifesto justifying their actions in supporting the legitimacy of slavery and the rationale for splitting with the northern group. His seventeen-page manifesto was accepted unanimously by the Presbyterian Church in the Confederate States of America on December 4, 1861. In his assessment of Rev. Thornwell, Dr. Jack Rogers, a Presbyterian minister and a long term faculty member at Fuller Seminary, states, "He (Thornwell) assumed that Africans were descendants of Ham, by nature inferior to whites, and therefore assigned by God to the status of slaves. Rogers quotes an assertion made by Thornwell, "There are, no doubt, many rights which belong to other men—to his master, for example—which are denied to him. But is he fit to possess them? The truth is, the education of the human race for liberty and virtue, is a vast Providential scheme, and God assigns to every man, by a wise and holy decree, the precise place he is to occupy in the great moral school of humanity."[25]

Thornwell continues his argument, "As long as that race, in its comparative degradation, co-exists, side by side, with the white, bondage is its normal condition. Indeed, as we contemplate their condition in the Southern States, and contrast it with that of their fathers before them, and that of their brethren in the present day in their native land, we cannot but accept it as a gracious Providence that they have been brought in such numbers to our shores, and redeemed from the bondage of barbarism and sin."[26]

Thornwell died in 1862. Before his death he wrote to his wife the following: "Every day increases my sense of the value of the principles for which we are contending. If we fail, the hopes of the human race are put back for more than a century." Rogers summarizes the racist perspective of Thornwell as follows: "The human race, for Thornwell, was structured hierarchically. For him, the well-being of the "inferior classes," such as Africans, depended on the power and benevolence of the ruling classes, which in this case meant southern white men." [27].

Robert Lewis Dabney

Dabney, an influential Presbyterian minister in the South, became the most outspoken supporter of slavery after the death of Thornwell in 1862. He served as a chaplain in the Confederate Army and then as a major to General Stonewall Jackson. While the civil war was in progress, he wrote a lengthy defense of slavery called, *A Defense of Virginia.* Like Thornwell, Dabney argued that blacks were subjected to slavery as "God's punishment" for the sins of Ham. The punishment is referred to as "Sins of the Fathers" to be passed down in perpetuity. After the Civil War, some southern clergy strongly voiced the opinion that African Americans be given full equality in the church, including ordination to the ministry. Robert Dabney vehemently objected and delayed any effort on the part of southern Presbyterian clergy to racially integrate their churches.

After emancipation Dabney continued to argue that slavery, though abolished by law, was correct. In an article, *Anti-Biblical Theories of Rights,* written in 1888, he criticized as radical, the social theory that asserts, "all men are created equal." He encouraged his readers to go back to the Bible, contending that, *The honest student, then, of the New Testament can make nothing less of its teachings on this point than that domestic slavery, as defined in God's word and practiced in the manner enjoined in the Epistles, is still a lawful relation under the new dispensation as well as the old.*[28]

For Dabney, the ancient story of Noah's flood, and the aftermath, fully explains why the posterity (future generations) of Ham are guilty today of a crime allegedly committed in pre-historic times. He cites the story of Noah in the book of Genesis Chapter 6:1 through Chapter 9:29. The following Biblical verses provide the gist of the well known story. I include the verbatim verses because we come across the same passages, and the same arguments to justify slavery in our travels south to Tierra del Fuego as Christianity was introduced to the indigenous peoples of the New World.

The Holy Bible Genesis Chapter 6:

[5] *The Lord saw how great man's wickedness on the earth had become, and that every inclination of the thoughts of his heart was only evil all the time.* [6] *The Lord was grieved that he had made man on the earth, and his heart was filled with pain.* [7] *So the Lord said, "I will wipe out mankind, whom I have created, from the face of the earth—men and animals, and creatures that move along the ground and birds of the air—for I am grieved that I have made them.* [8] *But Noah found favor in the eyes of the Lord.* [9] *Noah was a righteous man, blameless among the people of his time, and he walked with God.* [10] *Noah had three sons: Shem, Ham and Japheth.*

The Book of Genesis continues to describe the instructions of God to Noah to build his very large ark, and his task of bringing pairs of all living creatures on to his ark.

Genesis Chapter 6 (continued): verse [17] *I am going to bring floodwaters on the earth to destroy all life under the heavens, every creature that has the breath of life in it. Everything on earth will perish.* [18] *But I will establish my covenant with you, and you will enter the ark—you and your sons and your wife and your son's wives with you.* [19] *You are to bring into the ark two of all living creatures, male and female, to keep them alive with you.*

Genesis Chapter 7 describes the flood and ends with the following two verses, [23] *Every living thing on the face of the earth was wiped out; men and animals and the creatures that move along the ground and the birds of the air were wiped from the earth. Only Noah was left, and those with him in the ark.* [24] *The waters flooded the earth for a hundred and fifty days.*

Genesis Chapter 8 describes God's instructions to Noah after the flood waters receded, [15] *Then God said to Noah,* [16] *Come out of the ark, you and your wife and your sons and their wives.* [17] *Bring out every kind of living creature with you—the birds, the animals, and all the creatures that move along the ground—so they can multiply on the earth and be fruitful and increase in number upon it.*

Genesis Chapter 9 describes the rainbow as a sign of a covenant: [11] *I establish my covenant with you: Never again will all life be cut off by the waters of a flood; never again will there be a flood to destroy the earth.*[13] *I have set my rainbow in the clouds, and it will be a sign of the covenant between me and the earth.*

Genesis Chapter 9 states that all mankind come from the three sons of Noah: [18] *The sons of Noah who came out of the ark were Shem, Ham and Japheth.* (Ham was the father of Canaan.) [19] *These were the three sons of Noah, and from them came the people who were scattered over the earth.*

Genesis Chapter 9 describes the sin committed by Ham and the consequence: [20] *Noah, a man of the soil, proceeded to plant a vineyard.* [21] *When he drank some of its wine, he became drunk and lay uncovered inside his tent.* [22] *Ham, the father of Canaan, saw his father's nakedness and told his two brothers outside.* [23] *But Shem and Japheth took a garment and laid it across their shoulders; then they walked in backward and covered their father's nakedness. Their faces were turned the other way so that they would not see their father's nakedness.*

[24] *When Noah awoke from his wine and found out what his youngest son had done to him,* [25] *He said, Cursed be Canaan. The lowest of slaves will he be to his brothers.* [26] *He also said, "Blessed be the Lord, the God of Shem. May Canaan be the slave of Shem.* [27] *May God extend the territory of Japheth; may Japheth live in the tents of Shem, and may Canaan be his slave.*[28]

The Meaning of the Myth of Noah's Flood.

Friedrich Schleirmacher (1768-1834) is considered to be the father of modern systematic theology. He introduced the idea that theology is strengthened by integrating the best available data and theory from science into a coherent understanding of theology. He asserted that there are many supernatural elements in Scripture and in Christianity which defy reason and that there is no reason to accept such scripture and dogma as literal truth.[29] Other theologians have extended the liberal view of Schleirmacher. For example, Ernest Troeltsch (1865-1923) makes the observation that religious practice is widespread throughout human history and that religious belief is due to an inborn nature of mankind. While asserting that Christianity forms the best foundation for values in Western society, Troeltsch acknowledges that none of the core beliefs of Christianity can be backed up by rational or by scientific method.[30] What does this have to do with the story of Noah's Flood?

Noah's flood did not happen. There was no flood that wiped out all living things. There was no Noah's Ark. All human life does not go back to the three sons of Noah. It is a myth, not history. Worse yet the story of Noah's flood got transformed. It became a way to justify, with Biblical references, the great evil of slavery. It is interesting that Noah's anger was not expressed toward his youngest son, Ham, who somehow grievously offended Noah, but to Canaan, the son of Ham. As we have seen, according to Scripture cited above it was Canaan, who was the first to suffer from the "sins of his father." During the Atlantic slave trade, from 1441-1807, the millions of Africans captured and sold bore the stigma and the full brunt of the 'sins of the fathers.'[31]

The Hopi Indians under U.S Rule

Racism.

The writer Jack D. Forbes states that the European concept of race that was used to justify the capture and sale of non-whites for use as slaves had a direct bearing on racist policies that also impacted indigenous Americans. Racial stereotypes were reinforced by laws passed since the seventeenth century. For example, many states had laws prohibiting intermarriage between Native Americans and people of European ancestry. In many states Indians could not attend schools with white children. The important protections of traditional property rights and equal protection of the laws contained in the Fifth and Fourteenth Amendments to the United States Constitution did not apply to blacks (African Americans) or to Native Americans. Neither of these peoples could testify as witnesses in any action or proceeding in which a white person is a party. In addition they could not serve in the jury box, upon the bench or in the legislative halls.[32] The Hopi Indians, the focus of this chapter, experienced these racist policies as did all other Native Americans.

In a chapter entitled *Racial Destiny and the Indians,* the author Reginald Horsman succinctly captures the consensual racist beliefs within the United States that shaped American policy towards Native Americans:

The United States shaped policies which reflected a belief in the racial inferiority and expendability of Indians, Mexicans, and other inferior races, and which looked forward to a world shaped and dominated by a superior American Anglo-Saxon race . . . .

Indian Removal represented a major victory for ideas which, though long latent in American society, became fully explicit only after 1830. Political power was exercised by those who believed the Indians to be inferior, who did not wish them to be accepted as equals within American society, and who expected them ultimately to disappear. In shaping an Indian policy American politicians reflected the new ruthlessness of racial confidence.[33]

A similar assessment is presented in a widely used book by Thomas F. Gossett, *Race: The History of an Idea in America.* In a chapter entitled "The Indian in the Nineteenth Century" he states the following:

The nineteenth century was obsessed with the idea that it was race which explained the character of peoples. The notion that traits of temperament and intelligence are inborn in races and only superficially changed by environment or education was enough to blind the dominant whites. The Indians suffered more than any other ethnic minority from the cruel dicta of racism. The frontiersman, beset with the problem of conquering the wilderness, was in no mood to understand anything about the Indians except that they were at best a nuisance and at worst a terrible danger. The leading thinkers of the era were generally convinced that Indian traits were racially inherent and therefore could not be changed. The difference between the frontiersmen's view of the Indians and that of the intellectuals was more apparent than real. In general, the frontiersmen either looked forward with pleasure to the extinction of the Indians or at least were indifferent to it. The intellectuals were most often equally convinced with the frontiersmen that the Indians, because of their inherent nature, must ultimately disappear. They were frequently willing to sigh philosophically over the fate of the Indians, but this was an empty gesture. [34]

The racist views held by our government led to a number of laws enacted to enforce racist views that continue to impact Native Americans and, in essence, all Americans. They include the Indian Removal Act of 1830, and the Dawes Act of 1887.

The Indian Removal Act of 1830

Many Americans considered sending Indians who wished to retain traditional Indian beliefs and practices to the west into the newly obtained lands acquired from the Louisiana Purchase of 1803. In contrast, the Indians who chose to assimilate and did so could remain in their familiar lands, farm their land, and pass on their land to their heirs. At this point Indian removal was considered to be voluntary and require consensus of the tribe and individuals within the tribe.

In January 1817, under the Presidency of James Monroe, the Senate Committee on Public Lands endorsed the general policy of exchanging Indians' lands east of the Mississippi for lands west of the Mississippi. The policy explicitly called for such actions to be based on voluntary consent of the tribes. However, the state of Georgia wanted no Indians at all within their state. This included the Cherokee Indians who had assimilated to a large degree. Arguments shifted back and forth until Andrew Jackson was elected to the Presidency in 1828. He was eager to ban Indians from the southern states and won elections in the critical states of Georgia, Alabama, Mississippi and Tennessee by a wide margin.

The Indian Removal Act of 1830 passed in Congress and became law. Now whole tribes of Indians could be removed with military force. Any resistance meant the US army would be called to enforce the move. President Jackson addressed his plan of Indian removal in his Second Annual Message to Congress on December 6, 1830. It was, he stated, a positive—even benevolent act; in the words of President Andrew Jackson:

It gives me pleasure to announce to Congress that the benevolent policy of the Government, steadily pursued for nearly thirty years, in relation to the removal of the Indians beyond the white settlements is approaching to a happy consummation. Two important tribes have accepted the provision made for their removal at the last session of Congress, and it is believed that their example will induce the remaining tribes also to seek the same obvious advantages.

The Cherokees and the "Trail of Tears"

The Cherokees refused to move from their ancient and traditional lands. They were forcibly removed by the US armed forces, as directed by the United States government, during the fall and winter of 1838 and 1839. Approximately 4,000 Cherokees died during the forced march, which is known as the "Trail of Tears," an amount equal to one out of five members of their population. What happened to the Cherokees had an impact on all Native peoples in the United States. It meant that if the majority white population wanted traditional Indian land they would get it and the US government and military would assist in Indian removal.

Prior to the forced relocation, the Cherokees had been one of the largest Native American tribes that had become most nearly "assimilated" to US culture. The majority of the Cherokees spoke English, were literate and some adopted Christianity. Many owned their own houses, worked and paid taxes. They had developed a written constitution and members of the Cherokee tribe testified before the United States Congress. [35]

The Civil War and the Cherokee, Creek, Seminole, Choctaws and Chickasaw Tribes

With the outbreak of the Civil War in 1861, the impact on the five "Civilized Tribes" was profound. The Cherokee, Creek, Choctaw,

Chickasaw and Seminole tribes (with few exceptions) were the only Indian tribes who fought in the American Civil War. It was not their choice. These five tribes were all removed (expelled) from their ancestral lands by leadership of the Southern states. As stated above President Jackson sided with the Southern states to enact policies that resulted in the forced removal of any among the five tribes who refused to leave voluntarily.

All of the United States agents assigned to these five tribes were secessionists from the South and supported the Confederate military objectives against the Union. Consequently, these agents persisted in efforts to persuade the Indians to support the South and to join the Confederate army. Many of these Indians were opposed to fighting at all in this malevolent war, but eventually many of the tribes did form alliances with the South. This created conflict and dissension within the tribes. In the case of the Cherokee tribe, their chief, John Ross, initially urged his people to remain neutral. However, at the battle of Wilson's Creek, the Union army was defeated and suffered severe losses. Chief Ross was persuaded that the South would win the Civil war and expressed willingness to enter into a treaty with the Confederate forces. Chief Ross may have felt the decision was in the interest of self preservation for his tribe. The decision, however, increased tension within the Cherokee tribe and some of his tribe joined the North. The Indians of these five tribes suffered heavy losses in a brutal war fought without a Red Cross or anything close to medical care for the dying and wounded. No adequate medical care was available to wounded soldiers fighting on either side.

The Sand Creek Massacre (also known as the Chivington massacre)
     November 29, 1864

In 1851, the United States government and 10,000 Indians, among them the Sioux, the Cheyenne and the Arapaho gathered in the West at Fort Laramie and signed an agreement in which the Cheyenne and Arapaho and five other tribes were to hold a vast territory between the North Platte River and Arkansas River and from the Rocky Mountains to western Kansas. The Treaty of Fort Laramie was the first time the Indians agreed to live within specified boundaries.[35] However, in 1858 gold was discovered in the Rocky Mountains of Colorado. This brought a large number of white gold seekers who invaded and occupied Indian Territory within the boundaries established by the Treaty of Fort Laramie. In an effort to forge a peaceful arbitration ten chiefs of Cheyenne and Arapaho signed an agreement with U.S. officials known as the Treaty of Fort Wise. In the signed agreement about 93 percent of the Indian lands established at the 1851 treaty were taken away. When the new arrangement was explained to tribal members they were aghast. Many Cheyenne opposed the treaty modification and stated that the few chiefs who signed the treaty did not understand what they had signed. Conflict brewed. Two Cheyenne chiefs, Black Kettle and White Antelope, sought to maintain peace. They obtained permission to camp near Fort Lyon at Sand Creek and were assured by the U.S. government they would be safe. Black Kettle flew an American flag over the campsite, attended by approximately 800 Indians. Assured of peace most of the men went hunting, leaving behind about sixty men who were too old to hunt and many women and children.

U.S. Army Colonel John Chivington, who was also a Methodist preacher and known as "the fighting parson," led a combined force of 800 troops of the First Colorado Cavalry, the Third Colorado Cavalry and a company of First New Mexico Volunteers. They arrived at the Black Kettle campsite on the night of November 28. Without any provocation, on the morning of November 29, 1864, Chivington ordered his troops to attack. In the attack 160 Indians were killed, the majority were women and children. Fifteen members of Chivington's soldiers were killed, mostly by friendly fire, as many of Chivington's soldiers were drunk and fired their weapons impulsively. [36]

After the massacre, Chivington returned to Denver and proudly boasted of his victory and showed battle trophies in Denver's Apollo Theater and area saloons. The attack was reported in the press as a victory achieved over fierce opponents. However, as news carried to the East coast, many raised questions about a possible massacre. A military panel, the Joint Committee on the Conduct of the War, investigated the action. After a formal review the panel declared:

As to Colonel Chivington, your committee can hardly find fitting terms to describe his conduct. Wearing the uniform of the United States, which should be the emblem of justice and humanity; holding the important position of commander of a military district, and therefore having the honor of the government to that extent in his keeping, he deliberately planned and executed a foul and dastardly massacre which would have disgraced the verist (sic) savage among those who were the victims of his cruelty. Having full knowledge of their friendly character, having himself been instrumental to some extent in placing them in their position of fancied security, he took advantage of their in-apprehension and defenseless condition to ratify the worst passions that ever cursed the heart of man.

Whatever influence this may have had upon Colonel Chivington, the truth is that he surprised and murdered, in cold blood, the unsuspecting men, women, and children on Sand creek, who had every reason to believe they were under the protection of the United States authorities, and then returned to Denver and boasted of the brave deed he and the men under his command had performed.

In conclusion, your committee are of the opinion that for the purpose of vindicating the cause of justice and upholding the honor of the nation, prompt and energetic measures should be at once taken to remove from office those who have thus disgraced the government by whom they are employed, and to punish, as their crimes deserve, those who have been guilty of these brutal and cowardly acts.[37]

Despite the recommendation by the Joint Committee on the Conduct of the War, neither Colonel John Chivington nor any other participants in the Sand Creek massacre were brought to justice. Unfortunately, in 1909, a Civil War memorial was installed at the Colorado Capital in 1909 and lists the Sand Creek battle as one of the Union's great victories. This error was corrected in 2002 when a plaque was added which gave details of the massacre.[38]

However, a more appropriate marker was placed in 2007, when The National Park Service installed a stone marker to commemorate the tragedy. It is named the Sand Creek Massacre National Historic Site, and is situated on Big Sandy Creek in Kiowa County, Colorado. There is also a trail, the Sand Creek Massacre Trail in Wyoming, that follows the paths of survivors after the massacre. The trail passes through Cheyenne, Laramie, Casper, and Riverton en route to Ethete in Fremont County on the reservation. Every year Arapaho youth run the length of the trail in an effort to bring healing to their nation.

The site was dedicated April 27, 2007, and was attended by dignitaries and several hundred descendants of some of those who were massacred. Former U.S. senator Ben Nighthorse Campbell, who led the effort to give the massacre site a federal designation, spoke at the event as did the historian Patricia Limerick of the University of Colorado's Center of the American West. She said that the dedication of a National Park unit at the Sand Creek site "is the greatest testimony of the strength of a nation—that you are big enough and strong enough to acknowledge the cruelties and injuries of the past."[39]

The Dawes Act of 1887

In 1877 Lewis Henry Morgan published *Ancient Society: Or Researches in the lines of Human Progress from Savagery through Barbarism to Civilization.* He proposed there are seven stages of cultural evolution from lower savagery to civilization. In his framework no Indian society had ever achieved civilization, but in time all peoples would be civilized. Progress was inevitable. He asserted that two developments were critical: the first is the monogamous family, and the second is private property; without the concept of private property, a society's social, economic and political development would be stunted.[40] Morgan's ideas published in *Ancient Society* strongly influenced U.S. policy that governed Indian affairs. Carl Schurz, former commissioner of Indian Affairs, stated in 1881 that Indians were confronted with "this stern alternative extermination or civilization."[41] On the same note, Henry Price, commissioner of Indian Affairs, stated: "Savage and civilized life cannot live and prosper on the same ground. One or the other must die."[42]

In 1887 Congress passed the General Allotment Act, known also as the Dawes Act of 1887, named after the senator from Massachusetts, Henry Dawes. The act was an effort to break tribal connections and speed the development of Indians to be civilized. Indian Reservations (formed after the Removal Act) were to be surveyed and divided up among the Indians: 160 acres to each family head, 80 acres to single persons and orphans over eighteen years, and 40 acres to single persons under eighteen. The Dawes Act called for citizen status to be granted to all those given allotments who would then be subject to the criminal and civil laws of the state or territory where they lived. A second provision was to extend the nation's legal system to Indians; that is, Indians would be trained to monitor and enforce laws among tribesmen and given a badge of authority to carry out directives of the reservation agent. An additional area of the Dawes Act was that Indians would be "taught the knowledge, values, mores and habits of Christian civilization." [43]

The case for education came with a caveat: as older generations of Indians were unwilling or incapable of giving up tribal customs and becoming "civilized." The effort was focused on Indian children. Soon it became apparent that Indian children who learned the language, values and basic tenets of the Christian religion in school would lose it after spending time with their families and others within their tribe. The solution was to remove Indian children from their families and tribal connections and send them to off-reservation residential schools. The first off-reservation boarding school was located in Carlisle, Pennsylvania, and opened in 1879. The second was the Chemawa residential school which opened in Salem, Oregon, in 1880. (Incidentally, some children from Wrangell, Alaska, were sent to the Chemawa School in Oregon. The plan to send children far from home was to isolate Indian children from family and tribal connections to speed up their assimilation to "civilized" white culture. See Chapter 1.) By 1902 there were 25 such residential and off-reservation schools in the U.S.[44].

I concur with the conclusion given by David Wallace Adams in *Education for Extinction*. He writes:

In the final analysis, the boarding school story constitutes yet another deplorable episode in the long and tragic history of Indian-white relations. For tribal elders who had witnessed the catastrophic developments of the nineteenth century—the bloody warfare, the near-extinction of the bison, the scourge of disease and starvation, the shrinking of the tribal land base, the indignities of reservation life, the invasion of missionaries and white settlers—there seemed to be no end to the cruelties perpetrated by whites. And after all this, the schools. After all this, the white man had concluded that the only way to save Indians was to destroy them, that the last great Indian war should be waged against children. They were coming for the children.[45]

After the War and Forced Relocation: All is Forgotten

After the forced relocation with the associated deaths of many of the Cherokees, the Commissioner of Indian affairs, Nathanial G. Taylor, in his annual report of 1868 saw nothing but goodness and happiness for the Five Civilized Tribes, which had been rescued from paganism and savagery through Christian missionary efforts.

Taylor responded to a hypothetical question: "How can our Indian tribes be civilized?" He answered as follows:

History and experience have laid the key to its solution in our hands, at the proper moment, and all we need to do is to use it, and we at once reach the desired answer. It so happens that under the silent and seemingly slow operation of efficient causes, certain tribes of our Indians have already emerged from a state of pagan barbarism, and are to-day clothed in the garments of civilization, and sitting under the vine and fig tree of an intelligent scriptural Christianity.

Taylor continued his thoughts with specific reference to the Five Civilized Tribes who were forced from their ancestral lands just 30 years before his own appointment to the position of Commissioner of Indian Affairs. He makes no reference to their tragic removal:

School-houses abound, and the feet of many thousand little Indian children—children intelligent and thirsting after knowledge—are seen every day entering these vestibules of science; while churches dedicated to the Christian's God, and vocal with His praise from the lips of redeemed thousands, reflect from their domes and spires the earliest rays and latest beams of that sun whose daily light now blesses them as five Christian and enlightened nations so recently heathen savages. (Frances Prucha p. 349)

An American imposed reservation system:
The Navajo-Hopi Land Controversy

About one million, or nearly half of the total American Indian population in the United States, reside on reservations. The Bureau of Indian Affairs recognizes 287 land areas as federal Indian reservations. The Navajo reservation, at 16 million acres, is the largest federal reservation. It straddles portions of Arizona, New Mexico and Utah. Of significance is that it completely encloses, or surrounds, the Hopi reservation, which lies within the boundaries of the Navajo reservation.

Three of America's oldest continuously settled communities are the Hopi villages of Oraibi on Third Mesa, Shungopuli on Second Mesa, and Walpi on First Mesa. The San Francisco Peaks, Arizona's highest mountain, are sacred to the Hopi. The Hopi have a concept of land ownership that Hopi did not need to be physically residing on clan lands in order to claim rightful possession. In contrast the Navajo way of land ownership is that land not within Navajo clan boundaries could be settled and incorporated into Navajo territory. For example, a Navajo house, or Hogan, could be built on vacant land, a ceremony performed, and the land becomes Navajo. This has occurred numerous times when the "vacant land" was part of the Hopi reservation.

The treaty of 1868 limited Navajo land to a small rectangle of land, straddling the Arizona-New Mexico border. During the period from 1868-1991, the Navajo land base has been extended over 15 times at a cost of what Hopi claim to be rightfully theirs. In 1974 Congress enacted Public Law 93-531 and partitioned the 1882 Hopi Reservation. The Navajo tribe gained title to half of the Hopi Reservation, some 911,000 acres. In October 1992, the Hopi and Navajo tribes reached an agreement in principle. Navajo could remain on Hopi land for at least 75 years, and in turn the Hopis would receive about 400,000 acres of land around the San Francisco Peaks area in return for allowing Navajo to lease Hopi partition lands. However, Senator Dennis DeConcini and Governor Fife Symington, denounced the plan and undermined the agreement. To date the Hopi have received no replacement land for the loss of half of their reservation.

Endnotes Chapter 3. Hopi Indians

1. Roberts, David. *The PUEBLO REVOLT: The Secret Rebellion That Drove the Spaniards out of the Southwest,* Simon & Schuster Paperbacks, New York. 2004. p. 59.
2. Ibid., 63.
3. Ibid., 63.
4. Ibid., 63.
5. Ibid., 66.
6. Ibid., 72.
7. Ibid., 75.
8. Ibid., 76.
9. Ibid., 87.
10. Ibid., 88.
11. Ibid., 89.
12. Ibid., 102.
13. Ibid., 99.
14. Ibid., 99.
15. Ibid., 100.
16. Ibid., 116.
17. Ibid., 116.
18. Waters, Frank. *The Book of the Hopi,* Ballantine Books, New York. 1963. p. 310.
19. Ibid., 310.
20. Roberts, op.cit., p. 124.
21. Ibid., 126.
22. Ibid., 127.
23. Ibid., 245.
24. Ibid., 152.
25. Rogers, Jack. *Jesus, the Bible, and Homosexuality: Explode the Myths, Heal the Church. Westminster John Knox Press. Louisville, Kentucky. 2006. p. 20*
26. Ibid., 21.
27. Ibid., 22
28. Ibid., 22
29. **The Holy Bible. Genesis Chapters 6, 7, 8. 9. and 10.**

Slavery came to the New World along with Christian missionaries. The Biblical story of the flood that allegedly killed all life except for those animals and humans on Noah's Ark is a great and terrible story, but not true. The fact that Protestant and Catholic clergy, maintained it was true and then used it to justify slavery is perhaps the most devastating use of the Bible ever. From Chapter 4, Guatemala, through Chapter 8, Tierra del Fuego, slavery played a major and terrible part of the tragedy of the conquest.

30. Jacqueline Marina, ed. *The Cambridge Companion to Fredrich Schleirmmacher*. Cambridge University Press, Cambridge. 348 pages. 2005.

31. Troeltsch, Ernst. *Ernst Troeltsch: Writings on Theology and Religion*. Edited and Translated by Robert Morgan and Michael Pye. Atlanta: John Knox Press. 1977.

32. Pope-Hennessy, James. *Sins of the Fathers: The Atlantic Slave Trade 1441-1807*. Castle Books, Edison, New Jersey. 2004

33. Limerick, Patricia Nelson. *The Legacy of Conquest: The Unbroken Past of the American West*. Norton & Company, New York. 1987. pp. 179-221.

34. Horseman, Reginald. *Race and Manifest Destiny: The Origins of American Anglo-Saxonism*, 1981. Harvard University Press, Cambridge Massachusetts. pp. 189-190.r

35. Gossett, Thomas F. *Race: The History of an Idea in America*. Oxford University Press. 1997.

36. Deloria Jr, Vine. *Promises Made, Promises Broken*. In *Native Universe: Voices of Indian America*. Gerald McMaster and Clifford E. Trafzer, editors. National Museum of the American Indian, Smithsonian Institution in association with National Geographic. Washington, D.C. 2008.

37. Site of 1864 massacre of Indians dedicated—The Denver Post. http:www.denverpost.com/technology/ci_5774659. Posted 04/28/2007.

38. "United States Congress Joint Committee on the Conduct of the War, 1865 (testimonies and report)". University of Michigan Digital Library Production Service. http://quod.lib.umich.edu/cgi/text/t/text/text-idx?c=moa;idno=ABY3709.0003.001;rgn=full%20text;view=toc;cc=moa. Retrieved 2008-03-19. See http://en.wikipedia.org/wiki/Sand_Creek_massacre

39. Site of 1864 massacre dedicated—The Denver Post. Op.cit.

40. Ibid.

41. Adams, David Wallace. *Education For Extinction: American Indians and the Boarding School Experience.* University Press Kansas. 1995. p. 14.

42. Ibid., p. 16. Note: Carl Schurz did not recommend the extermination of American Indians, but felt that government policy must be implemented to bring them to the level of civilization of white Americans. There were white Americans who were expecting that Native Americans would become extinct.

43. Ibid., p. 15.

44. Ibid., p. 18.

45. Ibid., p. 57.

46. Ibid., pps. 336-337.

CHAPTER 4

The Spanish Introduce Christianity to the Maya of Guatemala

Volunteer in Missions (VIM)

I have travelled to Guatemala three times, in 1996, 2004 and 2008, as a "volunteer in mission" a program sponsored by the United Methodist church. The idea of the Volunteer in Mission (VIM) program is to give church members a chance to travel to other countries where the church is involved in relief work. Rather than put money in a collection plate to pay for church relief work, the person travels as part of a group to do relief work. In a country like Guatemala that has gone through a 36 year internal war (1959-1996), the church member can participate in setting up medical clinics, build houses to replace those destroyed in warfare and listen to survivors relate their experiences during nearly four decades of violence and destruction.

The volunteer will also work with Maya people who endured the severe internal conflict that killed about 200,000 Maya and left hundreds of thousands homeless and adrift. The background of the conflict relates to government policies that left the Maya landless, and to agricultural practices of foreign owners of Guatemalan farmlands. Malnutrition was rare during pre-colonial times for the Mayans, who raised beans, maize, squash, chili, pineapple, and such root crops as manioc and sweet potatoes. The ancient Maya also developed artificial ponds for the raising of fish. However, the export crops of coffee and banana which now dominate agriculture in Guatemala do not sustain life. For foreign landowners, beans and maize are not profitable export crops; but without their traditional crops the Maya people have experienced rampant malnutrition and hunger.[1]

As laborers on foreign owned plantations, the Maya people endured both coercive work conditions and malnutrition. For some Methodist VIM volunteers, the experience in Guatemala comes as a severe cultural shock. They become a witness to poverty and to a history of brutal military governance that has suppressed the Maya population.

A volunteer who participates in these programs pays his own way and contributes monies for the relief effort. An important requirement of a volunteer in the VIM program is that the volunteer signs an agreement, "I will not proselytize." The volunteer will not try to convert a Mayan or anyone to the Christian faith. On all of these trips there is ample opportunity to visit historic and cultural sites. Rev. Larry Monk led the three trips in which I participated. He coordinated our volunteer efforts with indigenous church leaders, particularly the Iglesia Metodista Nacional Primitiva de Guatemala, in advance of the trips. My first trip to Guatemala (November-December 1996) came before the signing of the Peace Agreement, which was signed in Oslo in late December 1996. Before the 1996 trip Rev. Larry Monk warned each of us not to mention the conflict while in Guatemala and not to bring any written materials such as books or newspaper articles (such as from the New York Times) that reviewed the conflict and the US involvement.

One of the goals Rev Monk instituted was for each volunteer to prepare and give a twenty minute presentation to the group of volunteers on some topic related to the long civil war in Guatemala and the VIM mission program. Two of my presentations that I gave in 2004 and in 2008 were entitled, 1. The introduction of Christianity to the Maya in the 16th century, and 2. U.S. foreign policy in Guatemala. This chapter includes some elements of my two reports, as well as details of our work projects, and information about historic and cultural places we visited such as trips to Tikal, Lake Atitlan, the Mayan ruins at Iximche, and the ancient city of Antigua.

In addition to my travels to Guatemala as a Volunteer in Mission, my wife and I visited the Mayan ruins of Chichen Itza in 2003 while on our way to travel in Cuba. We have also visited Mayan ruins in Belize several times. The long and troubled history of how Christianity was introduced to the remarkable Maya people starts in the early 16th century with the Spanish Conquistadors and the Catholic priests who accompanied them.

Spain: the Conquest of Guatemala and the Introduction of Christianity to the Maya

In the year 1514, a Catholic priest named Bartolome' de Las Casas gave a sermon at Sancti Espiritus, the Cathedral in Santo Domingo (Cuba), condemning the unjust and oppressive treatment of the Indians in the New World. He continued his opposition to unjust treatment of the Indians in the New World for the next 40 years. One of his efforts was to establish a colony in Guatemala called Verapaz, or the Land of True Peace. In this colony Indians lived and worked in a self-governing co-op and had the opportunity to learn about the Christian faith without coercion; i.e., conversion to the faith was not required.[2]

The Spanish conqueror of Mexico, Hernando Cortes, sent conquistadors led by Pedro de Alvarado to Guatemala in 1524. Alvarado defeated the Indians within the year 1524, and established a Spanish colony in Guatemala. The conquest was brutal. Alvarado used his influence to play one rival Mayan group against another. With the help of the Cakchiquel Mayan nation, he managed to defeat the Quiche Mayan forces of 72,000 men, led by Tecun Uman. Of the battle Alvarado proclaimed, "We commenced to crush them and scattered them in all directions and made the greatest destruction in the world, at a river Rio de Sangre."[3]. The river, named Rio de Sangre, translates as "Blood River." A legend states that 30,000 Quiche died in the battle.

Mayan groups from time to time battled the Spanish. The last major Mayan revolt was suppressed in 1697, when the Spanish conquered Tayasal, capital of the Itza Maya, and Zacpeten, capital of the Ko'woj

Maya. The long and short of it is that the Spanish systematically crushed with great violence any opposition by the oppressed Mayans. The peaceful effort by Bartolome' de Las Casas to influence the Maya people in the "Land of True Peace" was erased from Guatemala. He continued his influence, but not in Guatemala. The methods Spain used to introduce Christianity to the Maya people are comparable to the rigid authoritativeness, oppression, and cruelty used by Stalin to control the peoples of Russia and Ukraine in the 1920's and 1930's.

In other areas of Central America many indigenous populations also met catastrophic decline as a result of conflict with the Spanish conquistadors. For example, about one half-million Indians lived in Honduras at the time of first contact with Spanish rule in 1525. Spanish enslavement, military directed suppression, and European diseases reduced the population of Indians in Honduras to about 18,000 by the year 1590. Honduras is relevant because the Spanish initially ruled Honduras through their Spanish colony of Guatemala, which borders Honduras. Furthermore, Honduras played a part in the US overthrow of the democratically elected president of Guatemala in 1954.

Spanish Rule in the New World: The Burning of Books and Concepts of Requerimiento and Encomienda

The Burning of Books In an effort to rid the Mayan culture of any remnant of Mayan religion and Mayan spirituality, the Spanish implemented a zero tolerance policy akin to the Spanish inquisition in Europe. In the words of Bishop Landa, "We found a large number of books in these characters (Maya writing) and, as they contained nothing in which there were not to be seen superstition and lies of the devil, we burned them all, which they regretted to an amazing degree, and which caused them much affliction."[4] In addition to the book burning, a large number of Mayan priests were executed. In the eyes of the Church, Mayan priests were heretics. The Spanish did not appreciate the amazing invention of the Mayas, of syllabic writing, unique in the Americas. The loss of the written works of a major culture is a terrible loss to all humanity. The destruction of Mayan writing was complete. By the 1700s no Mayan had any memory or skill in Mayan literacy. The fact that the destruction was authorized by priests of the Roman Catholic Church remains a major sorrow. The Spanish viewed their actions, which amounted to cultural genocide, as preparing the Mayan people for the Christian faith. The profit motive was also part of the goals pursued by the Spanish. To ensure that profit would be realized from the colony, the Spanish implemented the policies of requerimiento and encomienda.

Requerimiento The Spanish Conquistadors came to the new world in the name of the King and the Church. Priests accompanying the soldiers, as they came upon Indian villages, read the **Requerimiento,** which stated the King of Spain's title to the New World (granted by the Pope).[5] The formal demand required that the Indians acknowledge the King's sovereignty and accept the faith. Refusal could mean death. The Spanish felt it their responsibility to destroy Indigenous religious symbols and temples. At times they required the natives to destroy their own sacred sites. Following the act of destroying their temple, the Indigenous people were then required to build a Catholic Church for their own initiation into the worship of the Christian religion. For example, the Spanish required Mayan workmen to destroy a Mayan temple and build with the stones the Monastery of San Antonio in Isabal in 1553.

Later, in 1618, Franciscan priests Bartolome de Fuensalida and Juan de Orbita visited the remote wilderness of central Petan. They attempted to convert the Mayan king of that area named King Canek. He declined, saying, "the time had not yet arrived in which the ancient priests had prophesied to them they were to relinquish the worship of their gods." In response the infuriated Father Orbita smashed an image of a Mayan God. Five years later the Itza people in the area killed a Catholic priest, several Spanish soldiers, and about 60 fellow Mayans who had converted to Christianity. In retaliation king Canek was executed and remains a martyr among Guatemalans who still practice remnants of the Mayan religion. He is considered a martyr among many in Guatemala because he chose death rather than accepting the Christian faith as it was presented to the Indigenous peoples of Guatemala.

Encomienda With the authority of the Crown of Spain, land was given to a Spaniard (usually a soldier) along with a number of Indians to work the land. This term **encomienda**, further defines the relationship between the Spanish and the Indian. The Spanish was a lord, the Indian a serf, or a slave, without legal rights.[6] This relationship persisted for centuries, and was ruthlessly enforced by the Spanish until Spain lost their influence in the New World.

Spain abruptly loses its colonial influence in the Americas

The Spanish navy was defeated by Lord Nelson in the famous battle of Trafalgar on October 21, 1805. As a result, Spain was no longer able to defend its interests in the New World.

The British quickly developed into a strong military power in Central America in the 19th century, and used its powerful navy to help the five Central American countries gain independence from Spain. This enabled Guatemala, Honduras, El Salvador, Nicaragua and Costa Rica to declare independence from Spain in 1821.[7]

With Spain out of power in the new world, the British and other European countries were then free to develop their own interests. The British took the opportunity to build railroads and develop substantial infrastructures throughout Central America. Also in the 19th century, Germany settled businessmen in Guatemala and used Native peoples to grow coffee. Although the Spanish military was no longer a factor, a substantial number of Spanish landowners remained. They were then joined by settlers from Germany, England and other European powers. As European settlement expanded in Guatemala, no provision was made to rethink land ownership. Native Mayan peoples remained landless, and were subject to work and live under terms established by Europeans.

The United States asserts its influence over the Americas

The Monroe Doctrine was delivered to the Congress of the United States by President James Monroe in 1823, and it established that no European country could develop new colonies anywhere in the Americas nor extend existing colonies.

In the 1850s Central America became a focus for wealthy Americans to gain financial profits from access to rich lands for agriculture and to profit from low labor costs and for a time to participate in the slave trade. William Walker, an American businessman, was an example of one who made huge profits by investing in Guatemala. Also the Vanderbilt Steamship Line prospered and developed infrastructure such as ports and railroad lines in Guatemala, making it feasible and economical to ship vast quantities of the main export agricultural crops of coffee and bananas to the U.S. The extensive slave trade in Central America ended with the conclusion of the U.S. civil war.[8]

James Blaine, U.S. Secretary of State, saw the future of US companies doing business in Central America. He focused on trade rather than seeking to annex territory. When Mexico threatened to invade Guatemala in the 1880s, Blaine warned Mexico. This was an early example of the US using military strategies to protect US interests. Blaine presided over the first inter-American conference in 1889. One outcome was the United States established a Commercial Bureau of the American Republics, the parent of the Pan American Union of the American States, to enable government and private business to coordinate their activities in the south.[9]

In 1898 the US military effectively crushed the Spanish military in the Spanish-American war and ended Spain's already declining influence in the Caribbean, Central America and the Philippines. Theodore Roosevelt became president in 1901 and declared that the United States was the "natural protector" of Central American affairs. United States companies continued to invest substantial funds in Central America, particularly Guatemala. The Panama Canal, under construction during this period, further strengthened the concept that the United States had the right to police the area.

President Theodore Roosevelt extended the meaning of the Monroe Doctrine. He declared that any weakness of the smaller Central American countries might tempt European nations to intervene. He declared the United States had the obligation to intervene militarily to stabilize any country in the Western Hemisphere to prevent foreign influence. Under this policy the United States sent armed forces into the Dominican Republic in 1905, into Nicaragua in 1911, and into Haiti in 1915. In all, U.S. marines entered the Caribbean about twenty times between 1898 and 1920.

Walter LaFeber writes that by the 1920s U.S. entrepreneurs, led by Minor Keith's United Fruit Company, ran the economy of the Central American countries, making those economies dependent on North Americans. He adds, "By 1920, the political and economic elites in each of the five countries understood that not only were they increasingly dependent on North Americans, but that the real Colossus of the North was willing and able to reinforce economic dependence with direct military and political intervention. Stability meant maintaining the status quo, which meant that two percent of the population in four out of five of the Central American countries controlled the land and thus the lives of the other 98 percent."[10]

What became entrenched was that for these five countries there was no clean break from the authoritarianism of the colonial period, starting in 1492, resulting in a continuing failure over the next five centuries to integrate Indian communities into the larger economy.

The U.S. Central Intelligence Agency organizes a military coup against the Guatemalan president, Jacob Arbenz in 1954.

The beginnings of the coup began in 1944 when a group of hard line conservative generals were overthrown by socially more progressive officers. The change was not peaceful. The crisis started when thousands of teachers, students and physicians marched in front of the Presidential Palace in Guatemala City. They protested the oppressive conditions of farm laborers in Guatemala, and demanded fair wages for public school teachers whose pay was $35.00 per month (U.S. equivalent). President General Jorge Ubico ordered his cavalry to charge. His cavalry opened fire with machine guns and hundreds of teachers and students were killed. Protests increased across Guatemala. President-general Ubico was forced out and the people of Guatemala selected a much beloved Guatemalan, Juan Jose Arevalo, to serve as president. He began to institute land reform. He was succeeded by Jacobo Arbenz Guzman in 1951, a president elected by the people of Guatemala.

In his inaugural address, Arbenz stated: "Foreign capital will always be welcome as long as it adjusts to local conditions, remains always subordinate to Guatemalan laws, cooperates with the economic development of the country and strictly abstains from intervening in the nation's social and political life." Arbenz aggressively began to institute agrarian reforms. Foreign commercial interests controlled more than 90 percent of the arable land in Guatemala. However, about 16 percent of Guatemala's privately owned farm land had not been developed; that is, no crops had ever been planted on those lands by their foreign landlords. The Guatemalan government, under the leadership of Arbenz, took over control of those lands and gave it to 500,000 Indians. This was an attempt through land reform to give poor Indigenous Guatemalans (mostly with Mayan ancestry) small parcels of farm land. United Fruit, the former land owner, was compensated based on their own previous assessment (for tax purposes) of the value of their land. The Guatemalan government offered a Q of 609,572 to United Fruit as compensation for the land expropriation. In response United Fruit claimed the Guatemalan offer was insufficient and demanded a Q of 15,854,849, or twenty times more than the offer of the Guatemalan government.

The CIA led overthrow of Jacobo Arbenz

Leaders of the US Fruit Company were furious about the loss of any of their land and asked the CIA to remove Jacobo Arbenz from office. President Dwight D. Eisenhower and Richard Nixon agreed. Before the coup, a new dictator for Guatemala was identified and selected. To create a rationale for the coup the CIA planted boxes of rifles with conspicuous Soviet markings near Nicaragua's Pacific Coast. Aircraft dropped bombs around the airstrip of Honduras, making it appear that Guatemala was attacking Honduras on orders from Jacobo Arbenz. Furthermore, planting rifles with Soviet markings suggested that Arbenz had communist leanings.

Through this military action the US overthrew the government of Jacobo Arbenz and installed military protectors for the private landowners.[11] After the CIA coup, hundreds of Guatemalans who had supported Arbenz were arrested and killed. Militia then rounded up Indians and transported them to work on the plantations. Disaffected military officers, who had worked under the more progressive regime of Arbenz, went underground and established small guerilla forces in remote areas of the mountains. They tried to recruit Indians in these areas to join a military force to fight the U.S. installed dictatorship. Few Indians responded by joining any such military group. The rise of military dictatorships since the U.S. led overthrow created the most severe level of violence in Guatemala since the early days of the Spanish Conquest. The Guatemalan army's officers were white and mestizo (mixed racial ancestry), who served as conscripts for the ruling class. Any dissent was treated as a threat to the stability of the nation. The United States supplied the military equipment to Guatemala, such as rifles, machine guns, helicopters and jeeps and trained their officers to prevent Guatemala from insurgency. The military dictators in Guatemala spoke of internal conflict in Guatemala as representing threats of a communist takeover.[12]

In 1978 General Lucas Garcia assumed power. His regime introduced government organized death squads that created extreme terror. Death squads operating under government sanction were spread throughout Guatemala, particularly in rural areas almost entirely inhabited by indigenous natives.[13] The death squads recruited indigenous Maya men in rural areas to participate in the government militias. Refusal to join the government militia often times meant death. Maya leaders protested by printing underground pamphlets explaining the horror. One such pamphlet stated the following:

We are being slaughtered like animals. The soldiers enter our homes and rape our daughters. They murder our old men and women and our sons who resist the draft. For years the military has raided our fiestas, kidnapping our young men and forcing them into the army. After their brain-washing techniques, the army's mad men own them. They can never again be re-integrated into the village of their birth. They have become cold-blooded killers. The person who directs this ever-present terror against us is the bloodiest, most repressive dictator ever to live, General Romeo Lucas Garcia. Will you help us to establish peace? Will you help us get rid of his government?

During the 1970's the generals made financial accords with large North American mining and petroleum firms. This served both to "legitimize" their ruthless repression of the population, and to enrich the powerful generals. In 1978 seven hundred Indian peasants in the area of Franja Transversa de Norte marched on the city of Panzos. They carried a letter of protest over the loss of their land and the violence they endured, expecting government officials to offer help and protection. Instead hundreds of the Indian peasants were killed by government militia and their bodies were buried in mass graves.[14]

In January 1980, a group of Indians traveled to Guatemala City to protest the violence in the countryside. They entered the Spanish Embassy knowing that the ambassador was an outspoken critic of human rights violations committed by the Guatemala military. While the Indians were meeting with the Spanish ambassador, the military broke in and opened fire against the Indians killing all but one of them. One of the men killed was the father of Rigoberta Menchu. There were widespread international protests, but the Guatemala government and its military were indifferent to all of it.[15]

As the repression and violence deepened, Indians who had initially avoided joining forces with guerilla groups began to join out of absolute desperation. By the mid 1980s there were an estimated 5,000 active guerillas and perhaps 250,000 sympathizers. Violence against the Indians increased and many Indians, sometimes entire villages, fled to Chiapas in Mexico. Others fled to very remote mountain areas, becoming internal refugees in their own country. A few managed to enter into the United States to seek refuge. However, the United States Immigration Service systematically rejected their claims that they were escaping oppression and persecution. Indians escaping from Guatemala were said to be "economic refugees" who did not qualify for refugee status. Churches in the United States who offered sanctuary to Mayans who fled Guatemala faced the possibility of legal action.

The terror for Guatemalan Indians increased under the government of General Rios Montt. He introduced the formation of Civil Patrol, which included thousands of Indians who had been coerced into spying for the government. They were to report anyone suspected of the slightest degree of harboring sympathies against the Guatemala government and the military. Failure to comply with the Civil Patrol was punishable by death.

During the 36-year war, 200,000 people including women and children died.[16]

A peace accord ended the violence in 1996.

Herman Paz Alvaredo, with a law degree helps resolve conflicts over land

Rev. Larry Monk has worked to establish relationships throughout Guatemala to help his volunteers gain an understanding of historical, cultural and economic factors that underlie the persistent poverty and oppression that continue in Guatemala. One such person is attorney Herman Paz Alvaredo. Alvaredo was Director of JADE, an organization of attorneys specifically working on land ownership issues. It was funded by Mercy Corps.

When Alvaredo spoke to our group in 2004 he told us that he had succeeded in helping resolve 46 conflicts over land holdings. This enabled 46 families to have title to a piece of land so they could eventually build a house and do subsistence farming. The tens of thousands of other potential land claims had not yet been resolved. Alvaredo helped put in context the difficulty in resolving land claims in Guatemala. He explained to us that after conquering Guatemala in the 1500s, the Spanish authorities assigned land to a Spaniard in such loose terms as, "Your land is from this tree to that hill over there and to that mountain." An individual Spaniard may have been given land equal in size to that of a large city, and given control of the natives who were then living on the land. The land was never formally surveyed; to this day much of the land in Guatemala is without official records showing boundaries or plot demarcations of land. Furthermore, as Spanish influence declined, much of the land came under the control of other

Europeans but remained unrecorded in any standard manner. The legal work done by Alvaredo was over land now "owned" by Germans who settled in the 1800s. Again, the land had never been surveyed; furthermore, some of the land had been mortgaged and was in control of the banks. An additional problem is that when land was assigned to indigenous farmers in the 1960's, the land was not assigned with reference to whether the indigenous farmer had ever worked that land or had ever even seen it. When returning Mayan refugees came back to Guatemala from hiding to take advantage of the "land reform," they met firm resistance from European-Americans who had occupied the land for generations and thought they "owned" the land. The government then issued court orders to remove the campesinos (Latin-American farm workers) from the land recently assigned to them. Armed conflicts resulted in the deaths of many campesinos.

Our group of VIM volunteers appreciated very much the presentation by attorney Herman Paz Alvaredo. He had driven three hours through mountainous roads to meet with us. We were left with an understanding of why the overthrow of the presidency of Jacob Arbenz in 1954 led to a situation in which meaningful land reform has been extremely difficult to enact.

Following the presentation by Alvarado we travelled to Chichicastenango. On the way we stopped at the Iximche ruins, and walked around the area. While admiring the ruins, I met and spoke with a Catholic Priest, named Padre Gardere. We exchanged e-mails and agreed to correspond regarding changes in Christianity in Guatemala. After viewing the Ixmiche ruins, our VIM group gathered for discussions. Larry asked two of our group to give their assigned and prepared talks. I made a presentation on "The CIA overthrow of the presidency of Jacobo Arbenze in 1954." Following my presentation and group discussion, another member, Beth, gave her presentation on "Mayan spirituality."

I had the opportunity to hear attorney Alvaredo again on my trip to Guatemala in March 2008. He reviewed some of the same issues and added some updates. One of the remarkable moments in his talk occurred during the question and answer period following his presentation. Rev.

Monk asked Alvaredo to reflect on the spiritual meaning for him of the history of Guatemala since the introduction of Christianity in the early 1500s. As he paused to reflect on the question of the spiritual meaning of the Spanish Conquest and the accompanying coercive missionary effort, I thought he might answer the question with a focus on the catastrophic loss of life of Mayan people due both to the military violence and to the widespread diseases introduced by the Spanish for which Indigenous peoples had no immunity. I thought he might focus on cultural genocide. I considered that he might relate the timing of the discovery of the New World in 1492, to the fact that the King of Spain, also in 1492, gave an order that all Jews convert to Christianity, or leave Spain, or be executed. It is unequivocal that during that period of time the missionary effort to spread Christianity to nonbelievers, especially Jews, in Europe was ruthless and coercive. That ruthless and oppressive pattern of missionary effort indeed continued on to the Americas starting with the "Discovery" in 1492.

Instead, after a pause, he said:

The Church needs to develop a new strategy. They have taken away our cultural heritage. (pause). If you are going to be a Christian, you must relate in some way to the Bible; however, keep in mind the Bible itself was written by the winners. The Bible was written from the point of view of the haves. It tells slaves to obey their masters. In the Bible heterosexuals won over homosexuals. The Church closes your eyes. Liberation Theology opens your eyes. We in liberation Theology are thinking of options for the poor.

I asked Alvaredo if the Vatican supports Liberation Theology and the numbers of Roman Catholic priests and nuns in Central America who support it. A Catholic himself, he answered *No!*

Liberation Theology in Latin America started within the Roman Catholic Church; however, as Herman stated, the Vatican has not endorsed the Liberation Theology movement and in fact has expelled some Catholic priests and nuns from the ministry who were committed to the movement. Dr. Harvey Cox, the Hollis Professor of Divinity

Emeritus at Harvard, states that the Liberation Theology movement in Latin America did not originate in privileged religious institutions. Instead the movement started among the very poor but religious (mostly Catholic) people. Cox describes the origin as follows:

> First, they read the gospels in small groups, often led by laypeople, in which they discussed ways to respond to the appalling conditions they lived in. Priests and nuns had originally organized these groups, called "ecclesial base communities" (co-munidades eclesiales de base, CEBs), to complement regular parish worship, especially in areas where clergy were in short supply. But they soon outgrew clerical oversight and took on lives of their own. They met in villages, small towns, and in the shabbier sections of the big cities.[17]

Father Gustavo Gutierrez, a Peruvian priest, is said to be the father of Liberation Theology. He was on the faculty at the Pontifical Catholic University in Lima, Peru, and served in a parish there. He also travelled extensively and blended his own indigenous roots, his passion for the poor and Christian theology as he understood it. Cox writes that Gutierrez was influenced by the writings of Pierre Teilhard des Chardin and also by the writings of Sigmund Freud.[18] The Vatican has condemned the writings of Pierre Teilhard des Chardin.

It has not been easy for Catholic priests in Latin America to be part of the Liberation Theology movement. In 1970 a young priest Father Rutulio Grande, who advocated for the poorest in El Salvador, was murdered by a death squad. Archbishop Oscar Arnulfo Romera, the Roman Catholic archbishop of San Salvador, officiated at the service for Father Grande. At the service parishioners asked the archbishop, "Will you stand with us as Father Rutulio did?" The archbishop embraced the message of Liberation Theology and spoke on behalf of the poor and oppressed. He refused to be silent about the violence endured by the oppressed. From his pulpit he made it a practice to announce each week the names of those who had been killed or who "disappeared." He warned members of the police and military that God forbade them from committing atrocities against the innocent peasants. In 1980 archbishop Romera was shot to death execution style. His death made him another martyr of Liberation Theology.[19]

Professor Harvey Cox states that Liberation theology is the most innovative and influential theological movement of the twentieth century. He states that the current spread of the Roman Catholic Church in Latin America is due almost entirely to the growth and influence of Liberation Theology. The movement is inspired by rethinking the Christian message from the point of view of the poor, and it has moved far away from the hierarchical structure of the Roman Catholic Church and its insistence on "correct creeds."[20] Cox had an interview with Cardinal Joseph Ratzinger in 1988. Cardinal Ratzinger had just returned from a trip to Africa and spoke with Cox about his consternation about the practice among Africans of blending Christian with indigenous local spiritual practices. Cardinal Ratzinger referred to this "syncretism" as the main source of "heresy" in the world today.[21] After the death of John Paul II in 2005, Cardinal Ratzinger became Pope Benedict XVI. I follow with interest news from the Vatican and words from Pope Benedict XVI.

Morning Devotion, March 26, 2008

Following the talk by Alvaredo and a brief discussion of Liberation Theology, Rev. Monk led the morning devotion by reciting the Biblical story of Lazarus, a poor man, who ate the crumbs that had fallen to the ground off a rich man's table. He asked us to consider from the point of view of liberation theology the question, "What would you do in the case of Lazarus?" As our group discussed the issue, we remembered that since the 1950's many Roman Catholic priests and nuns have supported the Maya people in Guatemala and have opposed the oppression and violence against them. This honorable effort, as stated above, was dangerous as numbers of priests and nuns have been killed throughout Central America. Nevertheless, a person advocating from the position of the Biblical story of Lazarus would have supported the proposed action of those Catholic Priests and Nuns and the Guatemalan government of Jacobo Arbenz, who campaigned against the oppression of his people.

Rev. Monk then asked us to consider the world view of the "powers that be," in a dictatorship like Guatemala, and asked, "What then would have been done?" The discussion among our group as we reflected on life in Guatemala produced a straight forward answer. A person advocating for Lazarus would be identified as an insurgent, or a terrorist. The military would be called in to evict both Lazarus and the insurgents who supported him. By their actions the military would have "restored order" and protected the lawful rights of the rich man. Such an action would have been comparable to evicting a leader such as Jacobo Arbenz, who had been overthrown by the CIA in 1954.

VIM Mission Projects

One purpose of VIM projects is to bring church members to countries like Guatemala to learn first hand the historical background and the nature of problems that the church is trying to alleviate. I will begin with an introduction to four projects that relate directly to massacres, without provocation, that created overwhelming suffering and despair in rural areas of Guatemala. The four VIM mission projects in the rural town of Chontala are the following: I. The Ruth and Nohemi Tailor Shop and Store, II. Widows of the Ruth and Nohemi Cooperative, III. The Building of a house in Chontola, and IV. The building, staffing and operation of health clinics.

Background: Killings in a Methodist Church at Chontala

In 1982 forty Mayan men, who were working in the fields of Chontala, were apprehended without warning and without a warrant. They were taken to a small rural Methodist church and shot to death. The church was then blown up.

When I visited this church for the first time in November 1996, I was part of a group of twelve "Volunteers In Mission." We were led by Rev. Larry Monk and his wife Linda. Also with us was Rev. Diego Chicoj Ramos. He invited us into the reconstructed church (rebuilt in the late 1980's) and discussed the tragedy and loss of life. He pointed out that some parts of the original church had been salvaged and installed in the rebuilding. He pointed out beams that showed gunshot holes, as well as evidence of fire and blast. He told us that the Chontola' massacre is typical of many, and "each community has its own account." (Cada pueblo tiene su propia historia.) Then he told us the story of the massacre.

One day in 1982 the military moved into Chontola, its mission to eradicate any guerilla presence in the community. They arrived about 5:30 a.m. and sealed off the village from the outside. Anyone who ventured up to the road was seized and thrown into the National Methodist Church. And about 4 p.m. as helicopters flew overhead, the military threw a bomb into the church, killing about 40 persons inside. Some accounts say the prisoners were machine-gunned first.

At one point, I walked along the road from Chichicastenango, coming to visit the congregation I served on an unpaid voluntary basis. A military officer told me, "You don't want to go in there." So I didn't, but the next day I did enter Chontola, and found the church destroyed, with only shrapnel-pocked steel beams standing and at least 16 of his congregation were now widows.

The military forbade gatherings of groups of people, so the congregation could not meet for some time. I continued ministering to the congregation family by family, walking one hour each way from Chichicastenango. The widows told me of their struggle to survive. They had to do the farming their husbands had done, plus care for their own children and those of their relatives who had been killed, and it was more than they could handle. So they asked me if there were any way the church could help.

After he told us of the tragic account, I asked Rev. Diego if there could be a small plaque on the door of the reconstructed church to announce in some way that the church was the site of a massacre.

He said "No! If we do that there would be more killing. We cannot bring attention to the government's involvement. We cannot criticize the government."

I then asked, "Instead, could there be a simple plaque, *God asked Cain, What have you done to your brother?*"

The minister answered, "We would not dare to do that!"

I. The Ruth and Nohemi Taylor Shop and Store.

Background Rev. Diego Chicog Ramos, the Guatemalan Methodist minister and a tailor (his work as a tailor provides his income), gave our VIM group a background of the violence and what the faith community has done to rebuild. I took careful notes so I will let his words tell you the story.

The Ruth and Nohemi project has its roots in the 1980's. At that time the army killed many people in our country. In 1982 the army blew up our Methodist Church in Chontala, with over 40 men killed. The army had a practice of taking over or destroying public buildings and putting people in them and blowing them up. The United States Methodist Board of ministry helped rebuild the church during the years 1984-1987. In 1986 the congregation was primarily made up of women. So, the women came to me and asked if there was anything I could do to help them. These women all had children but could not make do. I did not have anything, but I traveled to the Methodist headquarters and met with a man who was the equivalent of a Bishop. He, and others who met with us, told me that they had no money and no corn to give out. But they also said that giving money or corn is not the way to solve the problem. They explained, "If we could give the women food for a week, then next week they would have the same problem." They asked me to find out what the women could do to solve their problem. I returned to Chontala and told them the news. That was May 6, 1986.

The women talked about their skill in weaving. The church responded by supplying the women with 100 pounds of thread and a few chickens for them to raise. We asked the women to make things and to sell them at the market. However, the violence in the area was so severe that the Tourist Committee in Guatemala City prevented people from traveling to Chichicastenango, which is the big market.

Another problem was that the sons had no fathers, so the boys went to Guatemala City to find work. There was no work to be found, but many got hooked up with drugs, which added a new problem. So the mothers came to me and said, "What are we to do? Our husbands have been killed and our sons have left home?"

Diego Chicog looked at us and said, *I too was poor and when I was nine years old I began to work. At age ten I began to be a tailor, and I learned the craft very well. I told the women that I knew about tailoring and I could run a school on tailoring. We were able to take the fabrics the women sewed to make jackets, purses and other products. When this effort began, the boys stayed in their own communities and did not go to Guatemala City.*

But we found another problem—illiteracy. I asked the young boys, why don't you go back to school? They said, "We are twelve years old and older. If we go back to school, we would be with children who are six and seven years old." I told the boys that we would have them work during the day and we would provide schooling for them at night.

All of them agreed.

Another problem we had was the cramped quarters. We did not have a large enough building to set up an adequate tailor shop, and a place where the young students could live and work. In 1991 a woman came from a United Methodist Church in California. She said, "I have heard of the youth program here. Tell me about it?"

After I explained the program and introduced her to the young boys who were doing excellent tailor work to make jackets and purses, she told me she wanted to help. She went back to her church and made arrangements to sell our products. Her name is Carol Conger Cross. With the money we earned we began to build this building where we are in right now. We continue to make products and many of them are sold through churches in the United States.

II. Widows of the Ruth and Nohemi Cooperative

The Ruth and Nohemi Cooperative is located in the rural town of Chontola. The steep dirt trail leading to the cooperative starts at the Methodist Church (the one that was bombed) and is about one and a half miles long. When we arrived we were met by Maria Tomasa, who is head of the Ruth and Nohemi Cooperative. We saw the beautiful hand made products that the women had made. Each community of Indigenous people has their own distinctive pattern. We wanted to hear her story, so Maria, who speaks both a Mayan language and Spanish, spoke in Spanish and Rev. Monk translated for us. This is her story,

Good afternoon to all of you. Thanks to God and you for coming here. The history is very long, but I will not take all evening and night to tell the story.

This co-operative was formed in response to what happened here in 1980, 81 and 82. I was living here. My husband was killed by the Civil Patrol. People killed even a neighbor or someone with whom they had a grudge. This was done with impunity. The husbands of many women were kidnapped and never seen again. Some people fled to Guatemala City and saw on television what was happening in their community.

Some returned to our community after hiding for about five months. When they returned to this community they found their houses had been destroyed. For survival they lived all together in the school building. I had two children and, of course, my husband was dead. This was true for the other women also. Some other women and I went to meet with Diego to see what kind of help we could get.

Note: Maria repeated the story cited above about the "hundred pounds of thread," the raising of chickens and the success of selling their products. Maria then continued about the stresses endured by the community.

We started out with 20 women and at one time 22 women were making fabrics in our community. Now we are down to 14. The war was very traumatic. In some cases our women were forced to accompany (go with) the soldier who killed her husband and other men in our community. Many of the women who survived have not been able to be good care givers.

A member of our VIM group who was familiar with the 1996 Peace Accord, commented to Maria that the Peace Accord specified that victims of the violence would receive compensation. Maria stated that no one in her community received compensation. Rev. Monk interjected that President Efrain Rios Montt, who was behind the most severe atrocities, had been trained at the School of the Americas. Maria then told us that the Quiche Mayan group, of which she and her neighbors are a part, was one of the hardest hit during the Spanish Conquest in the 16th century. The river Rio de Sangre, meaning "blood river," where 30,000 Indians were killed is nearby. She stated, "Once again our area was one of the hardest hit during the violence under President Efrain Montt nearly five hundred years later in the 1980's."

After the presentation by Maria, and further discussion, all of us admired the colorful hand made products and purchased some of them.

III. The building of a house in Chontola

In preparation for our VIM trip in 2008, Rev. Larry Monk corresponded with Carla Gonzalez of the National Methodist Church ministries in Guatemala. She recommended a work project of building a small house for a family in need. There are pre-requisites for families receiving houses through the National Methodist Church. They must be poor and without a house of their own. However, they must have enough income to repay a loan (of $400-US equivalent-with no interest charged); the property must be in their name and not that of a parent or other relative. The National Methodist Church congregation had no one who would qualify, and so they found a member of the Church of the Nazarene who happens to be the son of the pastor of that congregation.

The fellow was totally thrilled with the news that he would receive a house: now he and his wife and five children wouldn't have to live with his parents, and would have a brand-new home of his own! He immediately set to work leveling the building site, 25 feet down the side of the hill below the Church of the Nazarene's new building. And he carried down to the building site each cement block we were to use: about 1340 blocks weighing 22 pounds each, 8 at a time!

On March 28, 2008, our VIM group traveled to Chontola to help build the cement block house for this young Mayan couple with five children. While helping this family the work effort gave those of us from the US a glimpse of current life in Guatemala that directly relates to the traumas of the recent past. Large numbers of Guatemalan people lost their houses and small farms in addition to the large numbers who were killed or forced out of Guatemala. The young father earns a living by making leather belts and selling them as a street vendor. He buys hides from animals slaughtered for meat, prepares the leather and constructs finished belts. He is also a minister, but like most Protestant clergy in rural Guatemala, he receives no financial compensation for his church work. Though voluntary, his commitment to church work involves substantial time, effort and thoughtfulness.

The house we were building was made of concrete blocks. The two room house would have 322 square feet. Each room measured 11' by 14.' One room contained a wood stove for cooking and heating. The house was not built to have electricity or water, and the floor would be a dirt floor. The small community had out-houses for toilet needs, and a water pump for neighbors to get water as needed on a daily basis.

The terrain where the house was being built was very steep, and it took the young man seven days working with shovels and a wheel barrow to level a space for his small house. Rev. Diego explained to us that in 1997 on a similar project in Chontola the volunteer workers along with Native Guatemalans uncovered six pieces of intact pottery as well as pieces of broken pottery as they were preparing a level place to build a small house. The pottery and fragments were taken to some experts in the field of anthropology who dated the artifacts to be from the period of 700 BCE. Out of respect for the culture and its history the pottery was taken to religious leaders who still practice the ancient Maya religion. These Maya shamans performed a ceremony and placed a piece of corn in each artifact. The pottery remains in Guatemala and I was among those who had the opportunity to hold and admire these pieces.

By 2004 16 concrete blockhouses had been built in Chontola through the VIM project. Our building project was in 2008.

IV. Medical—Dental Health Care Clinics.

As a consequence of many indigenous people leaving cities in Guatemala during the 36 year civil war to live in rural and mountainous parts of the country, there was a lack of medical and dental programs in these rural areas. The Volunteer in Mission program helps support two medical and dental programs, the Patulup Clinic and the Salud Y Paz Camanchaj Clinic.

The Patulup Clinic has its origin in a medical crisis that occurred in 1993. A woman became seriously ill and there was no medical care available in the rural community set in a remote mountainous area of Guatemala. Her husband, Juan Ixtan Calgua, picked up his wife and carried her about twelve kilometers on a trail to a clinic run by the Association Benefica Metodista in Chichicastenango. She was given medical treatment and recovered. Her husband was determined that members of this community would not experience that degree of desperation during a medical emergency again. Rev. Larry Monk took notes from his first meeting with Juan Ixtan Calgua in 1994 and he shared them with me on my first trip to Guatemala in 1996,

This started Juan thinking. What did the people of his village do when they got ill? The 1100 people in Patalup farmed the steep hillsides, and lived in adobe houses with tile roofs and no outhouses. They had no money for medicines or doctors. In fact, only 45 people in town were older than 40, perhaps because there was no health care. And Juan, as volunteer pastor of Patalup's Iglesia Metodist Nacional Evangelica Primitiva de Guatemala, felt God's call to respond to their needs for health as well as spiritual guidance.

So Juan began learning about medicine, including traditional medicine, using plants that grew locally, as well as Western medicine. He began visiting his neighbors and advising them on what plants would treat their illnesses. He started a campaign to get them to construct out-houses, and bring the prevalent intestinal problems under control. He began getting vaccine to vaccinate the Patalupans against tetanus and the most prevalent diseases. He converted his living room into a clinic, and he recruited other volunteers to join him as a Health Care Promoter. He organized them so that each promoter would visit each family in their area once a week, report any illnesses, and dispense what medications they could.

We first learned of the medical side of Juan's ministry while we were visiting with him at the Campamento Metodista in San Sebastian de Lemoa. So we asked, "what was his most pressing need for his clinic?" "Vitamins," he said. "We can get antibiotics from the hospital in Sta. Cruz de Quiche, another half hour north of Lemoa, if we need them. But vitamins will help prevent illnesses. We need Children's and adult daily vitamins."

So the next time we traveled to Guatemala, we brought vitamins. Over a hundred bottles of vitamins, from funds contributed by our congregations back home. And as Juan rode with us on the bus over the torturous road through the hills to Juan's home and clinic, he told us with tears in his eyes that we were the first non-Guatemalans to visit his village. He was overwhelmed by the donation of vitamins as he told us that these vitamins would supply everyone in his community for a full year.

Starting in 2001, the Executive Committee of the Methodist Church authorized the construction of a new church building and clinic by Juan's home. Juan and his father have donated the land for that building and for a two-story clinic behind it. Volunteer-in Mission teams have helped with the construction of the church building and the new clinic building. It has spaces for a dentist, a pharmacy, a waiting room, a doctor, a store-room, and a small kitchen.

The General Board of Global Ministries was impressed with what Juan has accomplished, and sent him to Bolivia for training in community health. Juan has offered other communities his expertise in setting up a Health Promoter program.

In November 2003, we asked Juan what his most pressing needs are now. The answer: basic equipment for his 12 Health Promoters. We brought him 12 copies of "Where There Are No Doctors" For each promoter we provided a stethoscope, a blood pressure cuff, an otoscope and a digital thermometer. A doctor has donated a glucometer to diagnose diabetes, which we brought in March 2004.

And the results of his efforts: The health of the community has improved. Women deliver healthier and heavier babies, and in the last year the midwives delivered 40 babies, and not lost one.

Larry Monk, memo from 2004.

Rev. Juan Ixtan Calgua continued his presentation to us (2008 VIM trip):

Jesus was concerned about the poor and oppression brought on by evil rulers. He said to his disciples referring to judgment day: The Lord said to those who are blessed by God, I was hungry and you fed me. I was thirsty and you gave me water. I was sick and you cared for me. I was in prison and you came to visit me. And his disciples said when did we do those things, and Jesus said when you have done these things to the least of these you did it for me."[22] *Juan Ixtan Calgua then looked at us, paused and said, "This is what you have been doing; you have followed that commandment of Jesus. We know that this effort has cost you a lot of time and money to help us get started with the clinic and our work.*

He then said,

I would like to introduce two people to you who have come to us from a Volunteer In Mission in Fairbanks Alaska. They are Dr. Susan Tate, a physician, and Amanda Traver, who is a nurse practitioner. They have volunteered to spend a full year helping us in our work.

Amanda Traver then spoke to our group about their work. She said that she and Dr. Tate came to volunteer in a rural setting in Guatemala to make amends for the violence that erupted following the United States role in overthrowing a democratically elected president in Guatemala in 1954 and the 36 year civil war that followed and brought so much loss of lives among the Maya people and so much devastation. Following her talk we had a nice lunch and a chance to walk around the community set at a very high altitude of 10,000' in the rugged mountains of Guatemala.

Lake Atitlan

On each of my three VIM trips to Guatemala, our groups spent several days at Lake Atitlan. This idyllic lake is a crater lake formed following an explosive volcanic eruption. In that sense the lake was formed in a similar manner as Crater Lake in Oregon, Yellowstone Lake in Wyoming, and Lake Taupo in New Zealand. Lake Atitlan is known internationally and is a destination resort that is popular for travelers from Canada, the U.S., Europe and Asia. On every VIM trip Rev. Monk makes arrangements for a geologist to explain the geological history of this lake.

Geologist Juan Skinner Alvarado presented a lecture entitled, *History of Lake Atitlan: Geologic Origin and Evolution.* His talk was accompanied by high quality digital slides. He told us that the vast number of heavily forested steep hills in Guatemala are weathered down remnants of ancient volcanoes. His main focus was the cataclysmic eruption of Mount Los Chocoyos about 158,000 years before the present. He stated it extinguished all life in Guatemala. The explosion covered the country with heavy layers of ash, pumice and debris, in places reaching depths of thousands of feet. The explosive eruption moved at 800 km per hour with temperatures exceeding 500 degrees Fahrenheit.

Lake Atitlan, created by the eruption of Mount Los Chocoyos, is about 128,000 years old (not 158,000 years) because it took about 55,000 years for the magna to cool. This beautiful lake has a maximum depth of 342 meters. Although Crater Lake in Oregon is twice as deep, Lake Atitlan covers a much greater surface area. The transparency is 11 meters and the water quality remains quite good, in large part, stated Juan Alvarado because traditional agriculture in Guatemala was based on low impact methods without the use of pesticides or chemical fertilizers (this has changed recently). For our trip the cataclysmic eruption of Mount Los Chocoyos about 158,000 years ago served as a metaphor for the cataclysmic consequences of the Spanish conquest and the oppression of the Maya people that continue to this day. I was reminded of the statement by the attorney Herman Paz Alvarado that "Guatemala is a land of eternal spring time and eternal violence."

. We stayed at a beautiful hotel with cabins with shore front views of the lake. The *Posada De Santiago,* was built over a three year period and completed in 1980. The cabins were built of rustic stone, bamboo walls with shutters and thatched roofs. There are trails in the area and canoes available for the guests on the lake. Each morning about 5:00 A.M. I made my way to the lake and paddled out with one of the canoes for an hour or so. I always saw indigenous fishermen catching the small fish that populate the lake. They fished from wooden boats hand hewn from logs.

We enjoyed our stay at Lake Atitlan, but a major reason for our visit to this beautiful place was to visit the site of a massacre against unarmed citizens by the Guatemala military on December 2, 1990. Prior to that December in 1990 there were numerous, but isolated, attacks against citizens by the military in the area around Lake Atitlan. Dave, the owner of *Posada De Santiago,* told us that in the ten year period leading up to December 1990 there were about 800 killings, including a Catholic priest and an additional 700 who disappeared. About the killings on December 2, 1990, Dave wrote the following passage to explain the massacre so that he does not have to retell the story a thousand times. To the question, "What happened that night?" He gives this account:

I was playing poker in Panajachel that night, so this is not a first hand account. Officers from the base, out of uniform, were drinking all day in the pueblo. They were asked to leave a cantina at about ten PM. They attempted to break into a merchant's house to, presumably, sexually assault his daughter. Neighbors responded to the man's cries for help and came to the family's aid. In a brief melee, a teenage boy was wounded in the arm by a pistol fired by one of the officers. The growing crowd of angry neighbors dragged the two officers to the police station and demanded that they identify themselves and be arrested. Most of the town's inhabitants were awakened by the noise and the ringing of the Catholic Church bells. Soldiers from the base, responding to the gunshots and noise, arrived at the police station, threatened the police with their machine guns, and led the drunk officers back to the base. A crowd of several thousand gathered in the plaza and brought the out-going and incumbent mayors to the base for an impromptu demonstration. There was a full moon when the white flag and flashlight bearing crowd arrived at the gate to the army base at about midnight. After asking for an audience with the commanding officer to present grievances and demands, the mayors were told to quiet the noisy crowd. One of the officers fired his pistol into the air. The young recruits took that as a signal and opened up on the crowd of unarmed civilians with their automatic weapons. Thirteen were killed, the youngest a child of nine, and twenty were wounded, some severely. Unlike many less public massacres, the bodies of the dead were still left lying on the ground in front of the base when later that morning both the national and international press arrived. The incident led to the army being expelled permanently from Santiago Atitlan two weeks later by then president Vinicio Cerezos. The massacre was cited along with the murder of Poptun inn-keeper Michael Divine later that month when the US Congress discontinued aid to Guatemala. One officer and three recruits were tried by a military court and given prison sentences. The first time the military has found soldiers guilty of crimes against civilians in this country. Their jail terms were between six and sixteen years.

On each of the three occasions that I have served as a VIM volunteer in Guatemala our groups have visited the site where the thirteen bodies are buried. We always paused to reflect on the massacre as but one small example of the 200,000 people (mostly Mayan) who were killed in the 36 year reign of terror. It should not be called a civil war, because only one side had weapons. I vividly remember standing in front of the humble stone marker for the young child, age nine, who was among those shot to death.

Los Romeritos: A day care center in Guatemala City

Los Romeritos is a unique day care center for low-income children providing schooling with a focus on art and drama, meals and health care in a secure environment. The young children who attend are children of "sexual workers" and other low income families of Guatemala City. The program was started by Megan Parkinson of the Oregon City United Methodist Church and Jamie Marcia, of Guatemala, who is trained in drama and the arts. In 2008, my third trip to Guatemala as a VIM volunteer, this portion of the VIM mission remains a highlight for me and to everyone who visits this amazing program. On my first visit to this program in 1996, Jamie Marcia met with our VIM group privately and out of the hearing of the children. He told us that the children were poor and the offspring of troubled women who live in difficult circumstances. Many, he said, were "sexual workers," that is prostitutes. The children wanted to "perform a little skit for us," and Jamie admonished us to be patient and supportive of their efforts as unpolished as they might be.

Instead of the children behaving as shy and withdrawn, they were exuberant and skilled. They put on a show that would have been the pride and joy of parents, grandparents and the public anywhere. One play designed and performed by the children was that of a woman "sexual worker" who was threatened by an unruly and potentially violent male. The part of the "sexual worker" was played by an eight year old boy dressed as a woman of the night. In the play the woman was able to escape the danger. I was amazed at the realism with which these children played out their inner lives. Should a Christian program allow children of prostitutes to attend a day care program? I am reminded of the story in the New Testament Book of John where Jesus was entrapped by his fellow-Jews into approving the stoning of an adulteress. Jesus suggested that the honor of throwing the first stone should be given to the man in the unruly mob who is without sin. The children who are part of this program would have been homeless "street children." Now at least part of their day is predictable, and they are provided with food, education and basic health care in a caring and supportive environment.

Ancient Maya Sites

The ancient civilization of Maya stretched well beyond the borders of present day Guatemala. On one of several visits to Maya sites in western Belize we visited the ancient city of Cahal Pech. A marker at the site states the following:

The ancient city of Cahal Pech was abandoned around 850 A.D. During the "Collapse" the Maya people vacated the older cities and moved to coastal regions of Belize, in highland areas of Guatemala, and throughout the Yucatan Peninsula. Their government changed from Divine Ruler to a confederation with multiple leaders.

At a small information center about the Maya sites we obtained a brochure to explain the background. One stated:

Unfortunately, Spanish colonization and new diseases introduced by the Europeans decimated thousands of these people. But the Maya are resilient and today there are over 8 million people (Maya) living in Guatemala, 3 million living in Mexico and thousands more in Belize.

Cahal Pech and other large sites stand as silent testimonies of their past achievements.

(I made a note in my journal about the complete lack of information about the catastrophic abuses inflicted by the Spanish conquistadors on the Maya people. Indeed new diseases were catastrophic throughout the Americas; however, the Spanish instituted a policy of cultural genocide in *all* of its conquests in the "New World.")

We also visited Xunantunich, a major Maya site in Belize, where we saw their ball court and replica friezes on El Castillo that honor Maya gods. The replicas protect the original friezes underneath. To reach Xunantunich we rode a hand-cranked ferry across the Mopan River which is a short distance from the Maya site. Nearby are a series of sacred caves, which Maya saw as a gateway to the underworld. The caves still contain ancient Maya pottery and human skeletons. While in Belize my wife and I joined our son Erik, his wife Rhea, sons Finn and Reed, and Rhea's parents on a horse back trek through the jungles and visited an ancient Maya city that remains buried under centuries of jungle growth. We learned that in Belize and Guatemala only 15 to 20 percent of ancient Maya ruins have been uncovered and explored.

At Tikal in Guatemala we climbed the Great Pyramid of Tikal's Lost World and enjoyed the vantage point 105 feet above the jungle floor. We admired Temple IV, the Lost World and the Grand Plaza, with its ceremonial courtyard and temples. We saw and photographed wild turkeys and howler monkeys.

I was reminded that members of our VIM group, who averaged age 70, did not teach the Maya whom we worked with how to build any more than a Methodist group on a VIM trip to Brazil would teach Brazilians how to play soccer. We helped strong, resilient and able Maya men and woman by showing compassion, understanding and support. Everyone of our VIM group felt that we got more out our interaction with present day Maya people than we contributed.

Léif G. Terdal

Thomas Berger in this book, **A Long and Terrible Shadow,** states: "the military campaign against the Indians is so far-reaching, pervasive and malignant that it amounts to genocide." (page 124) He reminds his readers that, "It is a violation of the Genocide Convention of 1948 to commit any of the following acts "with the intent to destroy, in whole or in part, a national, ethnical, racial or religious group, as such: (a) killing members of the group; (b) causing serious bodily or mental harm to the group; (c) deliberately inflicting on the group conditions of life calculated to bring about its physical destruction in whole or in part . . ."

Berger further states that, "Until Guatemala acknowledges that Indian land, Indian culture and Indian survival, and the refusal by Guatemalans to recognize their legitimacy, lie at the heart of the nation's trauma, there will be no resolution of the political and economic sickness that has afflicted the country for five centuries." (page 125) The death toll from violence following the 1954 coup exceeds 100,000.

A comparison and contrast of life for the Maya during the early part of the Spanish conquest and the current situation with North American companies and the United States government dominating the economy and the government of Guatemala.

Requerimiento The Indians were to acknowledge the King's Sovereignty and accept the faith during the period of the Spanish Conquest. Violence was severe against the Maya for any number of reasons including the simple reason of their not wanting to be subjugated to another power.

Thomas Berger reports that since the overthrow of an elected head of government in 1954 which was authorized and supported by the U.S. CIA, that the level of violence and death among the Maya equals or exceeds that which took place 500 years ago.

Encomienda During the Spanish rule land was given to a Spaniard (usually a soldier) and a number of Indians to work the land. This has been replaced by mega companies from North America that have vast land holdings. These mega companies require Indians to work for them; coercive practices, level of pay, and work conditions have been questioned as a throwback the inhumane and coercive practices in the time of the Spanish conquest.

Stephen Schlesinger wrote an article in the Washington Post September 30, 1996 concerning the CIA 1954 coup in Guatemala. He has information that the CIA has 180,000 pages of documents concerning the coup and that the CIA was aware they were funding a government militia that performed kidnappings, torture and executions on a large scale. The CIA has withheld the documents during 19 years of persistent efforts to require them to provide the documents. While the books may not have been burned, as was the case of the Maya books, there is a parallel.

Recommended Readings

Berger, Thomas. (1991). **A long and Terrible Shadow: 1492-1992.** University of Washington Press, Seattle, WA.

Carmack, Robert M. (ed.). (1998). **Harvest of Violence: The Maya Indians & the Guatemalan Crisis.** University of Oklahoma Press: Norman & London.

LaFeber, WAalter. (1984). **Inevitable Revolutions: The United States in Central America.** W.W. Norton & Company, New York.
sp

End notes for Chapter 4. Guatemala

1. LaFeber, Walter. (1984). *Inevitable Revolutions: The United States in Central America. W.W. NORTON & COMPANY*: New York. p. 115.

2. Berger, Thomas R. (1991). *A Long and Terrible Shadow: White values, Native rights in the Americas*. University of Washington Press. Seattle. pp. 1-17.

3. Carmack, Robert M. (ed.). (1998). *Harvest of Violence: The Maya Indians & the Guatemalan Crisis*. University of Oklahoma Press: Norman & London.

4. Alfred M. Turner, ed. and trans., "Landa's Relaction de las cosas de Yucatan: A Translation," Papers of the Peabody Museum of American Archaeology and Ethnology; Harvard University 18 (New York: Kraus Reprint Corp., 1996), p. 149.

5. Berger. Op. cit., p. 3

6. Ibid. pp.3-16.

7. LaFeber. Op. cit., pp. 25-28.

8. Ibid. p. 8.

9. Ib id. pp. 33-34.

10. Ibid. p. 81.

11. The New York Times. (9/19/1996). "Guatemala and Guerrillas Sign Accord to end 35-year Conflict." Article by Julia Preston.

12. Berger. Op. cit., p. 118.

13. Ibid. p. 118.

14. Krauss, Clifford. (1991). *INSIDE CENTRAL AMERICA: its People, Politics, and History*. Summit Books: New York. p. 36.

15. Ibid. p. 37.

16. The New York Times. (12/4/2009). "Court Papers Detail Killings by the Military in Guatemala." Article by Elisabeth Malkin.

17. Cox, Harvey. (2009). *The Future of Faith*. HarperCollins Publishers: New York. p. 195.

18. Ibid. p. 193.

19. I bid. p. 190.

20. Ibid. p. 195.

21. Ibid. p. 116.

22. The words spoken by Rev. Juan Ixtan Calgua are a paraphrase of Scripture: Mathew chapter 25, verses 35-40.

CHAPTER 5

Traumas confronting Cuba
for 500 years

Part I: Our Trip to Cuba

Our trip to Cuba, in February 2003, was different from our other travels in several ways. Our trips to Alaska and British Columbia (chapters one and two) were done entirely as independent travel. I would have loved to have travelled to Cuba on my own boat, as we travelled to Alaska and British Columbia. The distance between Florida and Cuba is only 90 miles. That is the same distance as from Prince Rupert, B.C. to Ketchikan Alaska, a delightful six hour trip that I have made many times. Furthermore, Cuba has many excellent harbors and coves, as well as good fishing. However, as a U.S. citizen independent travel to Cuba was forbidden by the U.S. government. Furthermore, taking a private boat from Florida to Cuba, a potential remarkable opportunity for adventure and travel, remains off-limits.

When Marge and I travelled to Cuba in February 2003, our trip was organized and conducted through the Center for Cross-Cultural Study Inc, the CC-CS. The program was named **Cuba: Key to the Americas.** The title is extremely relevant because Cuba and its islands were the first to have a substantial European settlement after

Christopher Columbus discovered the "New World" in 1492. Cuba was also the last colony of the New World that Spain lost. All other lands of the vast Spanish conquest from Mexico (including California) to Tierra del Fuego were lost during the 19th century as a result of bitter struggles for independence. Brazil, in contrast, shares its troubled history not with Spain but with Portugal. The CC-CS was partnered in the U.S. through Elderhostel in Boston, MA. Many universities in the U.S. contribute their expertise to their educational program including Willamette University in Oregon.

Our information packet contained substantial information about travel in Cuba. We were informed that Cuba is safe; that *Havana is one of the safest big cities in the world, far safer than any comparable European or American city. Violent crime is rare.* We found that to be true.

Broader issues of safety are always an issue when traveling abroad. What happens to a traveler visiting Cuba in case of illness? How about other emergencies? We were informed that,

Foreign visitors are carefully attended, and most hotels have resident physicians and are well supplied with pharmaceuticals. Still, if you regularly need medication, you must take adequate supplies for the duration of the program. Anyone needing emergency hospital care will receive it promptly.

In case of emergency, the Group Leader will be available 24 hours a day to assist hostelers. In the unlikely event of crimes or accidents, the police are helpful, considerate and persistent.

Furthermore, the American Interests Section, under the United States Department of State, is in effect a U.S. consulate and offers minimal services of registration and counsel.

Note: Two members of our group needed medical attention while we were in Cuba. Each received good care and at no cost to them.

Our information packet was explicit about the need to be careful about our authorization letter and our copy of the Elderhostel license for travel to Cuba. In bold print we were advised:

Please take ALL of the enclosed information with you to Cuba, especially the authorization letter and license, which are required for legal travel to Cuba. You may be required to present these documents upon re-entry to the U.S.

The beginning of our trip (after our departure from the U.S.) was Cancun, Mexico, on February 3, 2003. While there, Marge and I took a side trip to the Mayan ruins at Chichen Itza, Mexico.

Havana

The next day we flew to Havana and while there we stayed at the Hotel Sevilla. We had lectures on the history of Cuba before 1492 and the "discovery" and the long Spanish Colonial period. We learned that the original indigenous peoples of Cuba became extinct within one hundred years after 1492, although most of our group knew that part of the history before this trip. We had lectures on the Revolution of 1953-59, education, health care, ecology, and the rich history of music and arts in Cuba. We took field trips to Old Havana, and visited the Museum of the Revolution. This museum was of major interest to me. The museum is housed in a three story building intended to be the Presidential Palace. Construction began in 1913 and it served as the Palace for a series of presidents (considered corrupt by most Cubans) until the Revolution. Following the Revolution the palace was converted into the **Museo de la Revolution.** The rooms are divided in chronological sequence and a marked route permits a visitor to follow the battles and progress of the war. Hundreds of guns and other weapons are on display, as well as some very gruesome photos of rebel soldiers who had been captured, tortured and mutilated by Batista forces. At the rear of the building is the *Granma Memorial* which houses the preserved and maintained vessel that brought Fidel Castro, Che Guevara and other revolutionaries who fought for independence against Batista forces that defended foreign (U.S.) domination of Cuban politics, economy and society. Other displays in the museum show the successful defense against the ill conceived U.S. led Bay of Pigs invasion.

One afternoon we took walking trips to a farmer's market in Havana. The markets reminded Marge and me of farmer's markets we have seen in Ukraine, as well as in Guatemala. There were substantial amounts of fresh vegetables, fruits, fish and meat available. Many of the customers are tourists from Canada and Western Europe. Cubans are necessarily selective in what they can buy beyond that of their food rations. We also visited Earnest Hemingway's house. It is on a hill southeast of Havana. It is preserved as he left it. (He died of a self-inflicted wound in Idaho). His sport fishing boat—the *Pilar* is on the museum grounds. After a long and pleasant walking tour in the afternoon we had the opportunity for "dinner on your own" and a selection of many available restaurants and *paladars* (family run restaurants). Song and instrumental music are ever present in Havana, and during meals even in small restaurants musicians skillfully entertained.

While in Havana we walked about three miles a day. Much of the pavement is in a state of disrepair and we had to be careful going up and down hilly streets. Havana itself shows neglect and many historic, old houses (some three and four hundred years old) are sadly in disrepair and many had been torn down. In 1982 UNESCO's Inter-Governmental Committee for World Cultural and National Protection named Old Havana a **World Heritage Site** worthy of international protection. This was an important and well deserved honor and gives hope for restoration and preservation. During our walks, we saw children walking to and from school, and they seemed quite happy. We saw *no* examples of homelessness, or beggars. The people in Cuba are poor, but poverty is different in Cuba than in Brazil (next chapter), or in the United States. In Cuba in 2003 an average pay per month in U.S. equivalent was forty dollars a month. That was what a physician told me he earned, and what a young lawyer told me he earned. A worker at a sugar mill, or a professional baseball player, or a professional musician would have earned about the same amount. However, the dollar amount per month is not a good indicator of either wealth or poverty. Each Cuban receives an allotment of food independent of salary. Every Cuban family has a place to live, independent of rent money. Every Cuban has the right (and obligation) to get an education. Every Cuban has access to health care.

During our stay in Havana we had a chance to converse informally with some Cubans who had been contacted (and paid) by CC-CS for their time with us. Marge and I met informally with a young lawyer and a young woman. Both were fluent in English. Both were well educated and expressed a desire to travel to the U.S. and Europe. The lawyer said that his income as a lawyer does not quite match his expenses as a lawyer. He indicated the best way for him to earn more income is to drop out of the field of law and become a travel guide, where he would receive tips from Europeans or Canadians who visit Cuba. He spoke of friends of his who make more money as a taxi cab driver, than what they could earn as an employee of the government. He did state that with the collapse of the Soviet Union and communism in Eastern Europe, the economy in Cuba has taken a severe downturn.

On another topic, I did ask if he could tell me about the visit of Pope John Paul II to Cuba in January 1998. He said that the trip of Pope John Paul II was warmly greeted by Cubans and he described the response as one of joy. The crowds chanted such sayings as

| *Juan Pablo, amigo* | Juan Pablo, our friend |
| *el pueblo esta contigo* | the people are with you |

He added that Pope John Paul II gave a mass at Santiago de Cuba that was well attended and afterwards he travelled to Parqie Cespedes and the Caridad del Cobre church and visited the shrine where Cuba's patron saint, *la Virgen de la Caridad* (Our Lady of Charity) resides. Towards the end of his visit, the Pope gave a mass in Havana at the Plaza of the Revolution. Throngs of Cubans were present. During his visit the Pope criticized Castro's human rights violations and he criticized the U.S. embargo of Cuba as a form of violence against the poor people of Cuba. The young man said that the Pope called for Cuba to open itself up to the world, and for the world to open itself up to Cuba. This young man did not criticize Castro, or the Cuban government, but he felt free to speak about the visit of Pope John Paul II and he was clearly moved by the Pope's visit and his speeches.

One afternoon our large group broke up in smaller units of four or five people to visit families, and to enjoy a conversation with Cubans. Our "host" family had a small child. I was interested in the kinds of children's books and stories available for Cuban children.

That evening we went to the Fortaleza San Carlos de la Cabana, the largest fort in the Spanish Americas, and witnessed a cannon ceremony. I enjoyed looking at the cars in Cuba. Most were American cars like Chevrolets, Buicks, Studebakers, but also some classic cars. The newest

American car in Cuba was built in 1958, the oldest cars that I saw were 1930's vintage. My first car was a 1934 Chevrolet Master Deluxe with spoke wheels. I saw one like it in Havana. The United States, of course, does not export cars to Cuba. Furthermore, the price of any new U.S. car would be out of reach in Cuba.

Vinales Valley

After four days in Havana we left by bus to travel about 140 miles to Vinales valley in the Pinar Del Rio region of Cuba. On the way we stopped at a resort in Las Terrazas. This is a first rate eco-resort with nature trails, pristine streams, waterfalls and lakes for swimming. There are also ruins of 19th century coffee farms developed by French agricultural entrepreneurs after they were driven out of Haiti. After a lengthy stop at Las Terrazas we continued on to Vinales and settled in at the Hotel Los Jazmines.

The Valley is absolutely beautiful and features large, high limestone formations reaching up to 699 meters in height with caves overlooking fertile fields where the world's best tobacco is grown. We saw Cuban peasants working the tobacco fields with ox-drawn plows and carts. The limestone mountains that arise out of the fertile valleys are pine-forested. During the long period of slavery in Cuba, some slaves who escaped from sugar plantations hid in the caves of Vinales Valley. We enjoyed taking long walks along paths leading to tobacco farms and taking photos of tobacco farmers (*guajiros*) wearing straw hats, and their oxen working the fields. One member of our group who was passably fluent in Spanish spoke with some of the farmers who readily interacted and answered questions. The homes in rural Cuba were small but very pleasant and reflect the fact that following the Cuban revolution, a major focus was on improving the living conditions in rural Cuba. Literacy is very high throughout Cuba and health care is well distributed even to rural areas. Furthermore, the housing situation in rural Cuba is much improved over what it was during the long Spanish colonial period (when the workers were slaves) or during the period following the Spanish-Cuban-American war until 1959. In contrast following the revolution the major cities showed a serious decline.

Santiago de Cuba

Santiago de Cuba is in the Oriente region and it is Cuba's second-largest city. It was the capital until the mid-16th century. We visited the house of Diego Velazquez, the founder of Santiago, who arrived in Cuba with 300 settlers in 1511. The Spanish came in search of riches in gold, silver and spices. Santiago was built under colonial rule by African slaves and immigrants. It remains the city in Cuba most heavily influenced by African traditions. African religious traditions were severely suppressed during the Spanish colonial period, but African spirituality lingered on in secret. We visited the Museum of Religiousness which contains displays of African spiritual traditions brought to Cuba by slaves from Africa. We also visited the Basilica del Cobre church, home to Cuba's patron saint, and a place visited by Pope John Paul II in 1998.

Santiago is known as the "Cradle of the Revolution" because Fidel Castro launched his revolution here in 1953. We visited the Moncada Barracks where the first battle took place between Castro rebel forces and the Batista forces. This early battle was an initial defeat for Castro. We saw bullet holes in buildings that remain so that Cubans will not forget the struggle against the oppression suffered during the long Spanish colonial period and the oppression following the Spanish-Cuban-American war when the U.S. played a dominating role in the politics and economy of Cuba.

Preparation for Travel to Cuba

Prior to our trip to Cuba, we were advised by CC-CS to learn about local customs. We were advised to *learn as much as you can about the local laws and customs of the places you plan to visit. Good resources are your library, your travel agencies, and the embassies, consulates or tourist bureaus of the countries you will visit.* The advice given is always good when visiting a foreign country. In my case, I supplemented background reading to include information about the trips of Christopher Columbus and other explorers and to gain a perspective about the momentous events within Christianity in Europe that was to influence the introduction of Christianity throughout the Americas.

The second part of this chapter is based on background information about Cuba going back to the indigenous peoples of Cuba before 1492 and the impact of the "Discovery." The second section of this chapter will flesh out the meaning of the title of Chapter 5,

Traumas Confronting Cuba for the past 500 years: Foreign Missionaries and Slavery, Foreign Military, and Foreign Merchants and Slavery.

Part II. The tragedy of *how* Christianity was Introduced to Cuba

The focus of this section is not the communist revolution or about Fidel Castro; instead, the focus is how Christianity was introduced to the indigenous peoples of Cuba and the developments within the Christian church over the next four hundred and fifty years until the Castro revolution. I include information about government actions as well, because in Spain there was no separation between Church and State. We need to be mindful that throughout the period of their colonization of the Americas, the only religion permitted in Spain was Catholicism. That policy carried over to all Spanish colonies in the Americas. For three hundred years Spanish military ruthlessly suppressed opposition within the Spanish colony of Cuba, while Spanish merchants earned huge profits. Revolt was inevitable. Many uprisings were ruthlessly suppressed; however, the second of two revolutions in the nineteenth century was about to overthrow Spanish domination of Cuba. Then the U.S. Military and U.S. business interests intervened and Spain lost its last colonies—Cuba and the Philippines.

Christopher Columbus Discovers the New World

On August 2, 1492 a large number of ships left the seaport town of Palos, Spain, carrying thousands of Jews to the lands where Jews were accepted, even welcomed, including the lands of Islam in the Mideast and the Netherlands. About 60,000 Jews had already escaped from Spain and travelled to Portugal, where they were initially tolerated, though not welcomed. Many other Jews travelled, some by foot, to Eastern

Europe in lands now identified as Hungary, Ukraine and Poland, and still others to Italy. Jews who remained in Spain after August 2, 1492, were to be executed unless they embraced Christianity.[1]

Christopher Columbus was in Palos on that terrible day with his select crew of 39 officers and crew of *Santa Maria,* 26 of *Pinta* and 22 of *Nina.* Columbus wrote little of the Jewish expulsion from Spain, except that he expressed the wish to exclude Jews from any lands that he discovered.[2] On August 3rd, just one day after the final expulsion of Jews from Spain, Columbus and his crew set sail. This was a voyage of discovery; there were no soldiers on board the three vessels.

At 2 A.M. on October 12th a lookout crewmember on *Pinta* spotted land and sang out, *Tierra! Tierra!* The Admiral rose and named this island *San Salavador*—Holy Savior.[3]

The first people encountered were of the Taino branch of the Arawak language group.[4] Columbus recruited some indigenous guides and set off again. His indigenous guides had communicated the presence of a very large island they called Colba. On October 27, 1492, Columbus arrived at the island of *Colba* (Cuba). Columbus encountered natives in Cuba and spoke well of them, describing their innocence,

They are the best people in the world, without knowledge of what is evil; nor do they murder or steal. All the people show the most singular loving behavior and are gentile and always laughing.[5] Columbus also saw in the American Indians their potential as slaves. For example, Columbus wrote of the Taino Indians,

They bear no arms, and are all unprotected and so very cowardly that a thousand would not face three; so they are fit to be ordered about and made to work, to sow and do aught else that may be needed, and you may build towns and teach them to go clothed and to adopt our customs.[6]

Columbus believed he had discovered India and thus named the inhabitants "Indians."

In 1493 Columbus returned to Spain and quickly prepared to communicate with the Papacy of the lands he had discovered as was the custom in Europe at that time. Pope Alexander VI granted to Spain control of the lands that Columbus had discovered. On May 4, 1493, the Pope drew a line of demarcation along the meridian, 318 nautical miles west of the Azores. All undiscovered lands east of it would belong to Portugal; all to the west of it to Spain. Pope Alexander VI also ordered that the Indians be converted to Christianity.

Columbus wrote a long letter dated February 15, 1493, on board *Nina*. It was printed in Barcelona in mid-April 1493 and served as Columbus's official report to Ferdinand and Isabella about his First Voyage. The New York Public Library has a copy of this treasure.

LETTER OF COLUMBUS

Selections: First paragraph of text

SIR, since I know that you will take pleasure at the great victory with which Our Lord has crowned my voyage, I write this to you, from which you will learn how in thirty-three days I reached the Indies with the fleet which the most illustrious King and Queen, our lords, gave to me. And there I found very many islands filled with people without number, and of them all I have taken possession for their Highnesses, by proclamation and with the royal standard displayed, and nobody objected. To the first island which I found I gave the name Sant Salvador, in remembrance of His Heavenly Majesty, who marvelously hath given all this; the Indians call it Guanahani. To the second I gave the name Isla de Santa Maria de Concepcion: to the third, Ferrandina; to the fourth, La Isla Bella, to the fifth, La Isla Juana (Cuba); *and so to each one I gave a new name.*[7]

Toward the end of his letter, Columbus summarizes, with great optimism, the potential financial benefits of his discovery—including slavery.

In conclusion, to speak only of that which has been accomplished on this voyage, which was so hurried, their Highnesses can see that I shall give them as much gold as they want if their Highnesses will render me a little help; besides spice and cotton, as much as their Highnesses shall command; and gum mastic, as much as they shall order shipped, and which, up to now, has been found only in Greece, in the island of Chios, and the Seignory sell it for what it pleases; and aloe wood, as much as they shall order shipped, and slaves, as many as they shall order, who will be idolaters.[8] (note: The slave trade was considered legitimate if Christians were not the victims).

The introduction of Christianity to the Indigenous Cubans

Columbus's Second Voyage to America was authorized on May 29, 1493. The primary stated objective was to convert the natives. An additional objective was to establish a trading colony to pursue business transactions with the wealthy cities of the Asiatic mainland. A third objective was to continue the exploration. The fleet consisted of seventeen vessels and 1200 men. Of the 1200 men, only six were priests—a very small number considering that the stated primary objective was to convert the natives. The names of most of the vessels are unknown, and no official log or journal of the second voyage has survived. Personal diaries and accounts survived from three participants.[9] The fleet departed September 25, 1493, from Cadiz, Spain, and arrived at an island they called Santa Maria de Guadalupe on November 3, 1493.

Columbus settled on Isabella as a site to develop a trading colony. He, of course, was not in Asia. The natives had nothing of value to trade, at least not from the perspectives of the Spaniards. Furthermore, Isabella lacked fresh water and did not have a suitable natural harbor. The place swarmed with malaria-carrying mosquitoes. Many of his men became ill, and they found little gold. Up until May of 1494, there had been no unfortunate incidents between Spaniards and Cuban natives. Tragically, that changed. By February, 1495, the Spanish rounded up fifteen hundred Indian captives at Isabella. Five hundred were loaded up on ships to be taken to Spain. Columbus then gave permission to the Spaniards at Isabella to take as many natives for personal slaves as they wanted. Natives not "selected" were released. Cuneo, one of the three Spaniards who kept a personal record indicated that when released from the wretched conditions, the natives fled as far as they could from the Spaniards, and that "women even abandoned infants in their fear and desperation to escape further cruelty."[10]

SPANISH ATTIUDE TOWARDS SLAVERY

Morrison describes the attitude of the Spanish toward enslavement of indigenous peoples.

There never crossed the mind of Columbus, or his fellow discoverers and conquistadors, any other notion of relations between Spaniard and American Indian save that of master and slave. It was a conception founded on the Spanish enslavement of Guanches in the Canaries, and on the Portuguese enslavement of Negroes in Africa, which Columbus had observed and taken for granted, and which the Church condoned. It never occurred to him that there was anything wrong in this pattern of race relations, begun and sanctioned by that devout Christian prince, D. Henrique of Portugal.[11]

In March 1495 a native known as "Guacanagari" united remaining Indians and organized a revolt against the Spanish. The battles resulted in the death of very many indigenous peoples in Cuba and the revolt failed. The population estimated to be in the range of 250,000 to 500,000 in 1492 was reduced to 60,000 in a period of only 16 years i.e., by 1508. The morbidity for the indigenous peoples continued as reported by Morrison who writes, "Fifty years later, not 500 remained . . . . The cruel policy initiated by Columbus and pursued by his successors resulted in complete genocide."[12]

The Second trip of Columbus ended on June 11, 1496, as his vessels arrived back in Spain at the Bay of Cadiz. The second voyage had been a disaster for the indigenous peoples of Cuba. The voyage was not good for the prestige of Christopher Columbus either. Samuel Eliot Morison, author of *Christopher Columbus, Mariner,* provides a summary statement of the Second Voyage,

Two years and nine months had passed since the Admiral's great fleet of seventeen sail departed Cadiz, with hearts high and grandiose expectations of starting a valuable colony and locating the Emperor of China. From the point of view of the average intelligent Spaniard, all that had been a phantom, and Columbus now seemed to be an importunate and impractical dreamer. Cuba was no limb of China; anyone who talked with a member of the exploring expedition could see that. Isabella, instead of being a rich

*trading factory like Portuguese Mina on the Gold Coast, was a miasmic
dump which even the Columbus brothers were abandoning. Instead of the
promised gold mine of the Cibao, gold was diffused in small quantities over
the island and could only be produced by slave labor.*[13]

Columbus did make two more voyages and, until the day he died,
he believed he had discovered Asia. On May 19, 1506, he ratified his
final will, and declared his son Don Diego his principal heir. He died
on May 20th and his last words were, *In manus tuas, Domine, commendo
spiritum meum*—"Into Thy hands, O Lord, I commit my spirit."[14]

In 1509 King Ferdinand gave Christopher Columbus's son Don
Diego, the title of Governor of the Indies with the duty to organize an
expedition to continue the discovery and settlement of Cuba, and to
carry out the order of the Pope to convert the Indians to Christianity.
Don Diego Columbus appointed Diego Velazquez de Cuellar to lead
the expedition.

In 1511 four ships from Spain carrying 300 settlers, led by Diego
Velazquez de Cuellar, arrived in what is now called Cuba. They founded
a town they named Baracoa, and within a few years they settled six other
villas, named Bayamo, Camaquey, San Cristobal de la Habana, Sancti
Spiritus, Santiago de Cuba, and Trinidad. Some of these towns were
paved with cobblestones shipped aboard the Spanish ships as ballast.
The Spanish who settled these villas included soldiers, merchants and
priests. They were prepared to meet and interact with the indigenous
population who had lived on the island of Cuba for thousands of
years.

The Spanish named the indigenous peoples of Cuba *Arahuacos.*
Anthropologists refer to them as the **Taino.** They lived in thatched
circular huts that were sturdy and built to withstand the severe storms
that strike during the summer and early fall, with hurricane force
winds, tremendous rains and high seas. The Taino built canoes from
large trees which enabled them to fish in the rivers and ocean waters.
Columbus reported that the canoes were very large: *Some of these canoes
I have seen with 70 and 80 men in them, each one with his oar.*[15]. They
developed advanced farming techniques and raised yucca, corn (maize),

yams and peppers. Cuba had extensive forests at that time and many of the tree species produced fruits and nuts in abundance providing additional food. The Taino excelled as weavers and pottery makers. The indigenous population of Cuba at the time of the arrival of the Spanish is estimated to be between 250,000 and 500,000.[17], [18]. However, by 1511, the population had already been severely reduced as a result of both diseases and the atrocities resulting from the Second Voyage of Columbus.

The Spanish came in search of riches in spices, gold and silver. They viewed the indigenous people they met as godless and inferior.[19]. Through a system called requerimiento the Spanish made efforts to identify leaders among the Taino people and to force them to acknowledge the King of Spain as owner of the land and to convert to Christianity.

One priest named Bartolome de las Casas had looked forward to meeting the indigenous peoples. He was prepared to be a Christian missionary. However, he was stunned and outraged by the behavior and criminal acts of his fellow Spaniards who accompanied him and Velazquez. He recorded the following:

> *The Indians came to meet us, and to receive us with victuals, and delicate cheere . . . . the Devil put himselfe into the Spaniards, to put them all to the edge of the sword in my presence, without any cause whatsoever, more than three thousand soules, which were set before us, men, women and children. I saw there so great cruelties, that never any man living either have or shall see the like.*[20]

Murder committed by the Spanish on a large scale was the first brutal act that confronted the indigenous peoples of Cuba. The second brutal act of the Spanish was to enslave the Indians. Each Spaniard was given a large section of cultivated land and assigned, as his slaves, the Indians who lived on it. The system was called *repartimientos* and occurred throughout Spanish America.[21] Spanish colonists favored this policy because it gave them free labor, all the gold found on their land, and the value of crops harvested by the slaves, except for the portion that was deeded to the king. The Indians were worked to death. The life span of an Indian forced to labor by the Spanish was about seven years. As knowledge of the brutal treatment spread among the Indians, a resistance developed led by a Dominican-born chief named Hatuey. He rallied large numbers of the Taino population and attacked Baracoa, the first city founded by Don Diego Velazquez de Cuellar. The siege lasted three months but the assault of tens of thousands of the Taino people could not defeat the 300 or so armed Spanish.[22]

The rebellion failed and Hatuey was captured. He was tied to a stake in preparation to be burned to death. In the middle ages the punishment of being burned at the stake was intended to extinguish the alleged evil spirits that empowered the wickedness of the accused person. Before the fires were lit, a Catholic Priest gave Hatuey the promise that if he renounced his pagan beliefs and accepted the Christian God he would go to heaven, i.e., after his execution. If he refused, he was told he would go to hell after his execution. Hatuey asked if Christians go to heaven. When informed "Yes," he replied that if people as wicked as Christians go to heaven that he would not want to go there.[23] Hatuey did not "convert." He was burned to death at the stake.

In a period of less than one hundred years, the entire indigenous population of Cuba had ceased to exist.[24] There were no survivors, no more indigenous laborers to be enslaved by the Spanish, and no more indigenous peoples in Cuba to be "converted."

In my travels from Alaska to Tierra de Fuego, I have made it an objective to learn about indigenous groups and to meet descendents of those who first encountered the effort of Europeans to introduce Christianity to the indigenous population. My trip to Cuba was my first experience to learn that the entire indigenous population had ceased to exist. The term for this is genocide. However, Cuba is not the only area in the New World in which an indigenous population met complete extinction of their race of peoples as a result of the "Discovery."

When I have spoken to audiences about Cuba from my trip in 2003 and mentioned that the original indigenous population ceased to exist in a period of just one hundred years, I have received a range of responses. Among them are the following:

1. "You are wrong to say the Indians died out. The Indians did not die. Instead they abandoned their pagan ways and became Christian. Their culture and pagan beliefs died, as they should have, but not the Indians of Cuba. They were saved."
2. "The Indians died because they had no immunity to the diseases introduced by the Europeans."
3. Some said to me, "I object that you went to Cuba at all. By going to Cuba you unwittingly helped support the Castro regime. You should have followed the purpose and intent of the US embargo of Cuba and stayed away."
4. Others said in essence, "I am sure there were some problems, but overall the discovery and the introduction of Christianity and Western culture was a good thing."
5. Another person asked, "Why would the Spanish settlers treat the Taino peoples so badly as to bring them to extinction, when they needed them as Slaves?"

Time and time again Columbus asserted the primary objective was to convert natives.

And Your Highnesses will command a city and fortress to be built in these parts, and these countries converted; and I certify to your Highneses that it seems to me that there could never be under the sun lands superior in fertility, in mildness of cold and heat, in abundance of good and pure water . . . And afterwards the benefits will be known, and it will be attempted to make all these folk Christians, for that will be easily done, since they have no religion; nor are they idolaters.

And I say that Your Highnesses ought not to consent that any foreigner do business or set foot here, except Christian Catholics, since this was the end and the beginning of the enterprise, that it should be for the enhancement and glory of the Christian religion, nor should anyone who is not a good Christian come to these parts.[25].

However, the stated objective of converting the natives to Christianity was not accomplished. Morrison states,

Every colonizing power in America, down through the seventeenth century, followed this Spanish precedent of loudly and frequently declaring that its first motive was to bring Christianity to the Indians . . . . Performance in every instance . . . fell woefully short of promise.[26]

Columbus spoke casually of the destruction of natives who would not convert and confess the faith,

I maintain, Most Serene Princes, that if they had access to devout religious persons knowing the language, they would all turn Christian, and so I hope in Our Lord that your Highnesses will do something about it with much care, in order to turn to the Church so numerous a people, and to convert them, as you have destroyed those who would not confess the Father, Son, and Holy Ghost.[27]

The "wealth" of Cuba shifts from gold and silver to sugar, tobacco and slavery

By 1611, one hundred years after the first settlements in Cuba, the Spanish modified their plan for Cuba, the Crown Jewel of the Spanish in the Americas. It was clear that the value of Cuba was not in gold or silver. The Spanish, using slave labor to work mines, found little gold or silver. But the Spanish found vast riches in other colonies, particularly Mexico, Peru and Bolivia. Furthermore, in 1564 the Spanish reached the Philippines and took possession. The next year the Spanish discovered the Pacific trade winds. The trade winds enabled their ships to transport Chinese treasures to the west coast of Mexico. Slaves carried the cargo overland to the east coast of Mexico for shipment to Havana and then eventually to Europe. Havana, with its excellent natural harbors and seaports, became a transportation hub to receive the vast wealth from other domains of the Spanish empire. The wealth included revenue from Spain's participation in the slave trade.[47]

Slavery

Just three years after Diego Valazquez de Cuellar founded Baracoa in 1510, the Spanish began shipping slaves from Africa to Cuba. The importation of huge numbers of Africans for slavery compensated for the rapid extinction of the indigenous peoples of Cuba. As if they were beasts of burden, the black slaves worked mines for gold, cut sugarcane, and labored to build the cities with its mansions, fortresses and churches. As a result of the brutality suffered by the African slaves, their life spans were shortened. However, Africans lived longer under conditions of slavery than did Native Americans. To the slave traders there was no shortage of supply.

The majority of slaves brought into Cuba came from West African tribes including the Fulani, Hausa, and Yoruba.[48] Once they were brought ashore, the Africans were herded into barracks (*barracoons*). In Havana the barracks were close to the governor's summer palace, where they could be viewed and inspected prior to being purchased. No attention was paid to family relationships. Parents, children and siblings were separated. Slaves were not allowed to marry. However, slave owners chose strong males to mate with healthy slave women who often did not see their babies beyond a few hours after birth. The babies were cared for by wet nurses. The treatment of the slaves was brutal and inhumane; and efforts through Spanish legislation, such as in 1789, to improve the living conditions of slaves went unheeded.[49] In 1817 Spain and England signed a treaty to abolish the slave trade. However, this tentative step failed because neither country enforced the prohibition against slavery. The slave trade continued to develop and by 1840 slaves constituted 45% of the population of Cuba.

Sugar and Tobacco

In the 17th century Spain profited greatly from the cash crops of tobacco and sugar grown in Cuba, all produced and harvested with slave labor. Wealthy native-born Spanish, who settled in Cuba, funded planting of new lands for sugar harvest and profits multiplied more than tenfold by the beginning of the 18th century [50].

In 1740 Spain created a policy, known as the *Real Compania*, which gave them a monopoly on all trade between Cuba and Europe.[51] The prosperity of Cuba continued unabated and by 1760 Havana was larger and wealthier than New York or Boston, and graced with monuments, parks, public libraries and theaters.[52] Large and beautiful colonial homes with paved boulevards and street lamps graced this fine city, all supported by vast fortunes made in sugar and in the traffic of slaves.

Angered by the *Real Compania* policy which gave Spain complete monopoly in trade, England invaded Cuba with 200 war ships and 20,000 troops in 1762. After a 44-day siege the Spanish lost control of Cuba and the English opened the Island up to free trade and *expanded* the slave trade. Foreign merchants previously blocked from trading flowed into Cuba. However, within a year the British traded Cuba for Florida, thus returning Cuba to Spain. King Charles III, of Spain, continued the more liberal trade policy enacted by England.[53]

In 1791 about 30,000 French sugar planters escaped to Cuba from Haiti following the Haitian rebellion. The French contributed their superior knowledge of sugar production, which led to a vast expansion of sugar production and to a massive increase in the number of slaves brought into Cuba. In the period between 1791 and 1810, over 100,000 documented slaves arrived by official count, many other slaves were brought in undocumented.[54] With the end of slavery in the U.S. following the Civil war, Spain was not able to maintain slavery in Cuba. In October 1868 a wealthy plantation owner named Carlos Manuel de Cespedes freed the slaves on his plantation. Many other plantation owners also freed their slaves. Spanish plantation owners who maintained their slaves were angered and named the freed slaves *Mamabi,* a derogatory term meaning "despicable."[55]

The possibility of freedom from slavery became associated with independence from Spain who introduced slavery almost four hundred years earlier. Freed slaves and other Cubans who wanted independence united and fought against Spanish troops. The rebels captured the town of Bayamo. When Spanish forces moved in to retake the town, the rebels destroyed the town. Spain supplemented their forces with an additional 100,000 troops shipped in from Spain. Two rebel leaders, General Maximo Gomez and General Antonio Maceo, were very effective in leading rebel forces and made substantial progress in liberating much of Cuba. However, the long and costly war bogged down and in 1878 the rebel troops signed the Pact of Zanjon. The Ten Year War cost the lives of 250,000 Cubans and 80,000 Spanish. Vast sections of Cuba, including plantations and sugar mills, were destroyed, and other tracts of land were abandoned. The economy was devastated. During this period of near economic collapse, North American investors purchased large amounts of land and sugar plantations at very low rates. It was during this extended conflict that Jose Marti, a teen age boy, was arrested and imprisoned. [56]

The Final Cuban Revolution against Spain

The government of Spain had a simple and authoritarian policy about running its colony of Cuba. Only native born Spaniards were allowed to establish a business, occupy a public post or travel unrestricted, that is without military permission. Spaniards born in Cuba were called Criolles and were denied basic rights. Following Spain's losses during the Napoleonic wars in Europe, Spain was too weak to defend its New World Territories. By 1835 only Cuba and Puerto Rico had not gained independence. Jose Marti is the acknowledged leader of the cause of freedom for Cuba; he was not a military man but a poet. He was born in 1853, and from a young age, Marti devoted his writing and speech making to the cause. At the age of 16 he was arrested for "treason" on the basis of his writing. He was sentenced to hard labor at a rock quarry near Havana, and later sent to a prison in Spain. He was released in 1878, as part of amnesty after the ten year war, and moved to New York where he worked as a reporter for a newspaper. He established contacts with other leading Cuban exiles and led a movement to free Cuba, and specifically to train revolutionary fighters.[57]

In 1895 Marti was named General of the Army of Liberation. Later that year he returned to Cuba and joined an army of 6,000 Cubans who fought Spanish forces at Dos Rios. In that opening battle, Marti was killed. Later that year General Maximo Gomez and Antonio Maceo led an army of 60,000 Cuban rebels and fought effectively against the Spanish the full length of Cuba. The fighting continued at a very high cost in lives on both sides. Spain had suffered very heavy losses and may have been at the verge of surrendering to the Cuban rebels. General Gomez would have welcomed U.S. aid in supplying arms and ammunition; but he did not ask for U.S. troops. The general believed his rebel army was on the verge of victory.[58]

U.S. President William McKinley sent the warship—the USS Maine—to Havana to protect U.S. citizens in Cuba. On February 5, 1898 the ship exploded in Havana Harbor killing 258. William Randolph Hearst published a headline account of the sinking of the Maine in his newspaper and blamed the Spanish. He coined the phrase, "Remember the Maine, to Hell with Spain." One month later Congress declared war on Spain and the U.S. broadened the attack by also attacking Spanish forces in Guam, Puerto Rico and the Philippines. By July 1898 the U.S. had destroyed the Spanish navy and on July 17, Spain surrendered.[59]

The U.S. military occupied Cuba for four years. General Leonard Wood was in charge of the initial occupation. Under his leadership the U.S. financed and directed the construction of schools, the establishment of a postal system, a judicial system and improved health care. During this initial period the Cuban Constitution was written in Washington. The constitution included a clause known as the Platt Amendment, which gave Guantanamo to the U.S. to be the site of the major Guantanamo naval base. The Platt Amendment also declared that the U.S. had the right to intervene whenever the U.S. deemed necessary. When U.S. interests were threatened by unrest, worker strikes or open revolt the U.S. sent in troops. The U.S. installed a series of presidents with Thomas Estrada Palma as the first Cuban president. The pattern of U.S. involvement in the management of Cuba continued until 1959.[60]

U.S. Economic Interests Dictate U.S. Policy in Cuba

During the 400 years in which Cuba was under Spanish control, U.S. economic investments in Cuba were small. U.S. business investments began to develop after the Ten Year War ended in 1878 and increased dramatically following the defeat of Spain in the Spanish-Cuban-American War. U.S. investors expanded the production of sugar, tobacco and lumber, and soon controlled about 75 percent of the economy of Cuba. They increased the value of their investments by building up major infrastructure in Cuba including railroads, ports, roads and utilities.⁶¹ Several thousand U.S. citizens moved to Cuba to manage these investments.

The peak of the sugar boom was reached during the period from 1915-1920 when the price of sugar reached just over 22 cents a pound. As in Guatemala, the United Fruit Company was the single largest agricultural power in Cuba. As is the case of many commodities the price of sugar fluctuates. By 1921 the price of sugar fell to 3.6 cents a pound and fell much further to one cent a pound in 1925.⁶² The collapse of the economy brought on widespread hunger among the Cuban population and was accompanied with violence, assassinations and bombings. General Gerardo Machado y Morales was determined to protect U.S. investments and received substantial U.S. support for those efforts. He confronted the growing numbers of hunger marches, strikes and anti-government demonstrations with militant attacks and with severe repressive moves, such as arranging the assassinations of dissidents, shutting down schools and universities where faculty and students protested government actions, and prohibiting public gatherings. In the midst of the violence, a wide spread general strike brought the country to a point of chaos. In the on-going crisis, Machado lost control and left the country in the summer of 1933.⁶³

A young sergeant named Fulgencio Batista y Zaldivar assumed power in Cuba following the departure of General Gerardo Machado y Morales in 1933. Batista ran the government and became the most powerful man in Cuba until 1959. After he retired at the end of has term in 1944, Batista hand-picked Ramongrau San Martin to succeed him, and corruption and violence escalated leading to 64 political assassinations. Batista maneuvered again and placed Carlos Prio Socarras (1948-1952) in power, and violence and chaos continued throughout Cuba leading to street demonstrations, assassinations and the formation of gangster mobs.

In 1952 during this period of violence and instability, elections loomed in Cuba. Batista ran again as a presidential candidate, but he was immensely unpopular because he was associated with the two previous disastrous administrations. However, Batista implemented a coup, cancelled the election, dissolved congress and put himself in power. This was extremely unpopular in Cuba; nevertheless, President Harry Truman immediately recognized the Batista regime. Baker states that Truman made a serious political error: "Had Truman acted with greater rectitude there may never have been a revolution in 1959. Batista's rule was so widely hated that it unified the Cuban people."[64]

Fidel Castro

In 1952 Fidel Castro, a 25 year old lawyer, campaigned for a position in the Cuban Congress. He was recognized as a gifted orator and he campaigned against corrupt government. He was one of many Cubans whose future career in Cuban government work was upended when Batista unilaterally cancelled the elections scheduled for June 1953. Within 24 hours after Batista took power, secret police came to arrest Castro.[65] Castro was forewarned and managed to escape arrest; then he recruited a small group of other politically disaffected to join him in an effort to overthrow what Castro viewed as a violent, corrupt and illegal Batista government. Their first effort was an attack on the Moncada barracks in Santiago de Cuba. The goal was to capture weapons while the Batista forces were away during a national celebration on July 26, 1953. Castro underestimated the numbers of Batista forces present at Moncada, and his efforts were met with a hail of gunfire. Sixty-four of his compatriots were captured, brutally tortured, mutilated and killed. Batista published photos of the executed men and proudly announced to the Cuban nation that he had successfully quashed a rebellion. The Cuban people were not pleased but were horrified and most expressed revulsion at the gruesome photos.

Castro was soon captured and placed in a Santiago jail. Reporters were permitted to interview Castro and his account was broadcasted on national radio. Castro was amazed that he was given this opportunity to explain his position to the Cuban people. Apparently, Batista felt that the Cuban people would accept Castro's admission of guilt and support his (Batista's) rule. Instead, Castro's opportunity to speak to the Cuban people greatly increased his influence. He was able to point out his objections to the corrupt Batista regime, and to discuss his revolutionary goals for Cuba.

Castro and the 25 other survivors of the July 26 attack were transferred to the Isle of Pines (where Jose Marti had been previously imprisoned). The prisoners were allowed access to books and they planned goals for Cuba following a successful revolution. The press had access to the prisoners, and the stature of Castro increased. A nationwide campaign developed to free Castro. In May 1955 Batista yielded to pressure and freed Castro and the other Moncada prisoners. Within two months Castro fled to Mexico for his own safety. In exile he prepared a plan for a guerilla army to invade and free Cuba. In a remarkable move he sent a message to the Cuban congress asking their support of the revolution. He called for the 500 delegates to refuse working with Batista. The delegates agreed and loudly proclaimed their support of a "Revolution!" Castro then wrote Manifesto No. 1 to outline his revolutionary goals. Some highlights include the following:

The outlawing of the Latifundia, distribution of the land among peasant families.

The right of the worker to broad participation in profits.

Drastic decrease in all rents.

Construction by the state of decent housing to shelter the 400,000 families crowded in filthy single rooms, huts, shacks, and tenements.

Extension of electricity to the 2,800,000 persons in our rural and suburban sectors who have none.

Confiscation of all the assets of embezzlers acquired under all past governments.[66]

In July 1955 Castro met Ernesto "Che" Guevara, an Argentinean physician and revolutionary. Together they planned strategies for the Cuban revolution. To raise money for the revolution, Castro toured the U.S. and gave speeches to Cubans in exile and to American audiences. He invoked the writings of Jose Marti. Meanwhile, opposition to Batista continued in Cuba even without the presence of Castro.

To launch the invasion, Castro purchased a 38-foot wooden cabin cruiser named *Granma*. Overloaded with 82 people and military equipment and supplies the boat headed out of Mexico's Tuxpan Harbor and headed for Cuba. The Boat took on water and ran aground at Los Cayuelos in Oriente Province. On December 5 the small rebel force was sighted by Batista forces and attacked. The rebel army of 82 men was defeated and only 16 men survived, including Fidel Castro, Raul Castro and Che Guevara. The survivors regrouped and retreated to the Sierra Maestra Mountains. Peasants in those mountains supported Castro and the rebel soldiers. They supplied the small rebel group with food and shelter and brought supplies to them. A merchant in the Sierra Maestro Mountains told a reporter of the contrast between Batista forces and the rebels, "They (Batista soldiers) would receive bread, eat a chicken and take away a daughter if there was one, but the rebels were different: they respected everything, and this was the basis of the confidence that they gained."[67]

Batista attacked the Castro forces from the air with B-26 bombers and P-47 fighter planes supplied by the U.S. This further increased the peasants' support of Castro and his rebel forces. The U.S. government awarded the head of Batista's air force a Legion of Merit for its bombing raids in the Sierra Maestro Campaign.[68] The U.S. continued to give military equipment and support to Batista's forces, seemingly oblivious to the implications and world opinion. [69]

Castro's Revolution is Victorious, but Life Remains Hard

On January 1, 1959, Batista recognizing his defeat left Cuba for the Dominican Republic. On January 2, Castro delivered a televised victory speech. Castro quickly moved to implement reforms. In May 1959 Cuba enacted the Agrarian Reform Law. With this law, large sugar estates and cattle ranches were seized by the Cuban government. Most of the lands had been owned by U.S. business interests, but others were owned by Spanish, British, French, Canadian and Dutch business interests. The U.S. owners were not compensated for their losses; Cuba eventually compensated the business losses of the other five countries.[70]

Cuba, as an island nation, cannot survive without imports and exports. In 1961 President Kennedy instituted a trade embargo on Cuba that is still in effect. Cuba turned to the Soviet Union for oil, other supplies and a market to export sugar. That survival move brought Cuba into the communist block, and the idealistic goals for Cuba expressed by Jose Marti drifted into the background. The U.S. embargo failed, and the price was high for the United States. The United States lost tremendous amounts of good will across the world. Even our allies do not support the U.S. embargo of Cuba. In October 2010 the General Assembly of the United Nations voted on a resolution calling for the United States to lift its longstanding economic embargo against Cuba. The resolution passed by a lopsided vote of 187 to 2. The United States, and one other nation, opposed the non-binding measure. This was the 19th such resolution in a row. The Cuban foreign minister, Bruno Rodriguez Parrilla, expressed disappointment that President Obama has not acted on his promise to change relations with Cuba.[71]

A Failed Christian Missionary Effort

The Christian missionary effort to the indigenous peoples of Cuba failed. It was catastrophic to the entire population of the Taino people. Events in Europe going back to the fourth century contributed to the high level of intolerance and oppression that the missionaries unwittingly brought with them from 1492 and on (see chapter 9). Until the end of the Spanish-Cuban-American war the only accepted religion in Cuba was Roman Catholicism. The 1901 Constitutional Convention abolished the state-supported church and decreed freedom for all religious sects. Many writers, including Leslie Dewart, a Catholic author, state that the Catholic Church was identified with the colonial policies of Spain and showed little interest in the poverty and oppression experienced by many Cubans.[72] In addition, the Catholic Church was thinly served by priests. On a national level Cuba had 725 priests for a population of six million, one for every 7850 Cubans.[73] Priests served parishioners in the big cities like Havana and Santiago with great cathedrals, but were essentially non-existent in rural Cuba where much of the harvest of sugar and tobacco took place.

Roman Catholicism adopts Creeds that foster Intolerance

Cuba was the very first lands "discovered" by Columbus in the New World to bear the brunt of the order of Pope Alexander VI that natives be converted to the Christian faith. However, to understand the scope of the tragedy faced by the indigenous peoples of the New World, it is important to understand that the Spanish had developed an unconscionably brutal system of converting non-Christian Spaniards to the "true faith." Jews were the first to face this monstrous threat. As stated above, in 1492 Spanish Jews were ordered to convert to Christianity. If they refused they were required to forfeit all their valued possessions to the Spanish government and to leave without the option of returning. The Jews who "converted" faced a ruthless inquisition involving torture. If they refused the options of either converting or leaving Spain they faced the very real possibility of execution. Muslims also were forced to convert to Christianity, but not in the year 1492, but in 1499.

Endnotes for Chapter 5 Cuba

1. Morison, Samuel Eliot. (1983). *Christopher Columbus Mariner.* A Meridian Book, Little, Brown & Company, Boston, MA. P. 37.

2. Ibid. p. 38

3. Ibid. p. 50.

4. Ibid. p. 51.

5. Baker, Christopher P. (2000). *Moon Handbooks; CUBA.* Avalon Travel Publishing, Emeryville, CA. p. 22.

6. Morison, Samuel Eliot. (1942). *Admiral of the Ocean Sea: A Life of Christopher Columbus.* Little, Brown and Company. Boston, MA. P. 290.

7. Morison. *Christopher Columbus Mariner.* op. cit., p. 205.

8. Ibid. pp. 212-213.

9. Ibid. p. 72.

10. Ibid. p. 97.

11. Morison. *Admiral of the Ocean Sea,* op. cit., p. 291.

12. Morison. *Christopher Columbus Mariner.* op. cit., p. 99.

13. Ibid. p. 132.

14. Morison, *Admiral of the Ocean Sea, op. cit., p.* 669.

15. Ibid. p. 232.

16. Baker. op. cit., p. 21.

17. Ibid. p. 23.

18. This information was given by our guide who walked us through much of Cuba.

19. Baker. op. cit., p. 23.

20. Ibid. p. 23.

21. Morison. op. cit., p. 119.

22. Baker. op. cit., p. 23.

23. Ibid. p. 23.

24. The fact of the complete genocide of the indigenous peoples of Cuba is noted both in the book by Baker (op. cit. p. 23) as well as the book by Morison, i.e., *Christopher Columbus Mariner.*

25. Morison. *Christopher Columbus Mariner.* op. cit., p. 279.

26. Morison. *Admiral of the Ocean Sea.* op. cit., p. 71.

27. Ibid., p. 260.

47. Mattingly, Garrett. (1959). *The Defeat of the Spanish Armada.* Jonathan Cape. London. p. 86.

48. Baker. op. cit. p. 24.

49. Ibid. p. 27.

50. Ibid. p. 26.

51. Ibid. p. 26.

52. Ibid. p. 27.

53. Ibid. p. 27.

54. Ibid. p. 26.

55. Ibid. p. 29.

56. Ibid. p. 30.

57. Ibid. p. 31.

58. Ibid. p. 31.

59. Ibid. p. 31.

60. Ruiz, Ramon Eduardo. (1970) CUBA: *The Making of a Revolution.* W. W. Norton & Company. New York. p. 169.

61. Baker. op. cit., p. 33.

62. Ibid. p. 34.

63. Ibid. p. 35.

64. Ibid. p. 37.

65. Ibid. p. 37.

66. Ibid. p. 39.

67. Ibid. p. 700.

68. Ibid. p. 40.

69. Ibid. p. 40.

70. Ibid. p. 23.

71, 72, 73. This information was shared by our guides in Cuba.

(There are no endnotes 28-46 because that part of the text was revised and moved from Chp 6, Cuba, to Chp 9, 'Tis a Pity.)

Author Leif Terdal cruises and fishes along the Inside Passage in British Columbia to Alaska

Nellie Torgenson—granddaughter of last chief of Tlingit Tribe, Wrangell, Alaska—shares memories with the author.

Alaskan Natives (Tlingit) refurbish a Community Center in Hoonah

Chaco Canyon, New Mexico, was central to thousands of
Pueblo Indians between 850 and 1250 AD.

A Guatemalan widow whose husband was executed as were
200,000 people in a 36 year civil war. The violence reached its peak
under General Rios Montt

Tobacco farm in Vinales Valley, Cuba, produces best tobaccos in the world.

Barracks Museum in Santiago, Cuba, commemorates 61 martyrs killed on July 26, 1953.

The *Explorer* attracts attention from scores of mixed race people about 1500 miles up the Amazon River

Medical ship under a missionary program provides medical and dental services to rural Brazilians along the Amazon River.

Marge Terdal initiates craft activities on a VIM visit to a remote island along the Amazon River.

Leif and Marge Terdal admire a stone wall of an ancient
temple of the Incas at Machu Picchu

Charles Darwin and Robert FitzRoy travelled this
Canal in Tierra del Fuego.

CHAPTER 6

Portuguese Missionaries bring Christianity to the Indigenous peoples of Brazil

Our Trip up the Amazon River

We arrived in Manaus, Brazil on April 1, 2005, to take a river cruise of about 1200 miles up the Amazon River to Iquitos, Peru. Our ship was the *Explorer* built in Nystad, Finland. The *Explorer* was 246' long and had a cruising speed of 11 knots and a cruising range (before refueling) of 5,300 miles. The ship's capacity was 108 passengers with a crew and staff of 53. The ship was built under the direction of Eric Lindblad, who designed the *Explorer* to be the world's first expedition ship to take passengers to the Antarctic. This *Explorer* earned additional acclaim by being the first ship to take passengers through the Northwest Passage. Designed with safety in mind, the *Explorer* featured double hull construction with many sealed compartments. Should the ship hit an iceberg and develop a crack in the hull, the flooding would be limited to the specific compartments that were damaged. Furthermore, the crew was trained to deal with a range of possible emergencies, including the unlikely event of an accident resulting in the loss, i.e., sinking of the ship while in cold Antarctic waters.

During the life (or tenure) of the *Explorer*, the ship made continuous travel taking passengers to the Antarctic in November, then returning north in March. As the *Explorer* neared the Equator on its northward journey, it entered the mouth of the Amazon River and travelled up that greatest of rivers the distance of 2200 miles to Iquitos, Peru. From Iquitos the ship turned around and cruised eastward down the Amazon River to the Atlantic Ocean, where it headed north. It arrived in Norway in the summer and then on to Greenland, then to New Brunswick, Canada. From Canada the ship headed south again to Antarctica.

Many passengers depart the ship at Iquitos and head for Peruvian archaeological sites such as Cusco and Machu Picchu. The concept of travel on the *Explorer* is to take passengers to areas of the world where men and women first explored, starting in the fifteenth century, the unknown territories of South America and eventually the Antarctic. The fifteenth century explorers sought riches, new territories and the opportunity to spread the Christian religion as it was understood at that time. The ship has onboard an excellent library with books describing the history of exploration of the New World, accounts of major sea disasters during explorations and rescues at sea, wildlife, and extensive geographical maps.

At Manaus Marge and I were part of a group of 35 Elderhostelers who boarded the ship at 4:00 pm on April 2nd, 2005. Our cabin was on the main deck; it had two single beds, an adequate closet and a small bathroom. A small porthole gave us a view of the river and forest, but we spent little time in our cabin. There were now 74 passengers on board, 39 passengers of whom boarded in Belem at the mouth of the Amazon River, and spent five days to cover the 1000 miles to Manaus. We made a point of sitting with new people as much as possible to get to know the other passengers. We found that essentially all the passengers had travelled extensively to other countries and to at least several of the world's seven continents. One of the unique features of an extended trip up the Amazon River is that, unlike trips to Europe or Asia, this is not a vacation in which you visit museums and eat in outstanding restaurants, or visit sites of major battles. Instead, you encounter wilderness, people living in primitive settings, and learn some of the history of exploration and the conquest of the New World.

While aboard the ship, Marge and I had a chance to walk around the ship on deck. I asked permission to visit the engine room. My father was a chief engineer on ships and spent more time during his life of 75 years on a ship than on land. Many times while I was growing up, my father would come home for a short visit after an extended trip at sea. He had great pride in his work as "chief" with the responsibility to keep all the engines, the propulsion systems, the generators in working order. He believed that a ship's engine should last fifty years of continuous service if properly maintained, and then be replaced with new engines without there ever having been a breakdown. He supervised such an engine replacement on a fifty-year-old oil tanker that had operated on the Great Lakes.

During the first safety drill each of us was asked to put on our life jacket and to stand during an inspection while crew members checked each passenger to ensure that his/her life jacket was put on correctly. Later on, we had a second drill in which we responded to a "full scale" emergency call. For this drill we all appeared at our designated stations, put on our jackets and got into life-boats. I told Marge that if I were ever at sea during another sea disaster, I would like the next emergency to be on the *Explorer*. We both felt confidence in the crew and the ship.

While on board the *Explorer* we had lectures twice a day by scholars in the Magellan Theatre. A German geologist, Stefan Kreidel, gave talks on the geologic history of the Amazon River. Ed Hudson lectured on the history of European explorers who "discovered" America while looking for passage to India. Some of these early explorers got lost and then came upon the Amazon River and the vast jungle and wildlife with its insects, numerous birds, and small mammals, including many varieties of monkeys that lived most of their lives in trees. There are no large animals along the Amazon basin. The river floods beyond its banks so extensively that animals such as deer, which cannot live in trees, do not live within many miles of the Amazon. During our long journey from Manaus to Iquitos, Peru, Ed Hudson lectured on the twelve explorers of the Amazon River including Francesco de Orellana in 1541; Alexander Humboldt, 1799-1804; Theodore Roosevelt, 1913-1914; and Colonel Fawcett, 1906-1925. He also gave excellent lectures on the Brazilian Indians and their encounter with missionaries and colonists and the factors that led to their rapid demise.

Two lecturers, David Astanio and Doris Valencia, were bird experts and helped us identify the numerous birds seen along the Amazon River. All the lecturers combined their presentations on board the ship with opportunities to observe the focus of the lectures as we departed twice each day on rigid hull zodiacs to observe wildlife, features of the river, and people living and making a living along the river. In a very real sense every person on board was a student.

The Amazon River

By day one of our journey we were ready for some serious lectures about this fascinating river, as well as the vast variety of birdlife and the enormous diversity of plants and trees. The geologist, Stefan Kreidel, stated that the river is between 6400 and 7000 kilometers in length, and is fed by about 100,000 tributaries. Fifteen of these tributaries are longer than 2000 km. The Amazon drains about seven million square kilometers and contains one fifth of the world's above-ground fresh water. Sixty percent of the water evaporates along the way downstream and falls again as rain, which creates and maintains the vast Amazon rain forest. From Iquitos, Peru, to the Atlantic there is only 175 meters of altitude loss. As a consequence, the Amazon is a relatively slow-moving river, and during the flood season may extend 60 miles beyond its normal banks on each side of the river. The mouth is more than 200 miles wide, and within the mouth of the river is the island of Marajo, the largest island in the world in fresh water. Marajo is about the size of Switzerland.

The average depth of the river at Manaus is 10 meters; however, at high water during the peak of the rainy season, the depth at Manaus reaches 18 meters. The river banks change constantly as strong currents during times of flood cut some banks and fill others. If a ship gets stuck in a sandbar while going downstream, it can not back up with its own power. The tidal flow from the Atlantic Ocean affects the Amazon River as far as 650 kilometers upstream from the river's mouth.

A standard means of measuring the size of a river is cubic km of water flow per year. The Amazon, the world's largest river, has a water flow of 6,600 cubic km per year. The Congo River in Africa is the second largest river in the world with a water flow of 1250 km per year. The Mississippi, the largest in the United States, has a water flow of 580 cubic km per year.

Day-by-Day Itinerary

Our first morning on board the ship we were awakened at 6:00 AM and the ship anchored at 7:00 at the small river town of Bocado Anama. By 7:30 we had loaded into small zodiacs for our morning excursion. In this small river town we saw local residents going about their business. Some grew cacao plants and harvested their fruit or other natural growing plants such as jute fibers, manioc, and cacao plants. An important crop is Brazil nuts. Doris Valencia told us the shell of the Brazil nut is hard and does not deteriorate when the nut falls to the ground. The survival of the Brazil nut tree is dependent upon a species of rodent, the agouti. It is the only creature with the teeth and strong jaws necessary to penetrate the hard shell of the Brazil nut to get the nut out of the shell. Enough seeds fall to the ground after the rodents break open the nut to germinate and produce more Brazil nut trees. Another feature of the Brazil nut tree is that this tree cannot live in a flood plain. Its roots and trunk cannot survive being submerged for months at a time, as happens throughout the Amazon basin. The Brazil nut tree grows only in the comparatively few areas of low level hills along the river not submerged by annual flood waters.

Fishing and processing fish for sale were the major activities that we observed as we walked through this small river town. Ed Hudson stated that the people living along this section of the Amazon are a mixed blood people named Caboclo. We cruised up a tributary for about two hours and observed the vast and richly varied plant and tree life along the river banks as well as bird life. Back on board the Explorer, we continued upstream and in the afternoon stopped to visit a small river village with a population of three families. The small village had a school and s soccer field. While on shore we experienced our first heavy rain and sought shelter under thatched roofs. That evening the *Explorer* anchored again and we got into zodiacs for a night excursion. We saw a great Potoo, a bird similar to a large owl, several caimans and three boa snakes.

Birds of the Amazon

David Ascanio, the bird expert, gave a talk entitled the Complexity of the Amazonian Bird-life. He began his lecture by describing the enormous number of species of birds along the Amazon. There are about 9000 known species of birds in the world; in the section of South America known as the Neotropics, there are 3751 species. The Neotropics are an area within a band from about 25 degrees latitude north of the equator to 25 degrees south. The process that generated such species richness is still debated by biologists. One line of reasoning among biologists is that during the different ice ages the area now called Neotropics supported life well, whereas parts north or south were too dry and cold. When glaciers retreated some species moved out to return to their former habitat; however, many species may have gone through enough mutations to have successfully adapted to life in the tropics.

David gave some helpful suggestions for observing birds: note the colors of the bird, its size and shape, particularly its wings, tail and bill and how it is standing; notice behaviors such as foraging, mating, singing, nesting, hunting; listen carefully to the voice and compare it with sounds of certain species. He stated that the song of a bird is a more reliable indicator of species than the bones of a bird. He also discussed migration patterns: warblers migrate north between May and October and can fly long distances at a stretch. Hummingbirds can migrate long distances but do so for short distances at a time.

He also gave us information on how to identify the families of birds, then the species. For example, all birds of prey have short necks. He pointed out birds that we had already seen along the river, such as the Harpy eagle, which has a wing span over six feet and a claw as big as a human hand, and is powerful enough to catch and fly away with a monkey During his lectures many of our group asked questions about birds we had seen on our early morning or late evening bird-watching trips.

The *Explorer* enters the reserve of the Tikuana Indians

On April 6th we arrived at the confluence of the river Jutai and the Amazon, and entered the Jutai, which comes from the south. At this point, approximately 1800 miles from the mouth of the Amazon, the population is all Tikuana Indians. The ship staff had obtained permission from these indigenous residents to enter their reserve. We were told we had permission to photograph the site, native ceremonies, and residents. Some other groups of Amerindians in Brazil do not want any photos taken of their people. We were told not to give food to any person while on shore. The Indians are totally self-sufficient with food from the jungle.

The Tikuana Indians came to meet the *Explorer* in large hand-crafted canoes. Aboard the zodiacs, we circled through large numbers of Tikuana in their canoes, and I was able to photograph many with the *Explorer* in the background. As we entered their reserve, crew members brought offerings of school supplies, notebooks and pencils for the children. The Tikuana and another tribe, the Yanamomi, are the most numerous Amerindian tribes in Brazil. These two tribes have survived as "Indians." They refused to be "converted" and subjugated by missionaries and colonists beginning with the 16th century. These two tribes in Brazil are among a handful who continue to live in their historic lands and hold on to some of their indigenous language, customs, and spiritual practices.[1] Our visit with the small tribe of Tikuana Indians prepared us to be receptive to learning from Ed Hudson about the Indigenous peoples of the Amazon and what happened to them from the time of the "Discovery" and the "Conquest."

The Indians along the Amazon River were Hunters and Gatherers, not Farmers.

A fascinating, but troubling, lecture on board the *Explorer*, was given by Ed Hudson. His topic was *The Indigenous peoples of the Amazon*.

He began his talk with the startling statement that "You need to travel 1800 miles from the mouth of the Amazon River to locate the first tribes of Indigenous people who currently live along the river." As we were among the Tikuana Indians, we learned these people represented the remnants of tribal people who once lived in great numbers along the Amazon River. Ed Hudson stated that before the conquest, the Indian population of Brazil is estimated to have been between three and five million people. However, by 1755 the Indian population of Brazil had been virtually destroyed by forced labor, religious persecution and, most of all, by disease. Currently, the percentage of Indigenous natives is less than one half of one percent of the total population of Brazil. The Indigenous tribes in Brazil, Columbia, and Peru were a focus of many talks and discussions while aboard the *Explorer*, and are discussed more fully in the section **Missionary work among the Indigenous peoples of Brazil and Peru.**

The Tikuana Indians had refused to accept the European system of agriculture which, in fact, is not suitable for the areas along the Amazon River. The soil along the river and the vast Amazon basin is made up of deposited mud that is acidic and bereft of essential nutrients. Furthermore, the river floods extensively every year. As a consequence the Indians who had lived for thousands of years along the Amazon were hunters and gatherers.[2] The Tikuana Indians also refused to abandon the practice of cremation of their dead, a practice which the missionaries condemned. Finally, the Tikuana refused to live in enclosed villages directed by missionaries and colonists. When threatened to be enslaved, the Tikuana fought the Portuguese.

On Friday, April 8th, as we continued our travels up the Amazon River, our staff informed us we would have breakfast on board the *Explorer* in Brazil, lunch in Columbia and dinner in Peru. We had breakfast at 7:00 and the Explorer anchored outside of Leticia, Columbia, by 8:30. We went ashore by zodiacs to a rickety dock and walked carefully along a muddy board without railings until we arrived on a muddy street to walk to the center of town. Marge and I enjoyed walking around Leticia. We stopped at a craft store and purchased a mask made by Tikuma Indians. I also bought a blow gun, which Indians use to kill birds for food. I enjoyed standing around fish markets and admiring the large assortment of fish for sale. We saw piranha for sale as well as many pirarucu fish, which is said to be the largest freshwater fish in the world and often grows to 400 pounds and larger. The name pirarucu comes from the Tupi-Guarani language meaning "red fish." The fish is an air-breathing fish and needs to surface about every 15 minutes to gulp oxygen. Amazon natives hunt the pirarucu by spearing them as they rise to the surface to breathe. (Actually, the white sturgeon which inhabits the Columbia River in our Pacific Northwest, grows larger than the pirarucu, but the sturgeon spends some if its life in salt water.) Fish sold in these markets are sold fresh, on ice, and whole. The exception is that very large fish can be purchased by the kilo. The markets also sold live chickens (absolutely free ranging), fruits and vegetables.

Marge found an internet café and sent messages to about a dozen or so family and friends. We re-boarded the *Explorer* at noon, and proceeded about 90 miles along the Amazon River in Columbia before arriving in Peru. By evening we were in Peru, and the ship continued on its long journey. We were still a couple of hundred miles from Iquitos, Peru.

On April 9th the *Explorer* anchored and all the zodiacs headed out towards two small indigenous villages. The Indians were Boras and Witoto, who live in two separate villages about one mile apart. A cement sidewalk connects the two villages. These two small indigenous villages have a school, a health clinic and a community building. Boras Indians lived in the first village and about 20 men and women, in traditional costume and make-up, performed a dance and sang for us. We then had a chance to look at a large variety of crafts made by the villagers. Marge and I bought several masks and necklaces.

The second village was home to Witoto Indians. They also performed dances for us and showed us some of their crafts. I bought an indigenous bow and arrow set as well as a blow gun and darts that continue to be used by the natives in this village to hunt small animals and birds. These two small villages in a very remote part of Peru, along the Amazon River have a staffed medical clinic, a school, a community center and a paved sidewalk. Such modern facilities in a remote jungle are very unusual. We found out why they were placed there.

Ed Hudson told us that these two indigenous villages endured brutal treatment by officials and workers of the Peruvian Amazon Rubber Company, a British owned company. The company was started by a Peruvian named Julio Cesar Arana, who saw the continuation of extreme world-wide demand for Brazilian rubber. In 1906 he purchased, from the Peruvian government 12,000 square miles of land along the Putumayo River, which flows into the Amazon. The land was inhabited by Witoto Indians; Arana sent large numbers of employees to persuade the Indians to harvest rubber from the *Castilloa elastica*, a valuable tree which was abundant in the area. He also monopolized steamship travel to ship the products down river. In 1907 he raised substantial money for his company on the London stock market, and recruited over two hundred British subjects from Barbados as overseers. One year later an editor for a "news sheet" in the town of Iquitos stopped by the area and became an eyewitness to horrifying examples of enslavement of Witoto Indians and widespread cruelty.

Testimony obtained from workers of the Peruvian Amazon Company further provided evidence of widespread cruelty, rape, and murder by company workers against the Witoto Indians. British directors of the Peruvian Amazon Rubber Company agreed to send a commission of enquiry to the Putumayo. The commission of five members included the forty-six-year-old Roger Casement., who was British Consul-General in Rio De Janeiro. Casement had previously investigated atrocities in the Belgian Congo. In 1911 the commission released their report. The Indians were losing their language and culture to the dominant occupying power, and the report authenticated evidence of lingering deaths from starvation, death by hanging, mutilations, and being burned alive as well as instances of rape. Casement reported that his observations reminded him of the plight of American Indians and his own Irish compatriots.[3] Roger Casement returned to England and published the book, Blue Book on the Putumayo in 1912 and was knighted for it. Soon afterwards Sir Roger Casement declared himself in favor of Irish independence and fled to Ireland. He was captured and tried in London for treason and executed in 1916. John Hemming writes that little came of the formal enquiry; he states, "no one was convicted. Such was invariably the way in Amazonia. Even Julio Cesar

Arana, although disgraced in Europe, continued to live in luxury in the upper Amazon."[4] International pressure after publicity of the plight of the Witoto Indians, however, contributed to the building of the school and the health clinic shared by the two villages.

April 10th was our last full day aboard the ship. We had our wake-up call at 5:30 and departed in the zodiacs at 6:00. I chose to join two others and fished for piranha. Marge joined a group in a different zodiac and went bird watching. It rained hard, but consistent with policy, we did not go back to the ship because of rain—not even a tropical downpour. I caught five piranha and enjoyed a chance to admire the jungle; I kept one eye on birds and the other on the river while waiting for a fish strike. The piranha, a relatively small fish, is about the size of a large blue gill. The have remarkable teeth and they are not hesitant about attacking large mammals. The indigenous peoples along the Amazon never raised domestic animals. However, a substantial amount of the rainforests have been cut in recent years to raise beef cattle. A few cows have fallen into the Amazon or its tributaries and lost their battles with the piranha. The area we stopped to fish and bird watch is the place where Francesco Orellana entered the Amazon River in 1541 and travelled the very long distance (2200 miles) to the Atlantic Ocean. He met vast numbers of Indigenous peoples along the way.

Some Final Lectures aboard the *Explorer*

Ed Hudson gave his final and free ranging lecture on the *Explorer* in which he spoke of environmental damage by industry since 1500 and destructive practices applied against Indigenous peoples and to African slaves. Brazil became the world's leading exporter of sugar by 1630 and remained a leading producer and exporter throughout the 18th century. Coffee overtook sugar as the main export by the early 1800s. The harvests of these labor intensive crops were done by slave labor. As a result, by 1775 the indigenous population had ben virtually destroyed by forced labor, religious persecution, and disease. African slaves were imprted to Brazil as early as the 1540s and by 1680, African slaves numbered about 150,000. By 1800 there were more than 1,000,000 African slaves and the numbers continued to increase during the 19th century. The total number of Africans brought as slaves to Brazil was 4.8 million. No other country in the world had as many slaves from Africa as Brazil. Ed Hudson stated that the current population of Brazil is the following:

White, 54%; Black 6%; Mulatto and Cabulco 39%; Japanese .5%; and Indian .4% (less than one-half of one percent). Mulatto is a mixture of European and African descent, and Cabolco is mixture of Native Indian and European or African descent.

Ed Hudson ended his lecture by stating that the conquest was cruel and brutal, and he referred to an essay allegedly written by an Indigenous person about a "five hundred loan." The essay is entitled *An Indigenous Claim Against Europe.*

I, a descendant of those who populated America for 40,000 years, have come to meet those who found us only 500 years ago. The European Customs official asked to see my VISA so that I could discover those who discovered us.

The Archives of the Indies in Seville show that between only 1503-1600m 185,000 KG of gold and 16,000,000 KG of silver arrived in Spain from America. That gold should be considered as the first of many loans from America, for the development of Europe. If not, then taking it should be considered as war crimes giving us the right to demand immediate payment and indemnity for damages.

I prefer to think that such export of capital was just the beginning of the Marshalltezuma plan for guaranteeing the reconstruction of barbarous Europe after ruin, by crusaders against Muslims, who were the creators of Algebra, of polygamy, of the daily bath and other superior aspects of civilization.

To celebrate the 500 years of the loan, we ask, did the Europeans make good use of the generous loan to them from the International Indo-American Fund? We are sorry to say No! The funds were used to finance battles against the Turks at Lepanto, in creating an invincible armada, and to build a Third Reich and other forms of Mutual extermination. You have been incapable in 500 years to repay any capital or interest! Milton Friedman clearly said that subsidized economies never work. This obliges us, for your

own good, to demand repayment of the capital and interest that we have
generously waited for all these years.

But we will reduce the interest rate from the excessive 20-30 percent
you have charged for loans to the third world. We only demand return of
the precious metal plus only 10 percent interest. We give 200 years free so
we just charge interest over the last 300 years. We recognize that in the past
500 years Europe has not generated riches enough to pay the interest due to
the failures of your financial system. We are not too upset. But we demand
a signed letter of intent to commit you to an immediate privatization of
Europe permitting you to give us Europe complete as first payment of your
historic debt.

Then Ed Hudson quietly added the statement, "The year 1910 was
the lowest point of the Indians' long decline along the Amazon. Since
that time some populations have slowly decreased."

Missionary Work among the Indigenous Peoples of Brazil
The Portuguese Empire in Brazil

Pedro Alvares Cabral with his ships was on his way to India in the
year 1500. Strong winds blew his ships off course and brought him to
the coast of America. Cabral and his men explored the jungle with its
vast forests. They found an unusual tree called brazilwood (caesalpinia
echniata). Cabral named his discovery of the new land the *Land of the*
True Cross. They brought some of the logs beck to Europe, where the
deep red dye became popular and in demand. The profits from the
brazilwood tree were sufficient to justify the risks and costs involved in
the long ocean crossing. It was commerce associated with the brazilwood
tree that introduced Brazilian natives to the attention of the Portuguese
explorers and merchants. The Indians cut the brazilwood trees into
logs, transported them, and loaded them onto his ships. The wages for
the Indians were not money but tools such as knives and axes. With a
steel axe a person could cut down a tree in one hour that would take
one hundred hours with a stone axe. It is estimated that in a period of
150 years, 50,000,000 brazilwood trees were cut down and shipped to

Europe.[5] By 1530 the name of the new land was changed to Brazil, in recognition of the status of the tree with the valuable red dye.

Martin Afonso de Sousa founded the first Portuguese colony in Brazil on the island of Sao Vicente in 1532. Recognizing the potential riches of the new territory, King Joao III divided the coast of Brazil into 14 hereditary captaincies. John Hemming states that the coastal tribes quickly understood that the new invaders who brought with them remarkable metal tools had a dark side. Their native land was to be permanently colonized.

The godlike strangers with wonderful metal tools assumed a different aspect. They revealed themselves as uncouth invaders who were generally brutal, greedy and licentious. They violated all the codes of Indian behavior, scorned tribal customs, abused hospitality and attacked Indian beliefs. They had arrived to occupy the land of Brazil, and were interested in its native men only as labourers and women as concubines.[6]

The Arrival of the Jesuits

The first Jesuits, led by Fr. Manoel da Nobrega, arrived in Brazil in 1549, along with the first royal governor, Tome do Sousa. The Society of Jesus (Jesuits) was a new Catholic organization founded by a Spaniard, Ignateus Loyola in 1539 as a monastic order pledged to defend the Papacy against the Protestant Reformation. The members were highly dedicated and Brazil became the first foreign venture for the Society, which went on to expand and to develop an international scope. Before preaching to the Tupi people, the Jesuits learned the Tupi language and created a grammar for the language. The Guarani Indians spoke the Tupi-Guarani dialect. The Jesuits carefully studied the customs and habits of the natives.

Hemming writes that,

The first meetings between Indians and Jesuits were joyful affairs, with each side enthusiastic and delighted with what it saw in the other. The Indians found in the Jesuits the first Portuguese they could trust, men devoid of material greed, who returned Indian hospitality with honest friendship. It immediately became clear that the Fathers were the Indians' main allies against colonial excesses, in those bewildering times when barter was degenerating into slavery and the settlers were imposing their barbaric notions of law, trade and morality.[7]

Fr. Manoel da Nobrega wrote to the King that, *the conversion of these heathen is an easy matter. For they believe in nothing—they are a blank page on which one can write at will, provided one sustains them by example and continual converse. All the heathen of this coast want to be Christian, but they find it harsh to abandon their customs.*[8]

The major reason for the Brazilian Indians flocking to the Jesuits and becoming Christian was to avoid being enslaved by Portuguese colonists. These Indians were members of defeated tribes in the early phases of Portuguese domination and control of the vastness of Brazil. The Jesuits soon learned that the first 'conversions' did not hold, that the Brazilian Indians may have learned some Christian beliefs and practices but they did not abandon their pagan beliefs and practices. The missionaries were opposed to syncretism regarding religious beliefs; they were content only when an Indian rejected all traditional Indian spiritual beliefs and practices and adopted Christian beliefs as taught by the Church.

The Jesuits decided that they must move Brazilian Indians into permanent mission villages totally under Jesuit control. These mission villages were called 'aldeias'. Nobrega wrote that he desired the Brazilian Indians to accept Christian teaching and beliefs and *become capable of grace and entry into the church of God....For this to take place, I also wish...to see the heathen subjugated and placed under the yoke of obedience to the Christians, so that we could imprint on them all that we desire.... Nothing can be done with them if they are left at liberty, for they are brutish people.*[9]

Forcibly moving Indians into permanent mission villages represented a profound shock and adjustment for the Indians. Traditionally, tribal Indians within the tropical area of South America inhabited an area for a few years. They hunted and fished for subsistence and picked available fruits and vegetables that grew wild. The Indians raised no domestic animals and grew no crops. When local food availability became reduced, the tribe moved on. Their lives were enriched by centuries of traditional dances and ceremonies and ministrations of shamans.

Settlement into mission villages demanded a painful readjustment for the Indians. Hemming states, *Mission Indians had to change from being semi-nomadic hunters to subsistence farmers working permanent farms and raising European livestock. They had to learn that the land was no longer a free commodity like air or water, something so abundant that men could roam and hunt across it at will. If they now moved outside the mission boundaries they were trespassing on estates awarded to Portuguese colonists. The loss of freedom must have been suffocating.*[10]

The Indian practices of subsistence through hunting and gathering as well as their spiritual practices were all prohibited in the missions under Jesuit control. Worst of all, for the Brazilian natives, according to Hemming, was the contact with European civilization.

The King of Portugal ordered that Indians trace with colonists at regular markets. But in trading with the Indians it was all too easy for white men to drive bargains so hard that they amounted to exploitation. For the settlers the true purpose of the settlements was to provide a pool of native labor for the surrounding estates. Just as barter degenerated into slavery, this casual labor by mission Indians degenerated into forced labor in conditions indistinguishable from slavery. [11]

Hemming provides his assessment of the Jesuit effort to Christianize the Indians of Brazil:

The Jesuit mission system was by any measure the most important experiment in dealing with Brazilian Indians: it involved many more Indians, affected them more profoundly, and lasted far longer than any other attempt at co-existence between the races. The Jesuit fathers were heroic and unselfish men, acting from high moral motives. The discipline and routine of their missions would strike a modern European as suffocating monotony; but this regimentation had more appeal to Indians accustomed to an uneventful communal existence devoid of individual competition.

The Jesuits managed the lands and labour of their missions in such a way that their Society grew rich and they themselves lived comfortably. But their organization and discipline also forced the Indians to change from being carefree improvident hunters to efficient farm labourers. Most of the Indians' labour went to keeping themselves well housed, clothed and fed.

The intellectual life on the missions was more controversial. The Jesuits were brilliant educators, the best in the Catholic world; they ran colleges for white boys in the Brazilian towns, as well as the Indian missions. But, after some disastrous failures in trying to ordain Indians, they decided that the natives were inherently inferior. They contented themselves with patronizing tuition, sufficient for the mission Indians to recite and perform their religious offices but with no scope for intellectual stimulus or debate. Their aim was to turn out pious domesticated congregations, and they succeeded. Their education had nothing whatever to do with the Indians' environment. It deprived them of tribal skills without making them competitive in the harsh colonial world.[12]

Disease and Slavery

Hemming writes that early chroniclers, such as the priest Manoel da Nobrega, in the year 1550 wrote that the Indians of Brazil were healthy, strong and lived to an old age. Tragically, that changed abruptly and with profound implications for the indigenous peoples of the Americas. An epidemic struck at Bahia in 1552 and raged until 1561. Another epidemic emerged near Sao Paolo in 1554, and two years later an epidemic killed 8000 natives at a French colony at Rio do Janeiro. Other epidemics raged throughout the Americas. Hemming states that the *Indians had no immunity against a terrible range of Eurasian and African diseases. This factor more than any other has doomed American natives to probably extinction. Imported diseases have destroyed hundreds of thousands of natives throughout the Americas, and reduced their populations to levels at which they could not mount effective resistance or claim their lands on demographic grounds.*[13]

The epidemics that were lethal to the Indians were a severe setback to the missionaries. As they worked among the Indians to introduce Christianity, the natives died by the thousands from diseases that the missionaries were helpless to cure. A priest named Antonio Blasque corresponded with a colleague in Portugal and wrote: *You can imagine how one's heart was torn with pity at seeing so many children orphaned, so many women widowed, and the disease and epidemic so rife among them that it seemed like a pestilence. They were terrified and almost stunned by what was happening to them. They no longer performed their songs and dances. Everything was grief. In our aldeia there was nothing to be heard but weeping and groaning by the dying.*[14]

The Jesuits found it hopelessly difficult to explain to the Indians why such horrific catastrophes were befalling them. Many wept with the Indian survivors over their losses. Father Anchieta visited a stricken Indian village and wept with the Indians and encouraged them to bear their pain with patience.[15] The primary response of the Jesuits to the huge death toll among their aldeias was to fill their missions with new recruits of Indians from the interior of Brazil. They sent priests as well as converted Indians into the jungles to recruit Indians and take them through long journeys to live in enclosed missions—and face the planned extinction of their language, culture and indigenous religious beliefs and practices, and to endure the risk of unknown and lethal diseases.

Europe was not immune to widespread epidemics during the middle ages. In 1561 a plague struck Portugal, taking 40,000 lives in Lisbon alone. That plague crossed the Atlantic and led to outbreaks with deadly impact on Itaparica Island and spread from there to other locations in Brazil. The Indians, believing that the Jesuits were able to treat them, flocked to the Jesuit Fathers. The Jesuits worked without fixed times for sleeping or eating and worked tending the dying and giving last rites and burial for the dead. When one epidemic passed, another illness struck worse than the previous. The Jesuits had only the rudimentary medicine that was understood during the 16th century. They were in fact helpless.

Out of great fear some Indians fled missions. Hemming writes that Father Joao Pereira "was almost killed by his Indians in 1564 when he tried to stop them fleeing from the epidemics."[16] The priests sought to baptize Indians and remove them into mission settlements, even though the mission settlements were among the hardest hit by the epidemics. By 1732, the Guarani missions numbered thirty, with 141,252 Christian Indians. Two years later a smallpox epidemic killed 30,000 Indians in a period of only a few months. A short time later other epidemics killed more Indians.[17] It is puzzling that the Jesuits continued the policy of removing Indians to mission settlements while being aware that the epidemics were probably imported by Europeans and that the mission settlements were among the highest risk places to contract the Plague. Hemming summarizes the Jesuit response to the epidemics as follows

The Jesuits were intelligent enough to appreciate that the epidemics were probably imported by Europeans, and that they struck hardest at converts congregated into mission settlements This did not deter them. Throughout the two centuries of their presence in Brazil, they always have believed that it was better for Indians to be baptized but dead than heathen but alive and free. But it often seemed that what really mattered was pride in maintaining the mission system. The Jesuits became obsessed with their personal soul-count.[18]

The enslavement of Indians was already fully established in Brazil, and 40,000 Indians worked as slaves for Bahia planters. The epidemic struck them and played to favorites among "converted" Indians on Jesuit missions or vast numbers of enslaved Indians. In many areas there were not enough healthy Indians to get water or tend crops. This resulted in the death or many Indians from starvation after failing to plant manioc. Some Indians fled from the plantations where they were enslaved to escape the epidemics.

Proposed End to Enslavement of Brazilian Indians

In 1570 the Portuguese King Sebastiao, on the recommendation of the Jesuits and the current royal governor of Brazil, Mem de Sa, issued a law which prohibited the enslavement of Indians. The law stated that Indians "may on no account and in no way be enslaved."[19] The anti-slavery law provided an exception and permitted enslavement of Indians who habitually attacked Portuguese or other Indians. King

Sebastiao was killed in a crusade into Morocco in 1578 and two years later King Philip II of Spain, the most powerful monarch in Europe, was declared ruler of both Portugal and Spain. The new King was less concerned about the rights of Indians, and the colonists had no desire to do the hard work on their plantations

Sugar was the source of major profit to the colonists in Brazil. The agricultural economy was labor intensive and the colonists readily enslaved Indians in spite of ongoing protests from the Jesuits. Slavery became institutionalized and the far-off governments of Spain and Portugal did nothing to interfere. Forced labor of the Indians on plantations, as well as the Jesuit missions, greatly increased the risk for diseases lethal to the Indians.

The Holy Inquisition visited Brazil in 1591. Hemming writes: *The standards of the Holy Office were truly amazing. The Inquisition was not concerned that these raiders had illegally enslaved thousands of natives. The offences they were obliged to confess were: trading European weapons to Indians, practicing Indian ceremonies, and most serious of all, eating meat during Lent while they were off on their long expeditions.*[20]

Tomacauna

Domingos Fernandes Nobre was born to a Brazilian Indian mother and a Portuguese father. At the age of 18, he lived like an Indian among tribes until the age of 36. He was known to the Indians as "Tomacauna." In 1572 he sided with the Portuguese as a leader of slave raids. In one extended raid in 1572 he lured 7000 members of the Tupiguen tribe, even children and the aged, to Portuguese slave markets.[21] In 1576 Nobre led a five-month expedition to capture slaves on the orders of Joao Brito de Almeida. He continued his expeditions to enslave Brazilian natives and was authorized by Governor Lourenco de Veiga and funded by a wealthy plantation owner named Fernao Cabral de Ataide.[22] He was ordered to appear before the Inquisition. However, Nobre had a strong defense, an official license to "descend heathen."[23] (The term "descend heathen" refers to the approved practice during the colonization of Brazil of moving Indians from the jungles to introduce them to Christianity and civilization.)

The Jesuits found themselves in an untenable situation. They were adamantly opposed to the enslavement of Indians. The Brazilian Indians understood that the Jesuits were on their side, but the Indians did not understand that the Jesuits were powerless to assist them. Manoel da Nobrega described the untenable situation of the Jesuits as follows: *Their only knowledge of justice is to come to us, as to fathers and protectors, seeking the shelter of the Church. But we, because we have already learned our lesson and do not wish to cause scandals or get ourselves stoned, cannot help them and do not even dare to preach about it. As a result because of the lack of justice, (the Indians) remain slaves and their masters remain in mortal sin, and we lose credit among all the heathen because of their (disappointed) hopes in us.*[24]

The enslavement of Brazilian Indians continued because it was condoned by the colonial authorities. Furthermore, the extreme death rate of Indians continued because they had no immunity for the diseases introduced by the Europeans and there was no known cure. Hemming refers to the Native Brazilians as enduring *a demographic catastrophe: cultural shock, a demoralization that caused social disintegration and a collapse of the birth rate; deaths from battles, massacres and sheer overwork; but the biggest killer by far was disease. Otherwise healthy Indians had no genetic defense against new diseases imported from across the Atlantic. They died in the tens of thousands from epidemics of smallpox, measles, tuberculosis or influenza.*[25]

Jesuit Missions Continue to Grow but Face Conflicts

In 1610 two Jesuit priests, Fathers Simon Maceta and Jose Cataldino, founded two large missions: Our Lady of Loreto and San Ignacio-Mini. These two missions served as a religious base and were surrounded by very large Jesuit controlled plantations which grew and prospered financially. Soon eleven more Jesuit missions were established between 1622 and 1629.[26] The Indians who worked the Jesuit plantations and responded to the missionary efforts were Guarani. Members of the Guarani tribe took some of the early Portuguese settlers to see the magnificent Iguacu Falls. Nearby colonists saw that the Guarani were effective workers and captured large numbers of them to work for

Portuguese landowners on their fields. Many Guarani fled but they were pursued and led back in chains and suffered physical punishment. Fighting broke out between Guarani and Spanish settlers, and the Jesuits had to convince the Guarani that they were missionaries and not agents for the colonists. However, many Guarani distrusted the Jesuits because the colonists who enslaved the Guarani came soon after the Jesuits entered their lives. Hemming states that two effective Jesuit priests, Antonio Ruiz de Montoya and Simon Maceta, were able to develop great and effective missions. These two Jesuit priests convinced the Guarani that their missions opposed the greedy colonists. The Guarani responded eagerly and contributed their own expertise, and with the Jesuit effective management and leadership their crops flourished. This led to many Guarani emerging from the vast forests of Brazil near Iguacu Falls to join the Jesuit missions. The Guarani tribe was very large and numbered over 400,000 at the time of contact.[27]

The Guarani were sedentary and agricultural before the time of contact (or conquest). They grew corn (maize) used manioc in their diet (the root from which tapioca is prepared), and made use of ample supplies of game and fish. They had been able to develop agriculture because they lived far south of the Amazon River, where vast flood plains made agriculture unfeasible. The Guarani people lived in communal houses, large enough to accommodate 10 to 15 families each. They were expert in pottery and wood carving. They were not known as a warrior tribe, in contrast to tribes such as the Paiagua (discussed below).

Bandeiras: Expeditions to Enslave Brazilian Natives

A large number of Portuguese settlers in Brazil became aware of the wealth that centered on the Jesuit missions with fast farms worked by co-operative Guarani. In the small town of Sao Paulo, below Rio de Janeiro in the South of Brazil, population 2000 in 1600, groups of men explored the vast forests and rivers of South America. Their expeditions became known as bandeiras; the bandeirants had large farms but they were too poor to afford African slaves. The men of Sao Paulo travelled extensively through the jungles of Brazil, encountering hordes of insects, snakes, Indian warriors, and flooded jungles in search of Indians to enslave and to bring back to their farms in Sao Paulo. The Jesuits were disturbed and amazed by this activity. A Spanish Jesuit who witnessed this act of enslavement in the 17th century wrote: "These Portuguese suffer incomparably more to win the bodies of the Indians for their service than I do to win their souls for heaven. For they are always on journeys on foot that are long and difficult. They lack all necessities of this life, suffering hunger, exhaustion and nakedness, always on guard against a thousand ambushes, with bodies and souls constantly in danger—all to catch four Indians, who run off or die on them the next day."[28]

The Expeditions were long in duration, often covering several years. For example, Nicolav Barreto took 300 men from Sao Paulo and many Indians over a two-year period and returned with over 3000 Indian captives to be sold as slaves. Traveling with the bandeiras were Catholic priests. Their function was to administer the last rites to dying bandeirantes—not to interfere with their slaving operations.[29] The Jesuits were opposed to these priests, but it is important to recognize the degree to which the enslavement of indigenous peoples was considered normal.

The Jesuits were opposed to the enslavement of indigenous peoples of Brazil; however, no authority was opposed to the enslavement of Africans. With the vast reduction in the population of the indigenous Indians of Brazil, the Portuguese increased the numbers of Africans being shipped to Brazil for enslavement. The number of black slaves in Brazil increased from 150,000 in 1680 to over a million by 1800. In all nearly five million blacks were shipped from Africa to Brazil to be enslaved. No other country enslaved as many Africans as Brazil. However, the bandeirantes continued to travel to further and further outreaches of Brazil to enslave natives. The Cost was an issue. A plantation owner paid ten times as much for an African slave as for a Brazilian Indian.[30]

Transportation to and from Africa was time consuming and expensive. The African slaves were not as vulnerable to diseases as the Brazilian Indians. Furthermore, a Brazilian Indian could escape into the jungles and have a chance of survival. African slaves, unfamiliar with the jungles of Brazil, would have no chance of survival after an escape.

Of all the Brazilian tribes the Guarani in southern Brazil were the most responsive to Christian missionaries. However, the Jesuits were helpless when a powerful group of armed bandeirantes launched a series of raids against their Jesuit missions in an area that is now part of Paraguay. They captured thousands of peaceful Christians (indigenous natives) and led them into slavery.

Portugal broke off its subservience to Spain with the Proclamation of the Duke of Braganca in 1640. He was proclaimed King Joao IV of Portugal in 1640. One who signed the act of Acclimation to validate King Joao IV was the bandeirante Antonio Raposo Tavares. The bandeirantes continued their expeditions to enslave indigenous peoples of South America without hindrance, except continuing protests by Jesuits. The bandeirantes developed vast estates where great harvests of sugar, wheat, corn, beans sand cotton enriched the owners. Other colonists profited from their great herds of cattle, pigs, sheep and horses on vast estates. In 1639 Spanish Jesuits travelled to Europe to protest against the bandeirantes and obtained a Bull from Pope Urban VIII. The Pope reiterated a statement that any form of enslavement of Indians was prohibited and all Indian slaves were to be freed.

The Jesuits were successful in obtaining a strong statement from the Pope that enslavement of the natives was prohibited. Unfortunately, the citizens of Rio de Janeiro evicted the Jesuits, effective 13 July 1640. The Jesuits were eventually permitted to return but only on condition that they not interfere with the enslavement of the natives.[31]

In a period of 130 years 2,000,000 Brazilian Indians were killed or carried away and enslaved.[32] Many Brazilian Indians fought against the bandeirantes, but were out gunned. Hemming summarizes the outcome as follows:

All such killings and robbings have been tolerated in a kingdom as Catholic as Portugal for years. (The killers) continue as before without any enquiry or trial or punishment, not even mildly shunned by public disfavor: nothing but total public immunity. Such was the climate of opinion in seventeenth-century Brazil. The bandeirantes today are honored

as pioneers, explorers and patriots; but their main purpose was the capture
of Indians, and they were merciless man hunters.[33]

Gold: Untold riches for Portuguese and untold sorrows for Native Brazilians

Gold was discovered along the Itaverava hills in 1694. Large numbers of Portuguese explorers searched for gold, and in 1701 the gold field of Ouro Preto was discovered, the greatest gold mine in South America. Forced labor of Indians continued although prohibited by Papal decree. Large numbers of Indians were captured and rushed off to the mine fields to work as porters, hunters and mine workers. As vast profits were realized, more gold-seekers crossed the Atlantic from Portugal. Many African slaves were also forced to labor in the gold mines. A percentage of the profits went back to Portugal, enough to make King Joao V one of the richest kings of Europe and graced with a magnificent palace. Great churches were built in Brazil and Portugal from profits from the gold.[34]

The Brazilian gold seekers were assisted inadvertently by natives in the jungles of Brazil. For example, women of the Goia tribe wore leaves of gold as ornaments. These women were captured and made to show the places where the gold was found. The Goia tribe then left out of fear of the colonists. Hemming states the tribe no longer exists and there is nor record or memory of them.[35]

Another tribe that was familiar with gold, but not its value to Europeans, was the Paiagua. Members of the tribe had gold and traded it to the Portuguese for a fraction of its value. In 1725 a group of about 200 Portuguese and their African slaves travelled in search of gold. They entered an area of the Paiagua and were attacked and annihilated. Only one Portuguese and one black escaped. In 1728 another expedition of Portuguese entered into an area controlled by the Paiagua tribe. The expedition was attacked and all of the Portuguese and slaves were either killed or taken as prisoners. On June 6, 1730, a flotilla of Portuguese travelled with black and Indian slaves and 900 kilos of gold. Hundreds of Paiagua tribesmen met them and fought them for over five hours. The Portuguese recorded the attack as "they covered us with such a dense cloud of arrows that it obscured the sun."[36] The Indians killed many of the Portuguese, took prisoners and threw the gold into the river. In September the victorious Indians took their prisoners to the Spanish town of Assuncion and offered to ransom them. The Indians readily accepted such items as a tin plate in exchange.[37]

In 1734 a punitive expedition of Portuguese forces led by Manoel Ruiz de Carvelho was sent to defeat the Indians. A long and tragic series of attacks continued and by 1780 the Paiagua were essentially annihilated. A remnant of the tribe currently survives on an island reservation at Asuncion.

The gold mines of Cuiaba continued on and needed labor. Slaving expeditions continued into remote areas of Brazil to transport workers to the gold mines. A missionary, Agostino Lourenco, in 1752 gave this report on the treatment of Brazilian natives who were captured and enslaved for gold mining.

Fifty or a hundred men would arm themselves and, leaving guards on the sandbank, would plunge into the sertao and attack the first Indian village they encountered. They would put the rest who did not escape into chains and shackles, destroy or burn the houses, ravage the fields, kill the animals and return triumphantly to their Long Island. There they would divide the vanquished among the victors and send them to Cuiaba and Mato Grosso under contract of sale. Many Indians perished here like beasts, felled by an axe or as targets for arrows or guns, and a great multitude from ill-treatment and illnesses The women paid with their lives and honour in the same way. [38]

The Treaty of Madrid

Before his death in 1750, King Joao V of Portugal created and signed an agreement with King Ferdinand VI of Spain to define the boundaries of their South American empires. For Portugal, the boundary of concern was Brazil. This treaty elaborated, extended and clarified the Treaty of Tordesillas of 1494. (That treaty was created by Pope Alexander VI on June 7, 1494, in Tordesillas, Spain. The purpose was to divide colonizing rights for all newly discovered lands between Spain and Portugal to the exclusion of other European nations.) The Spanish government had achieved vast wealth from their colonies of New Spain (Mexico) and Peru. The Portuguese had also achieved vast wealth from their colony of Brazil. Of interest is that the extended exploration by bandeirantes into far reaches up the Amazon River and into the vast jungles of Brazil in search of slaves assisted King Joao's ability to claim those vast areas of South America for Brazil. It is ironic that the activities of slave hunters contributed to establishing the framework for the Treaty of Madrid, which became official January 13, 1750.

One consequence was that Guarani Indians of the seven Spanish Jesuit missions east of the Uruguay River were ceded to Portugal by this treaty. The Uruguay River became part of the boundary between Spanish and Portuguese possessions. The implication for the treaty writers was simple. The Spanish Jesuit missions and their Indians had to move across the river to the area now defined as Spanish territory and leave behind all their houses, churches and their large and productive plantations. The Guarani Indians were given no choice; they were to complete their move by August 1754. Some Guarani Indian leaders and Jesuit priests met with boundary officials and pleaded with them to let them remain in their lands: According to Hemming: *For all the lands that they had boldly come to demarcate were neither the dominions of Portugal nor the conquest of Castile. For it was the Indians who had preserved themselves, not for years but for centuries in the peaceful possession of those vast lands. Although they might consider them barbarians in their lack of civilized manners, they should not judge them to be novices in their exercise of arms.*[39]

The Guarani Indians refused to move across the river. On February 6, 1756, a joint Spanish and Portuguese armed force met and attacked a large force of Indians on the Campos dos Milhos. The Indians took some heavy losses and fled. On February 10th an armed force of about 1800 Guarani was confronted again with a joint Spanish and Portuguese army. In a brief battle at an area called Caibate over 1400 Guarani were killed and 127 were captured. The Spanish and Portuguese lost only three dead and 26 wounded. More battles continued through March and April. By June 8, 1756, all seven missions had surrendered.[40]

Expulsion of the Jesuits

Both Spanish and Portuguese authorities blamed the Jesuits for the intransigence of the Guarani Indians who lived on the seven Jesuit missions. In effect, the Jesuits were blamed for the Guarani war. For a very long time colonists in Brazil were angry with the Jesuits. Much of the anger was the protracted opposition of the Jesuits to enslaving Brazilian Indians. Anger increased when officers involved in the Guarani war reported very prejudicial comments about the Jesuits. Henning writes:

There was growing hostility to the secretive Society of Jesus. The officers of the army that conquered the Seven Peoples made envious reports of the efficiency and luxury of the missions. They contrasted the missionaries' palatial residence with the Indians' simple huts. They described 'all the mills, ovens, factories and everything that those extraordinary men used to have for their convenience and comfort, so that they lived as abundantly as lords.' The Indians' huts were small and uniform. 'Two families live in each house and make their fire in the middle of it. Because of this, these aee so blackened that they are worse than negroes' slave quarters. These people are thus placed in the greatest misery that one can imagine, sleeping in hammocks and skins.[41]

While describing the alleged poverty of the Guarani Indians on the Seven missions in contrast to the alleged wealth and luxury of the Jesuits, military officers offered no comment as to why the Guarani were so loyal to the Jesuits. Furthermore, neither the military officers nor the colonial governors had any idea as to why the Guarani, or any Indian, would view their land as sacred and resist to the point of death any pressure to be forced to permanently leave. The beautiful area the Guarani were forced to leave is near the site of Iguacu Falls. The National Park and the waterfalls, one of the seven natural wonders of the world were declared by UNESCO in 1986 to be a Natural Heritage of Humanity. My wife and I visited this beautiful area in 2005 before our Amazon River trip.

The strong opposition to the Jesuits continued and the King of Portugal persuaded Pope Clement XIV to issue a Bull, dated April

1, 1758, to order a full scale reform of the Jesuits. The restrictions were severe--the Fathers were forbidden to engage in commerce, hear confessions, or preach. In 1760 all Jesuits were declared expelled and forced to evacuate their colleges, mission villages and leave Brazil. In 1767 the Spanish King ordered the expulsion of the Society from all his dominions. Following the expulsion of the Society of Jesus from the dominions of both Spain and Portugal, Pope Clement XIV in 1773 declared the Society extinct.[42]

In 1768 a force of 100 troops came to the missions to enforce the expulsion of the Jesuits. The Jesuits submitted without resistance; with tears streaming down their faces they left their work of two centuries of devoted sacrifices and went down to the ship which carried them away from Brazil. The Missions became part of Paraguay and were turned over to Franciscans, who had not earned the love and respect of the Indians. Indians left by the thousands to return to the forests. By 1800 the cattle, sheep and horses had disappeared; the plantations were overgrown with weeds and brush; and the splendid churches were in ruin.[43] In Paraguay Guarani tribes still exist but in vastly fewer numbers than before the time of contact.

This chapter was not intended to be a complete history of Brazil, but a brief history of the introduction of Christianity to the indigenous peoples of Brazil. By 1760 the Indians of Brazil had been introduced to Christianity and other aspects of European culture over a period of two and one-half centuries. For the Indians of Brazil it was catastrophic. My wife and I returned to Brazil in 2010 to serve on a Volunteers in Mission work project in Manaus, Brazil

Volunteers in Mission (VIM) Manaus, Brazil, June 5-17, 2010

Volunteers in Mission (VIM) is a program organized by the United Methodist Church. The purpose is to give church members a chance to travel to other countries (or states in the US) where the church is involved in relief work. Volunteers who participate in these programs pay their own way and contribute money for the relief work. Volunteers sign an agreement, "I will not proselytize." On the trips that we have participated in there is opportunity to visit historic and cultural sites, including vibrant and colorful markets, and on the visit to Brazil, a soccer game. Two issues of continuing concern in Brazil are poverty and crime.

Our group was led by Rev. Dr. Lowell Greathouse, a Methodist minister from Portland, Oregon, who now serves as Assistant to the Bishop; and by his brother, Gordon Greathouse, who lives in Belo Horizonte, Brazil. Gordon works with the Shade and Fresh Water program of the Methodist Conference of Brazil and is an executive with UMC in Brazil. The Shade and Fresh Water program is dedicated to support the vast numbers of families who have moved from rural areas of Brazil to the cities, leaving behind the support of extended families. Many face serious and prolonged poverty. Gordon is concerned about helping them understand what Christianity means in terms of support for one another.

Our group of 21 arrived in Manaus, Brazil. We were divided into two work projects. Marge and I and nine others worked on a church construction project; the other group re-painted the interior of another small Methodist church. Both work projects were based on recommendations by local Brazilians who have a connection with the United Methodist Church. The construction project was an on-going effort to expand an existing very small concrete room whose space was so limited that only 15 people could attend a church service. The new church will seat about 140 people. Previous VIM groups, with substantial help from local people in the area, had built a large aluminum roof and concrete slab for the floor.

Brazilian clergy who worked with us included the following: Deoniso Agnelo dos Satos, a District Superintendent; Lunalva Lucia Riberio, the woman minister who will be pastor of the "construction church"; Runilda, the woman pastor who was the original pastor of the construction church; and Aguusto, a pastor fluent in English who is pastor the other church where other members of our VIM were working, along with Brazilian volunteers, in repainting the church.

Finally, our VIM effort was helped substantially by the knowledge and assistance of Andressa Relica Ramos, a lawyer working on human rights issues, especially concerning poverty. She was available every day and her valued assistance to us was as an unpaid volunteer.

Church Construction Project

When we arrived on the scene of the church construction project, there were no walls at all, just a large concrete slab for a floor about 40' by 70' and an aluminum roof. First we needed to clear the grounds of rocks and old bricks. Following that, each day was the same as the next. As a truck came in with a large load of bricks, we unloaded and stacked them. One group mixed sand, mortar and water to make cement. Others carried bricks to those of us who were brick layers. As the walls increased in height, two of us were assigned to building strong support posts to reach from the concrete floor to the roof. This was accomplished by stringing 10'steel rods together with wire and then building wooden forms around them. The forms were then filled with concrete.

About ten local Brazilians worked with us throughout the effort. Some brought along their children. One delightful girl, about three years old, loved to carry one brick at a time to help. Her brother, age four, carried two bricks at a time. The young mother was very gracious and assisted in many ways. One Brazilian teenage boy, named Igor, had a broken arm in a cast and helped, as well as he could, by carrying bricks and mixing mortar with his good arm and hand.

About noon each day a few church women came with food and we took a 30-minute break to eat. Some who brought food stayed afterwards and helped out. Water was brought in 5-gallon jugs. None of the Brazilian volunteers spoke English, and my wife and I and others of our VIM group did not speak Portuguese. However, there was a sense of comradeship, of shared interest and purpose. Gordon Greathouse, who is fluent in Portuguese and English, provided overall instruction and reflections to all of us, alternating between the two work sites. We ended work about 5 PM each day and returned to our 'hotel' to shower, eat dinner, and have a devotion period and discussion. There were brief downpours most days and the temperature during the day was in the low 90s with humidity about the same. It is no wonder that Brazilian natives, like the proverbial king, wore no clothes.

On the second day at the work site, Runilda (former pastor of the tiny church) invited Marge to join her on a tour to visit some of the families of the church congregation. Runilda and Marge communicated in Spanish. They walked about six blocks and stopped at the homes of church members. At one stop an older woman and a younger one offered Marge a chair and turned on an electric fan to cool the room as they talked. At another home, the mother was away working. Two middle-age men in the room neither spoke nor acknowledged their presence. Also present was a teenage girl, and a 4-year-old girl. Runilda said the mom and dad are alcoholic, and other relatives who live with them are drug addicts. The house was crudely built but there was a TV. Back at the work site Marge chatted with Gordon about her visit to homes of church members.

After five work days, we stopped to participate in other events during our two-week VIM project.

Conversations with Andressa Relica Ramos

Andressa spoke to our group at some of our evening meetings and provided historical background of Brazil's independence from Portugal. In 1807 Napoleon's French troops invaded Portugal. One year later King Joao V and his court escaped from Portugal and moved to Brazil. After the defeat of Napoleon the Portuguese court returned to Portugal. The son of the king remained in Brazil and declared independence in 1822, and this was done peacefully. In contrast, all the countries that were colonies of Spain achieved independence after painful and tragic periods of war.

Brazil is the fifth largest nation in the world in terms of land mass. With a population of 177 million, Brazil is the largest Catholic nation in the world. John Allen, author of a chapter entitled "The Catholic Church will Grow Worldwide by Becoming Less Centered in Europe" and published in *The Catholic Church: Opposing Viewpoints*, agrees that Brazil has the largest Catholic population in the world with 149 million Catholics. Mexico is second with 92 million and the United States third with 67 million Catholics. Andressa stated that Catholicism in Brazil has become syncretic, with strong influence from African traditions including Macumba, Candomble and Umbanda. Allen agrees that Catholicism in Brazil has become syncretic with substantial influence from African traditions. Furthermore, Allen states that local control has spurred growth in all the Christian traditions in Brazil. He states that Protestant groups together represent 15% of the Brazil population and that the Pentecostal church is growing rapidly. The churches in Brazil grow by encouraging 'quickest possible transition to local or indigenous leadership."[44] He asserts that the continuing growth of Christian churches in Africa, South America and Asia is unrelated to current Western missionary efforts.

Although poverty is rampant, Brazil is not a poor country. Andressa explained the contradiction, stating that Brazil has the tenth largest economy in the world. However, she stated, "One percent of the people in Brazil own 90 percent of the wealth." She pointed out that Brazil ranks eighth in the world for most income inequality; the US ranks 33rd. While there is very serious poverty in Brazil, the situation has improved in recent years. She credited the effective policies and leadership of Brazil's President, Luia Inacio Lula de Silva. At least 25 million Brazilians have moved up from what she called "staggering poverty" to where they can now aspire to the working class. Edward Glaeser, in an article published in *Forbes Magazine*, states that Rio De Janeiro has a poverty rate—defined as living on less than a dollar a day—of around 9%, while the northeast section of Brazil, including Manaus, has a poverty rate of 55%.[45]

From my own observation, the extensive poverty I saw in Brazil is more severe than in Cuba, where people indeed have a very low income, but all have housing, food, health care and effective education programs. Andressa told us that violent crime, drug and gang wars, and prostitution are serious problems in Brazil. Sao Paolo, which had a population of 2000 in the year 1600, now is the world's third largest city, with a population of 20.3 million. The homicide rate per year is very high with 3400 murders in 2009 in Sao Paolo, compared with 471 for New York City with a population of 19.4 million.[46] As stated earlier in this chapter, Sao Paolo was the center of the slave trade of both indigenous Brazilians and Blacks from Africa. The black population of Brazil is second only to that of Nigeria. When slavery was abolished in Brazil in 1888, Brazil's population was more than 50% of African heritage. The government of Brazil paid for 4 million Europeans to immigrate to Brazil, which boosted the white population to be slightly higher than African American.[47]

Touring the Opera House and Watching a Soccer Game

Tuesday, June 15, 2010, was essentially a national holiday in Brazil. Brazil's soccer team was scheduled to play the North Korean soccer team at the opening of the World Cup Soccer event in South Africa. Gordon Greathouse told us that it was important to witness the game in order to appreciate the importance of soccer to all Brazilians. Every community has an arena with very large television screens, some about 90 feet wide and 20 feet wide. The screen can be seen from hundreds of yards away. With powerful loud speakers, the announcers of the game can be heard a mile away. By 2:30 that afternoon we were in a large arena in Manaus with a huge screen. My wife, who had never before seen a soccer game, took careful notes:

This is what I learned. The game has two halves of 45 minutes each. There are no time outs. At the beginning the opposing team players were polite. In the first half North Korea did a great job of defense; Brazil controlled the ball most of the time. At the end of the first half the score was 0-0. In the second half Brazil finally scored two points and put in some of its reserve players. North Korea scored one point. Thousands groaned when Brazil missed a goal and cheered and hooted loudly when Brazil scored. I quietly cheered for the underdog, North Korea, and even clapped quietly when they finally scored. There was dead silence when North Korea scored its one goal, except for my quiet little clap. Then the game was over.

We heard many times that Brazil will host the 2016 Olympics in Rio. Brazilians are wild about sports. The estimated cost of upgrading its electrical grid for the 2016 Olympics is $260 billion.[48]

On another day our VIM group visited the large plaza in the center of Manaus with its beautiful Catholic cathedral and famous Opera House. Both face a monument in the plaza, honoring Cabral, who "discovered" Brazil. The Opera House was built between 1881 and 1896. The construction started with black slave labor. When slavery ended in 1888, there was a labor shortage which slowed the final completion of the structure. The cost of this beautiful building had to be enormously expensive. The Opera House was designed by expert European architects, and most of the material was shipped from various countries in Europe across the Atlantic and then 1000 miles up the Amazon River. We admired its outstanding architecture, artistry and workmanship.

Our tour guide explained that sap from the rubber tree, Hevea brasiliensis, was known by Indians prior to the voyage of Christopher Columbus. Indians used sap from the rubber tree to make balls. Early explorers in Brazil used the sap to make waterproof boots and clothing. In 1839 Charles Goodyear found a way to harden rubber to make it suitable for tires, using a process called vulcanization. This was first used for bicycle tires. When automobiles were developed the demand for rubber soared. Manaus became the world center for rubber harvest and for shipping the product to Europe, Asia, and North America. Profits soared. By 1912, 190,000 men were employed in the rubber business, most gathering sap from trees. Our guide said that some English men, without permission from Brazil, took seeds from the rubber tree and successfully transported them to Malaysia and then to other British colonies, including India. By 1926 the export of rubber from Brazil ceased, and the country suffered a catastrophic depression. The continuing and huge world demand for rubber was now supplied by British colonies in Asia. Following. the economic disaster when the demand for Brazilian rubber stopped, the opera house was boarded up. It was not re-opened until the late 1970's.

Excursion by Medical Boat

One Saturday we boarded a medical missionary boat and sailed down the Rio Negro River and up the Amazon for about an hour and a half to Sao Sebastian, a small village on one of the numerous islands in the Amazon River. The medical boat, ten years old, was donated by the head of World Vision, when World Vision obtained a larger replacement medical-hospital ship. On board we inspected the fully equipped dental office, medical exam office and waiting room. The boat also has a pharmacy. This boat travels from Manaus to rural outlying communities, where the staff has established relationships. The physicians, dentists, and other staff volunteer their time and expertise. The cost of operating this boat in terms of fuel, maintenance, and other overhead expenses averages about $10,000 per week while in use.

At Sao Sebastian, our group interacted with children and their families with extended play activities for children, including games, singing, and craft activities. Lowell Greathouse read from a remarkable children's book, *God Has a Dream*, written by Desmond Tutu. The parents and children enjoyed the activities, and this event showed us the rapport that the program has established with families in rural, outlying communities.

Church Services

During our stay in Manaus, we attended three Protestant church services. I will describe one service, which is representative of the others that we attended. About one half hour before the designated time for the service, five young musicians were on stage near the pulpit and playing robustly---their percussion instruments and guitars all amplified. The words for the songs were displayed on a large screen. About 150 people entered and joined in with active, loud, joyful singing for about 40 minutes. This was followed by scripture reading. A soloist then stood in front of the pulpit and began to sing. Suddenly, a woman near the back of the church stood up and joined the singing. Improvisation was clearly part of the service. Church members felt free to clap their hands or comment to signal their reaction to the service. Members also stood up and used cameras with flash to photograph events whenever they wished. Our group of 21 was introduced to the congregation, and each of us made a brief comment, which was translated into Portuguese. The sermon focused on both the Good Samaritan parable and the story of the woman, who after hearing Jesus, wanted to drink from a well from which she would not thirst again. The minister said that Jesus had the presence that created the feeling among those who heard him that they were close to God. That is the meaning of "Son of God," said the preacher. The service lasted just short of three hours

I commented to Gordon and Lowell Greathouse after the service that the center of Christianity seems to be no longer in North America or Europe. In South America the churches are focused on Liberation Theology and are faith-based rather than creed-based. I was also impressed that the Methodist church services we attended were also clearly influenced by African spirituality. Church attendance is growing in Brazil, while declining precipitously in Europe and North America.

Final "Ceremony" at the Church Construction Site

On our last day we returned to the construction site for a small 'ceremony," including lunch and a discussion of future plans for the church. The church would have a small apartment for the minister, who would receive a monthly salary of $300 (US equivalent). Numbers of local people gathered as well and were given a chance to speak Gordon translated for us. I was especially touched by a middle-aged woman who said she welcomed the church in the area because of its poverty and high crime rate. She hoped that the church would provide a sense of hope to the neighborhood. She was the one who had initially approached the District Superintendent about her anxiety for her neighborhood. This led to the Superintendent contacting Gordon Greathouse to begin the process of involving VIM.

End notes for Chapter 6. Brazil

1. Hemming, John. (1987). *Amazon Frontier: The Defeat of the Brazilian Indians*. Harvard University Press: Cambridge, Massachusetts. p. 32.
2. Mann, Charles C. (2005). *1491: New Revelations of the Americas Before Columbus*. Alfred A. Knopf: New York. p. 290.
3. Hemming. (1987). *Amazon Frontier*. Op. cit., pps. 309-311.
4. Ibid. p. 312.
5. From Ed Hudson's lecture on board the *Explorer*.
6. Hemming, John. (1978). *Red Gold: The Conquest of the Brazilian Indians, 1500-1760*. p. 69.
7. Ibid., p. 98.
8. Ibid., p. 99.
9. Ibid., p. 106.
10. Ibid., p. 104.
11. Ibid., p. 105.
12. Ibid., p. 116.
13. Ibid., p. 140.
14. Ibid., p. 141.
15. Ibid., p. 146.
16. Ibid., p. 143.
17. Ibid., p. 134. Also, see *CATHOLIC ENCYCLOPEDIA: Guarani Indians*, Editor Kevin Knight. http://www.newadvent.org/cathen/07045a.htm
18. Hemming. (1978). *Red Gold*. Op. cit., p. 145.
19. Ibid., p. 151.
20. Ibid., p. 155.
21. Ibid., p. 156.
22. Ibid., p. 157.
23. Ibid., p. 156.
24. Ibid., p. 157.
25. Hemming. (1987). *Amazon Frontier*. Op. cit., p. 5.
26. Hemming. (1978). *Red Gold*. Op. cit., p. 253.
27. *CATHOLIC ENCYCLOPEDIA: Guarani Indians*. Op. cit.
28. Hemming. (1978). *Red Gold*. Op. cit., p. 246.
29. Ibid., p. 249.
30. Ibid. p. 149

31. Ibid., p. 279.
32. *CATHOLIC ENCYCLOPEDIA: Guarani Indians.* Op. cit.
33. Hemming. (1978). *Red Gold.* Op. cit., 380.
34. Ibid. p., 381.
35. Ibid., p. 384.
36. Ibid., p. 397.
37. Ibid., p. 398.
38. Ibid., p. 404.
39. Ibid., p. 470.
40. Ibid., p. 473.
41. Ibid., p. 474.
42. Ibid., p. 480.
43. CATHOLIC ENCYCLOPEDIA: *Guarani Indians.* Op. cit.
44. John L. Allen Jr. "The Catholic Church Will Grow Worldwide by Becoming Less Centered in Europe." pps. 199-208. In, *The Catholic Church: Opposing Viewpoints.* Book editor, Noah Berlatsky. Greenhaven Press. New Haven, Conn. (2011)
45. Edward Glaeser. "NEW LANDS OF OPPORTUNITY: If you are alive today, there is a one-in-eight chance that you are living in a slum in the developing world, desperately—often successfully—trying to improve your lot." Forbes, 5/9/2011, Vol. 187 Issue 8, p102-112.
46. Daniel Fisher, Naazneen Karmali and Gady Epstein. "URBAN OUTFITTER: Siemens Chief Peter Loscher is betting n Explosive growth among the world's megacities. Even shantytowns need electricity and clean water." Forbes, 5/9/2011, Vol. 187 Issue 8, p80-98.
47. Hemming. (1987). *Amazon Frontier.* Op. cit., p. 471. An account of Brazil paying substantial funds to pay for white Europeans to immigrate to Brazil is developed more fully in a documentary aired on Public Broadcasting. The title of the program is *Black in Latin America: Brazil: A Racial Paradise?* The program was produced, directed and narrated by Professor Henry Louis Gates Jr. Aired, Tuesday, May 3, 2011.
48. Daniel Fisher, Naazneen Karmali and Gady Epstein, "URBAN OUTFITTER: Forbes. Op.cit. p.94.

CHAPTER 7

Spanish Conquistadors and Christians Take Down the Incas of Peru

April 11, 2005, we were anchored on the Amazon River just off Iquitos, Peru. We were up early in the morning, finished packing our bags, ate breakfast, thanked the staff of the *Explorer* and were on the deck ready for departure by 7:00 am. A river boat pulled along side the ship, unloaded luggage, and began taking passengers the short distance to the dock at Iquitos, Peru, then made return trips until all were taken to the dock at Iquitos. This was done in a very efficient manner. I was impressed with the number of large ocean going ships at Iquitos, having arrived from ports in Asia, the Americas and Europe. No other river in the world carries ocean going ships this far, about 2200 miles upriver, from its salt water port at the Atlantic Ocean.

A bus took us for a tour of Iquitos on the way to the airport. There were many 3-wheel "taxis," heavy street traffic with lots of noise and air pollution. At the airport we checked in and were soon on our way to Lima. After arriving in Lima we took a three-hour bus tour of downtown Lima (population 9 million; tallest building 35 stories, a lovely old section with colonial buildings and a plaza). Lima, being on the west coast of Peru, is dry with annual precipitation of less than two inches (desert conditions). However, Lima benefits from an outstanding irrigation system, carrying abundant water from melting snow from the Andes, and the city has beautiful gardens, shrubs and well kept lawns. We appreciated a tour of the Cathedral, Iglesia de Santo Domingo. This cathedral, finished in 1755, replaced the previous church destroyed in an earthquake in 1746. The body of the ruthless Francisco Pizarro rests in a chapel to the right of the main entrance. We also visited the Monasterio de San Francisco, one of the oldest continuously used churches in Lima. It survived the 1746 earthquake. Inside is a catacomb that contains the remains (bones) of tens of thousands of corpses. We heard from our guide that the nobility and the rich were buried in the floors of the churches or in side chapels, while the peasants were buried in large pits full of lye within the catacombs.

The next morning all 18 passengers from the *Explorer* who planned to continue on a second Elderhostel to Cusco and Machu Picchu got up very early, ate breakfast and were taken to the airport by 4:30 for the 6:00 AM flight to Cusco. The Lima airport is modern, attractive and run very efficiently.

Cusco

Arriving in Cusco, we checked in at the Novotel Hotel, built on the remains of a palace from the Inca era. Doris, our bird expert on the *Explorer,* introduced us to Peter Frost, who was to be our guide in Cusco. Frost led us on a walking tour of Cusco and explained the complex and tragic history of the conquest. The Incas had created an empire comparable in size to the Roman Empire. It stretched from the modern Ecuador-Colombia frontier to the Rio Maule in southern Chile. In the west it was bounded by the Pacific Ocean, and to the east by the Amazon forests. As the Inca spread their boundaries they incorporated the accumulated culture and knowledge of earlier civilizations. They created a powerful state and ruled millions of people with a strong central state, while being tolerant of variations of sacred beliefs and practices.

Frost reviewed the history of the conquest and explained that Pizarro had a triumphant entry to Cusco on November 8, 1533. The Spanish were hugely impressed by the great structures of Cusco. One who was present wrote a message to be delivered to the king of Spain: "We can assure your Majesty that it is so beautiful and has such fine buildings that it would be remarkable even in Spain." Frost explained that Cusco was no ordinary city. It was an elite settlement with special ceremonial and administrative functions. Cusco was a holy city, with the greatest temple of the Inca Empire located within it. UNESCO has declared Cusco a World Cultural Heritage site.

Nevertheless, for two years the Spanish plundered the wealth of Cusco and abused the natives, but left the buildings intact. Then, a puppet Inca of Pizarro, Manco II, escaped and returned on May 6, 1536, with between 100,000 and 200,000 Indians and began a six-month siege of Cusco.[1] (Note: Manco II had been installed by Pizarro, because he was of a tribe who had initially fought against Atahualpa, and he agreed to support the Spanish in their conquest. In that sense he was a *puppet* Inca leader.) In the intense fighting, everything that could burn in Cusco was destroyed, and the Inca warriors were defeated suffering overwhelming losses. Frost told us that the Spanish then dismantled the fine buildings in Cusco to build Spanish style colonial buildings. Captive Inca workers, under duress, provided the labor to construct the colonial buildings. Had the Spanish conquered a primitive society and introduced the marvels of an advanced civilization, they could be proud. But plundering an advanced civilization was hard to explain to the people back home. Frost states:

Moreover, evidence that the Inca civilization was highly advanced provoked discomfort among the Spaniards; it complicated the task of justifying the destruction. And so the dismantling of Inca Cusco began soon after Manco's rebellion. Inca cut stones were re-used higgledy-piggledy in new construction, while the buildings of Sacsaywaman served as a public stone quarry.[2]

After the defeat of the Inca Manco, and his large force of Inca warriors, Cusco became the focus of a civil war among the Spanish. Some of Pizarro's men formed a faction against Pizarro to get a larger chunk of the spoils of Cusco. They fought among themselves. During the fighting between one Spanish force against another, survivors of the Inca Manco II rebellion took advantage and made another bold attempt to drive away the Spanish. The Inca warriors again lost.

In 1650 a violent earthquake wrecked the newly built Spanish colonial buildings in Cusco. The Inca walls and foundations stood firm; however, the newly constructed colonial buildings suffered severe damage.[3] In 1780 another Inca rebellion, led by Tupac Amaru II, attempted to drive away the Spanish. It failed and Tupac Amaru II was executed in the main square of Cusco, in the tradition of executions established by Torquemeda. Executions performed during the long periods of the Spanish Inquisition were brutal, and public, and were accompanied with great ceremony.[4]

During the times when we were not in lectures or on walking tours, Marge and I enjoyed walking about in Cusco, particularly the main square. The northeast side of the square is dominated by the Cathedral built over a former Inca palace. Frost had told us that the construction of the cathedral was started in 1550 and completed about one hundred years later. Most of the labor was by Inca craftsmen. Inca artists were schooled by Spanish priests and Spanish artists, and the 400 or so colonial and religious paintings in the cathedral were done by trained and supervised Inca artists. Frost pointed out some paintings in which Inca spiritual symbols and imagery were blended into Christian religious paintings. These are examples of syncretism.

The Qoricancha

While Pizarro held the Inca king Atahualpa prisoner in Cajamarca, awaiting his execution, Pizarro sent three of his Spanish soldiers to Cusco to locate the Temple of Qoricancha and loot the gold. The three Spaniards were unable to persuade any Inca natives to help plunder their sacred temple. The temple was vast and it housed 4000 priests and attendants.[5] Stretching hundreds of meters down to the confluence of the Tullumayo and Saphi rivers, the temple also served as the Incas' principal astronomical observatory. The royal astronomers were known as *Tarpuntaes*. They studied celestial bodies, noted the advance and retreat of the sun to measure the solstice and equinox dates, and predicted eclipses. Their work was vital to schedule sacred rituals and to guide the planting of crops. The three Spaniards made no notes or drawings of the Qoricancha. They plundered it. They took 700 gold sheets, each weighing 41/2 lbs. A gold altar weighed 190 lbs, and anther piece contained 120 lbs. of gold.[6] After additional members of Pizarro's party arrived in Cusco, the looting continued at an expanded rate. Then the Spaniards destroyed the Qoricancha and built with Inca labor, under duress, the monastery of Santo Domingo, now controlled by the Dominicans. We saw a room that the Dominicans designated as the *Sacrifice Room*, which may lead some visitors to think was an Inca sacrificial altar. Frost referred to the act as one done by shameless individuals. The Inca did not sacrifice humans. In their rituals they did sacrifice animals. The Spanish missionaries who claimed the Incas sacrificed humans distorted their religious beliefs perhaps in an effort to justify the missionary effort to suppress, or wipe out, the Inca spiritual and religious traditions.[7]

The Qoricancha may have been the most important Indigenous temple in all the Americas. Its destruction was a violent act, a suppression of a people's heritage. Although on a different scale, I was reminded of the Pueblo kivas in our own Southwest, USA. In the 16th century the Hopi Indians were forced to destroy their sacred kiva and were then forced to build a Catholic church over their sacred site. (chap. 3) Furthermore, I was mindful of the Mayan temple in Guatemala that was destroyed in the sixteenth century and replaced by a Catholic monastery, built with captive Mayan labor. (chap. 4)

Sacsaywaman

The vast ruin of Sacsaywaman overlooks the city of Cusco. The limestone blocks along the outer walls are the grandest of any Inca site. The largest stone in the outer wall of Sacsaywaman stands 8.5 meters high and weighs 361 tons. It is perfectly fitted to the stones next to it.[8] Frost states, "This is one of the most astounding megalithic structures of the ancient world."[9] Sacsaywaman was plundered by the Spanish for several hundred years as a stone quarry. No buildings remain. And yet, every visitor to Cusco should see it, to view the vast size and careful cuts of the remaining stones. Sacsaywaman was the site of the rebellion of Manco and his troops in 1536.

Onward to Machu Picchu

Before leaving Cusco I asked our guide, Frost, if he could recommend some readings to delve further into the history of the Spanish explorers and the missionaries who "discovered" and conquered Peru. He recommended the book *The Conquest of the Incas* by John Hemming because it provides a major contribution to modern knowledge and theories about the Incas and the conquest.

We left Cusco, the capital of the Inca Empire, around 8:00 am and prepared ourselves for a day long bus tour in areas surrounding Cusco on our way to Machu Picchu. Our first stop was at an agricultural college about 20 miles outside of Cusco. A woman faculty member gave us a tour of the experimental gardens and crops and explained ongoing research projects on the many varieties of potatoes, corn and other crops. She explained that ancient Inca tribes were in the area at least 20,000 years ago and successfully developed agricultural practices to accommodate the four vastly different ecological areas of Peru including the Pacific coast, the highlands, the mountain areas, and the Amazon jungle. In each of the four areas the Inca developed specialized techniques to survive and flourish. The coastal area of Peru, up to the Pacific Ocean, is a very dry desert; yet the Inca developed irrigation systems to bring water to that desert region. The Inca also developed effective systems to terrace and irrigate the steep mountainous areas of Peru.

The Inca engineered new varieties of crops long before such innovations were practiced in Europe. For example, they developed over three thousand varieties of corn; and they developed the potato from a native plant that prior to its genetic modification was poisonous. As we walked along the experimental gardens our guide pointed out finer points of Inca agricultural developments and answered the many questions from our group. She commented on the ways the Inca developed effective means of preserving and storing food to prevent famine during periods of drought.

Our next stop was at a roadside exhibit of llamas and alpacas. We had a chance to observe them and feed them grass, which they eagerly snatched up. The roadside exhibit gave us a chance to ask questions about the use of these animals. We saw many in Peru. In a small gift shop there was a variety of locally made products including sweaters, hats and clothing made from alpaca hair. We purchased a lovely hand-woven alpaca table runner. The design in the weaving represents corn, eyes, flowers, rivers and mountains. Our next stop was at a small town which featured a large outdoor market like that of Chichicastenango in Guatemala. Indigenous farmers and ranchers come from afar to sell locally made items and foods. Popular items for purchase among our group were alpaca sweaters, duffel bags, jewelry and pottery. Tourists were free to photograph scenes of the market, including the attractive clothing worn by the indigenous women and children who were selling items and manning the booths.

Machu Picchu

Shortly after departing from the outdoor market we arrived at our hotel, the Machu Picchu Pueblo Hotel—Inkaterra, a former nun's convent. The hotel is run ecologically and has gardens with hummingbirds, and an array of flowers and tropical plants. After lunch we had a two hour lecture on the Incas given by Ruben Orellana—an expert on the Inca civilization and the conquest. He spoke of many negative outcomes resulting from the Spanish conquest of Peru and the Inca civilization. The Spanish conquest was brutal and the Christian missionaries suppressed Inca religion. Spain became (for a while) the richest country in the world, and Catholicism became (and remains) the dominant religion in South America. However, many indigenous peoples became alienated and impoverished.

From our hotel we took a short 20 minute bus ride uphill to Machu Picchu. Elizabeth, our guide, provided substantial information about the function of the various structures and levels of quality of construction. The most beautifully cut rocks were designated for structures of worship and royalty. Rubble and rough cut rocks were used to construct terraces and houses for servants and farmers. A middle group of people, including merchants, also had structures of cut rock, but not at the exquisite level used for the magnificent Sun Temple.

After the lecture tour we climbed to the highest point for an overview of the entire site of Machu Picchu (Old Mountain), with Wayna Picchu (New Mountain) in the background. We also viewed the beautiful Urubamba River, which is a tributary of the Amazon. The entire site is beautiful and reminded me of a theme evident across religious indigenous sites from Alaska to Tierra del Fuego. When establishing a place to worship God or the gods, the indigenous peoples chose a site in nature that is in its own right a place of great beauty. Then, as they built a place of worship, they built it with the greatest of care, with the best materials, and with the best architecture and designs that were available. They chose the priests who were entrusted to lead worship and to perpetuate the religion with great care. If music were part of the traditional form of worship, then music as well would be at the level of best practice available within their society. Peter Frost in writing about Machu Picchu states, "Even today, the most jaded visitor cannot fail to sense the extraordinary beauty and power of the setting."[10]

Christianity, Inquisition Style, Takes down the Inca of Peru

Hemming writes that Francisco Pizarro, familiar with the fabulous riches plundered by Hernan Cortes from the Aztec empire in Mexico, set his dreams on further conquest in Peru. He had learned from Cortes how to subdue an empire. First, a conquistador must have superior weapons. Pizarro had an ample supply of horses, which the Indians had never seen before the arrival of the Spanish. The mighty horses carrying armed Spanish warriors were much feared. His soldiers had the world's best swords from Toledo (Spain) and they wore state of the art armor. Second, Pizarro understood the importance of capturing the head of the State. Third, he learned from Cortes the importance of identifying dissension among tribes and clans and using discontented ones to help fight against the strongest. Finally, he employed the artful use of deception, by announcing he came in peace.[11]

On November 16, 1532, Atahualpa, with a large army but with primitive weapons, approached a large square in the town of Cajamarca. He had come to meet a group of men never before seen in his empire.

Through an interpreter who had taken the side of Pizarro, Atahualpa was assured that no harm would befall him or members of his army.

The Inca king was transported on a litter carried by about eighty men who wore head garments made of gold and silver. Friar Vicente de Valverde, of the Dominican order, approached Atahualpa and delivered the Requirement, consistent with the policy established by the royal council in any conquest before a military attack. Friar Valverde, in his role as a priest, explained his function as one to proclaim the Christian religion, and he presented a Bible to Atahualpa. The Inca king examined it briefly and threw it down on the ground. Another author, Hubert Herring, states that the Inca king understood nothing of the "strange gibberish" given by the priest other than the demand for his submission.[12]

A Spanish warrior named Mena recorded that Valverde shouted: "Come out! Come out Christians! Come at these enemy dogs who reject the things of God. That chief has thrown my book of holy law to the ground!"[13]

With that as a signal Pizarro launched his force of 168 soldiers into the crowd of unarmed Indians. John Hemming devotes several pages to the massacre and concludes that perhaps six or seven thousand Indians were killed and that many more had their arms cut off or had other serious wounds. Hemming summarizes the outcome as follows:

The sheer rate of killing was appalling, even if one allows that many Indians died from trampling or suffocation, or that the estimates of dead were exaggerated. Each Spaniard massacred an average of fourteen or fifteen defenseless natives during those terrible two hours.[14]

The Famous Ransom

The captured Atahualpa noticed that the Spaniards were interested solely in precious metals. Atahualpa concluded he could buy his liberty. When asked how much he would give for his freedom, Atahualpa said he would give a room full of gold. The room measured 22 feet long by 17 feet wide and he would have it filled to a height of 8 feet. It took several months for Atahualpa's loyal subjects to gather gold jars, pots, tiles and other pieces to fill the room with gold objects. In addition, silver objects were also gathered and filled an area twice as large. While subjects were gathering the precious metals, Pizarro sent news to compatriots in Panama and asked for reinforcements to push deeper into Peru. Atahualpa was assured his life would be spared and he would soon be released to return to Quito, the land that his father had left him, provided that he committed no treason. Atahualpa met or exceeded every aspect of the ransom requirement. Much of the gold and silver and precious objects can be seen in Spain today, including some priceless objects in museums. Gold and silver from Peru is also evident in the construction and decoration of the magnificent Catholic Cathedrals and Monasteries of Spain.

The Public Execution of Atahualpa

On July 26, 1533, Atahualpa was brought out from prison and escorted to the middle of the square at Cajamarca. Trumpets blared and the square was surrounded by Spaniards and large numbers of shocked Inca natives as well as Atahualpa's associates. Atahualpa was tied to a stake, and was about to be burned to death. Pizarro's secretary, Pedro Sancho, wrote an account of the proceedings. Atahualpa was *brought out of his prison and led to the middle of the square, to the sound of trumpets intended to proclaim his treason and treachery, and was tied to a stake. The friar* (**Valverde**) *was, in the meantime, consoling and instructing him through an interpreter in the articles of our Christian faith. The Inca was moved by these arguments and requested baptism, which the reverend father immediately administered to him. His exhortations did (the Inca) much good. For although he had been sentenced to be burned alive, he was in fact garroted by a piece of rope that was tied around his neck.*[15]

With these last words, and with the Spaniards who surrounded him saying a credo for his soul, he was quickly strangled. May God in his holy glory preserve him, for he died repenting his sins, in the true faith of a Christian. After he had been strangled in this way and the sentence executed, some fire was thrown on to him to burn part of his clothing and flesh. He died late in the afternoon, and his body was left in the square that night for everyone to learn of his death. On the following day the Governor ordered all the Spaniards to attend his funeral. He was carried to the church with a cross and the rest of the religious ornaments, and was buried with as much pomp as if he had been the most important Spaniard in our camp. All the lords and chiefs in his service were very pleased with this: they appreciated the great honor that had been done to him. [16]

Hemming states that, "Far from appreciating the great honor of Christian burial, Atahualpa's immediate followers were stunned by his death." [17] Hemming supports his statement by referring to another Spaniard who wrote the following: *When he was taken out to be killed, all the native populace who were in the square, of which there were many, prostrated themselves on the ground, letting themselves fall to the earth like drunken men.* [18]

With the death of Atahulpa, the 600 year Inca Empire came to an end. [19]

Francisco Pizarro Selects then Directs Inca Puppets to "Rule" Peru.

Pizarro gathered Inca leaders from throughout Peru and instructed them about their duties to lead the native population in the new era. He informed them that he had been sent by Emperor Charles to bring them the true religion. All would be well if they would submit peacefully to the Emperor and his God. This declaration is known as the Requirement. His speech to the chiefs was recorded as follows,

The governor presented himself to the assembly dressed as finely as he was able in silk clothing, accompanied by the royal officials and some hidalgos from his army who attended in their best clothes to add to the solemnity of the ceremony. He read (the Requirement) *all this out to them and had it proclaimed word by word through an interpreter. He then asked them whether they had fully understood it and they answered that they had. The Governor then took the royal standard in his hands, raised it above him three times, and told them they must do the same. The caciques all dutifully raised the royal standard, to the sound of the trumpets. They then went to embrace the Governor who received them with great delight at their prompt submission. When it was all over the Inca and the chief held great festivities. There were daily celebrations and entertainment with games and parties which were generally held in the Governor's house.* [20]

Among the Inca leaders was Tupac Huallpa, whom Pizarro selected to be the new Inca ruler, but a ruler under absolute Spanish control. His appointment was consistent with the policy established by Cortes in conquering Mexico, a policy of forming allies among dissenting factions of the Indigenous tribes. Tupac Huallpa was from the Huascar faction, who had previously opposed the rule of Atahualpa. While the native leaders celebrated the apparent restoration of Inca rule, the Spanish made preparations for the conquest of central Peru.[21] Pizarro was sufficiently confident of success that he delayed his military attack and left proudly for Spain.

He arrived in Seville on January 9, 1534, with treasures that were astonishing in quantity, value and sophistication. Hemming states that "Post-Renaissance Europe was dazzled by the discovery and sudden conquest of an unimagined empire of such brilliance"[22] The treasures unloaded in Seville included, *thirty-eight vessels of gold and forty-eight of silver, among which was one eagle of silver whose body had a capacity of two cantaras (eight gallons) of water; two huge urns, one gold and one silver, each of which could hold a dismembered cow; two golden pots each of which could hold two fanegas of wheat; a golden idol the size of a four-year-old boy; and two small drums.*[23]

After his highly successful trip to Seville, Pizarro returned to Cajamarca to ready his men to conquer the Inca stronghold in Cusco. On August 11, 1534, Pizarro, and his two generals, Diego de Almagro and Hernando de Soto, and their men marched out of Cajamarca. They began a travel of 750 miles to reach Cusco. Pizarro and his troops were unaware that historical forces in Peru were acting strongly in their favor.[24] Two Inca tribal groups had fought against each other in a long and disastrous civil war, leaving the Inca forces drastically weakened and unable to mount a coordinated defense against the Spanish. This weakness was apparent when the Spanish troops were attacked by Quitan Incas, a force of about six hundred soldiers. This was the first major resistance by the Incas in 17 months since the Spanish occupation. In the ensuing battle the Inca forces were shattered and suffered large losses. Indians who tried to escape were pursued by

Spanish warriors on horseback and killed. The Spaniards took a good haul of gold and silver and women.[25] While the battle was proceeding, the young Inca Tupac Huallpa, who supported Pizarro and the Spanish forces, unexpectedly became ill and died. Pizarro had difficulty in selecting a candidate to replace the dead Tupac Huallpa.[26]

In the history of Peru before the Spanish conquest, Andean tribes worshipped many deities. There was no one dominant pagan religion. Instead, even in times of war the Incas showed tact in dealing with the deities of conquered tribes.[27] The ancient Inca policy of toleration of tribal religious beliefs ended abruptly with the Spanish conquest.

After the initial victory the Spanish marched from Jauja to Cuzco. They were greatly assisted by traveling on roads and bridges that surpassed any comparable roads in Europe. The area is made up of high mountains, steep canyons with rivers below. The rivers are as much as 6,000 feet below the mountain tops. The Inca highway through the area is remarkable with stone steps, which eased travel on very steep mountainous terrain. Well constructed bridges spanned the rivers at critical points. A most challenging task for the Spanish forces was to cross the gorge with their horses on a long suspension bridge along the canyon of the Apurimac River. The area was the subject of Thornton Wilder's novel, *The Bridge of San Luis Rey*.[28] Horses, then and now, are not fond of suspension bridges that sway in the wind.

The terrain was extremely difficult for the Spaniards who also faced extreme conditions of cold and heat. After crossing the Apurimac River, the Spanish were attacked by Inca troops who managed to kill six Spaniards, and wounded eleven. The battle became known as the battle of Vilcaconga. After the battle, on November 13, the Spanish brought a captive, Inca general Chalcuchima, to a public square. He had previously witnessed the brutal death of Atahualpa. When he was arrested by Francisco Pizarro and placed in chains, Pizarro confronted the Inca general and announced the following: *You have seen how, with the help of God, we have always defeated the Indians. It will be the same in the future. You can be certain that they will not escape and will not succeed in returning to Quito whence they came. You can also rest assured that you yourself will never see Cusco again. For as soon as I arrive where Captain (de Soto) is waiting for my men, I shall have you burned alive.*[29]

Hemming records the death of Chalcuchima as follows: *At Jaquijahuana on the evening of Thursday 13 November* (1533), *he was brought out to be burned alive in the middle of the square. Friar Valverde tried to persuade him to imitate Atahualpa in a deathbed conversion to Christianity. But the warrior would have none of it. He declared that he had no wish to become a Christian and found Christian law incomprehensible. So Chalcuchima was once again set alight . . . As he died he called on the god Viracocha and on his fellow commander Quisquis to come to his aid.*[30] As in the case of Atahualpa, Chalcuchima was executed with great fanfare in the middle of a public square with Spanish and distraught Incas watching. The execution was modeled after public executions that took place in Madrid and many other public squares throughout Spain.

Executions in Public Squares in Spain during the Period of the Discovery

The Plaza Mayor of Madrid: a scene of public executions

The Plaza Mayor of Madrid is the central focus of this fine city. When we visited Spain in 2011, our hotel, actually named *The Plaza Mayor,* was one block from this Plaza and we visited the Plaza several times each day. The Plaza has many park benches and crowds of people visit. It is common that all the park benches of Plaza Mayor are occupied, often by international tourists. I was intrigued that each park bench was decorated by sculptured portrayals of public executions. The victims who were shown garroted were not rapists, thieves or murderers. They had been convicted of religious crimes. The public display of the executions at the Plaza Mayor was meant to be a warning: to new converts (particularly Jews) to the Christian faith. Even the slightest remnant of a belief in the Jewish faith, or in any other non-Catholic religion was anathema to the Spaniards. I was anxious to photograph the scenes of executions portrayed in the Plaza Mayor, as unpleasant as they were. Since all the benches were occupied taking a photo was difficult. I asked two people if they could get up for a minute while I photographed the sculptured images on the park benches. They kindly agreed and we chatted for a while. The woman, named Thase, is from Peru. She is a graduate student at Brown University and her major is focused on the history of Spain and Portugal and the discovery and conquest of Brazil and Peru. Her companion is also a graduate student at Brown. I explained my interest and we agreed to correspond to share information and perspectives about the conquest of the New World and corresponding suppression of indigenous religions, particularly concerning Brazil and Peru. I then photographed scenes of executions for "religious crimes" that were part of a terrible and brutal period in Christianity.

After several visits to the Plaza Mayor I inquired about purchasing books about the inquisition and the conquest of the New World. I was unable to obtain any book about the Spanish Inquisition, the Discovery of the New World, The Conquest, or the Missionary effort to the Indigenous Peoples in the Americas in any of the museums in Spain that we visited. Spain has world class museums; however, Spain continues to have unresolved issues about the Discovery. In a commercial book store, I did obtain a book entitled, *A Traveler's Companion to MADRID*, edited by Hugh Thomas. The book contains verbatim letters, articles and stories written by tourists to Madrid over the past four hundred years. A number of the articles pertain to the Inquisition and to executions. I was struck by an account written by a French woman tourist to Madrid of her witness to a public execution in Madrid in 1680, at the Plaza Mayor. The author of the letter was Marie Gigault de Bellefonds, the French Ambassador's wife. Her account was in a letter to a friend and later published.

An Eye Witness Account of a 1680 Execution: a Product of the Spanish Inquisition

On the last day of June we had here in Madrid something that has not been seen for 48 years: a general auto of the Inquisition, in which was conducted, with great ceremony, the public trial and condemnation of several people guilty of crimes against religion, who had been gathered from all the Inquisitions of Spain. For this function, a large stage in the Plaza Major of Madrid was erected, where, between 7 in the morning and 9 at night, people were looking at the criminals and listening to their sentences. Eighteen obstinate Jews, both men and women, two apostates and one Mohammedan, were condemned to be burned; fifty other Jews or Jewesses, arrested for the first time and repentant, were condemned to several years in prison and to wearing what is called a sambenito, which is a yellow cassock with the red cross of St Andrew before and behind; ten others guilty of bigamy, sorcery and other misdemeanours, appeared in large paper hats, ropes around their necks, candles in their hands: the punishment for these things is usually flogging, the galleys, or banishment.

The following night, those who had been condemned to the fire were burned outside the town, on a specially raised mound, where these wretched creatures, before being executed, had to suffer a thousand torments; even the monks who were present there burning them with small flames from torches in order to convert them. Several people, who had climbed on to the mound, struck them with swords and the populace showered them with stones.

Those who had never been brought up on this Spanish preoccupation, which causes people to treat this ceremony with veneration, found it strange that, during the performance (the Inquisitor was placed much higher up than the King and on what seemed a throne), the King, from morning till night, had before his eyes these criminals and all the tortures as an entertainment, and that in his presence, and right next to him, some of the criminals were maltreated by the monks who beat several of them at the foot of an altar to get them to kneel down by force.

One saw the Grandees of Spain acting as sergeants since, besides the servants of the Inquisition who led forth each guilty person, those who were condemned to the fire were led on to the pyre by two Grandees of Spain, who held them. One saw extremely ignorant monks impetuously haranguing these Jews, without giving them any sort of reason for destroying their religion, while some of the criminals replied with as much knowledge as coolness, and others were gagged for fear they should speak. They appeared at all these moments, right up to their death, with a bearing worthy of a better cause, and some even threw themselves on to the fire. These tortures do not greatly diminish the number of Jews to be met with in Spain and especially in Madrid where, while some of them were being punished so ferociously, others are employed in finance, well considered and respected and nevertheless recognized as being from Jewish families.

Shortly after this execution, a certain Don Ventura Dionis obtained the title of Marquis, from the King, for 50,000 'ecus. His father had given even more for the order of St James and it was known that his uncle was one of the elders of the Synagogue in Amsterdam. There are quite a lot in the farms and in the King's receiverships, where usually they are let alone for a while until they are rich enough to be pursued. They are made to pay considerable sums to avoid the final victimization, which makes one think that this great apparatus for judgment of a few wretches is more the result of ostentation on the part of the inquisitors than a real religious zeal.[31]

I have included this digression from Peru to Madrid, Spain, in order to point out that the cruelties suffered by the Amerindians of Peru did not start with Francisco Pizarro, but is representative of the intolerance and brutality within the Christian Church as practiced in Europe at the time of the great explorations and discovery.

Pizarro Marches on to Cusco

As Pizarro and his small but well equipped army marched onward they were greeted by some as liberators, because Spanish warriors had killed the Quitans who had opposed the local Inca rulers in the area between Jauja and Cuzco. This is one example in which Pizarro took advantage of the recent history of conflict among the Inca. Locals even turned over Quitan prisoners to the Spanish, who had been captured during the Inca civil war. On the other hand, other Inca forces during their retreat employed a scorched earth policy by destroying suspension bridges and burning food stores to hinder the Spaniard's advance. In one attack by native forces against the Spanish, about 600 Inca Indians were killed, at a loss of about five Spaniards and some horses. Through out the war the casualties suffered by the Inca were vastly greater than Spanish losses.

As the Spanish campaign proceeded to within sight of Cusco, they expected a fierce fight from the Inca warriors; however, no further resistance materialized. On Saturday, November 15, 1533, the Spanish army with Pizarro at the head entered the great city without any further opposition. [32]

The Looting of Cusco

Pizarro may have been a high risk warrior who was willing to face great danger with daring and flair; however, he supervised the looting of Cusco in an orderly manner with strict supervision.[33] Ninety two pages of documents remain as to how the treasures were located, melted down and distributed. The value of the gold and silver was even greater than what was taken from Cajamarca. Hemming describes the looting as follows:

The sack of Cusco was one of the very rare moments in world history when conquerors pillaged at will the capital of a great empire. It was an event to fire the imagination of every ambitious young man in Europe. Francisco Lopez de Gomara wrote that, on entering Cusco, 'some of them immediately began to dismantle the walls of the temple, which were of gold and silver; others to disinter the jewels and gold vases that were with the dead; others to take idols of the same materials. They sacked the houses and the fortress, which still contained much of Huyna-Capac's gold.' In short, they took a greater quantity of gold and silver there and in the surrounding district than they had in Cajamarca with the capture of Atahualpa. [34]

The Temple of the Sun, located a few hundred yards south of the main square, was the greatest prize. It contained a golden enclosure and many precious objects representing llamas, women, as well as pitchers, jars and other objects made of gold. The Temple of the Sun was plundered. This architectural and cultural jewel, destroyed with abandon seriously wounded the Inca Culture. Gustavo Gutierrez, a Peruvian Catholic priest, records that towards the end of the 16th century some Spaniards expressed empathy with the suffering of the Amerindians of Peru.

Guaman Poma de Ayala tells us that he was moved by their plight and set out to scour the Incan empire 'in search of the poor of Jesus Christ.' His mission led him to 'settle among them for thirty years and I went everywhere to see and promote justice and help for the poor.' Faced with the injustices and indigence that he saw and heard of Guaman Poma explains: 'My God, where are you? Will you not hear me and help your poor? Because I myself am helpless!'[35]

The Temple, with modifications, is now the colonial church of Santo Domingo. The pain of the Amerindians of Peru remains. Gutierrez writes that several centuries after Guaman Poma another author, Jose Maria Arguedas, put these words in the mouth of Ernesto, the character who represents him in his novel *Deep River:*

> *Afterwards, when my father rescued me and I wandered with him through the towns, I found that people everywhere suffered. Perhaps the Maria Angola (the Cathedral Bell) mourned for them, here in Cusco. I had never seen anyone more humiliated than the Old Man Pongo (unpaid Amerindian Servant). At every stroke the bell became more mournful and its sound Penetrated Everything.*
>
> *Maria Angola (The Cathedral bell) made of gold and Amerindian blood, mourns and causes others to mourn. Its sad sound floods and penetrates everything. In that same cathedral is the Lord of the Earthquakes; his face resembles the faces of the most despised among the Amerindians, and in it is concentrated a vast sorrow.*
>
> *The face of the crucified Christ was dark and gaunt, like that of the Pongo (unpaid servant) . . . . Blackened, suffering, the Christ maintained a silence that did not set one at ease. He made one suffer; in such a vast cathedral, in the midst of the candle flames and the daylight that filtered down dimly, the contemplation of Christ caused suffering, extending it to the walls, to the arches and columns, from which I expected to see tears flow.* [36]

Others were also contemplative and mournful

A Catholic priest named Cristobal de Molina, who was present during the 16th century conquest, also condemned the brutality of his fellow Spaniards, expressing empathy for the tragedy suffered by the Inca people.

Their only concern was to collect gold and silver to make them selves all rich . . . without thinking that they were doing wrong and were wrecking and destroying. For what was being destroyed was more perfect than anything they enjoyed and possessed. [37]

After the defeat of the Inca, their population declined sharply. Native provinces that were estimated to have about 40,000 inhabitants at the time of discovery were reduced to about 4,000 by 1540.[38] Severe population losses occurred wherever there were significant presence and impact by the Spanish. Hemming cites a Spanish contemporary observer named Fernando de Armellones, who stated:

We cannot conceal the great paradox that a barbarian, Huayna-Capac, kept such excellent order that the entire country was calm and well nourished, whereas today we see only infinite deserted villages on all the roads of the kingdom.[39]

In part, the population loss of the Incas can be attributed directly to combat loss and injury during the war against the Spanish conquistadors. However, Hemming states that many other factors contributed as well. For example, once the Spanish took control of Peru they neglected to maintain the carefully constructed public works of the Incas. Irrigation canals fell into disrepair. Agricultural terraces on all the hillsides were left unattended and became unproductive, and great storehouses of grain were looted and not replenished. Large herds of llamas were destroyed at a faster rate than they could be replenished. Famine in Peru became widespread because the agricultural policies of the Inca were carelessly and recklessly neglected. A Spaniard named Pascual de Andagoya wrote to the King of Spain in July 1539. He told of marauders who roamed Peru after the defeat of the Incas.

But what is worse is that the Indians are being totally destroyed and lost. Someone—an official of your Majesty—told me here that it was not in fighting for one side or the other that fifty thousand souls died in Cuzco. They begged with a cross to be given food for the love of God; and when they were given none they threw the cross on the ground. One man in Cuzco collected 200,000 fanegas (five fanegas equals eight bushels) of maize from the Indians and was selling it in the native market. The soldiers and citizens took all the Indians' cloth and food and were selling it in the square at such low prices that a sheep (llama) was sold at half weight. They were killing all the (llamas) they wanted for no greater need than to make tallow candles. The Indians are left with nothing to plant, and since they have no cattle and can never obtain any, they cannot fail to die of hunger.[40]

Pizarro implements the notorious policies of Encomienda and Repartimientos

Pizarro awarded vast tracks of land to his conquistadors, and the natives who lived on those lands were entrusted to the new Spanish landlords. The land given to a Spaniard was named encomienda and the requirement for natives to work the land or pay tribute to the Spaniard was named the repartimiento i.e., the share. In turn the Spanish encomendero (who owned the land) was charged with instructing the natives in the tenets of the Holy Catholic Faith. [41]

The policy was often abused. One writer, Bartolome de Vega, is quoted by Hemming as stating that in one case Indians of Parinacocha had to carry their tribute over two hundred miles to Cuzco.

They sometimes have to carry five hundred fanegas (800 bushels) of maize. Fifteen hundred Indians to transport it, with three carrying one fanega and they carry all the things required by the assessment: wheat, maize, cloth, bars of silver, etc. Indian men are loaded with it, and so are the women, the pregnant ones with their heads on their swollen bellies and those who have given birth with their babies on top of the loads . . . Since Peru is such a mountainous country these people climb with their loads up slopes that a horse could not climb. They go sweating up the hillside with their loads, and it is heart-rending to see them. The Indians often take two months to deliver the tribute to their encomendero, including the outward and return journey and the time spent in the Spanish city. [42]

Hemming states that under Inca leadership (before Pizarro) the Indians were required to work for the state. Work projects included working on infrastructure along the Inca Empire as well as agriculture and harvest of various crops. The Indians were supported by the Inca state while at work, and during famine or periods of hunger the food was distributed back to the natives. Under the Spaniards none of the harvest was held in store for the natives. Hemming states, "The Peruvians had been torn from the shelter of a benevolent, almost socialistic, absolute monarchy into the cruel world of feudal Europe."[43]

The encomendero was obligated to convert natives to the Catholic faith. Hemming reports that oppressive encomenderos selected priests of similar character.[44] When natives of Peru were not satisfactory workers for the Spanish colonists, the Spanish brought shiploads of blacks from Africa, thus extending the slave trade.

After the Conquest the Inca adopt Christianity

Hemming states that "The Peruvians took to Christianity remarkably well. They found no difficulty in exchanging the official Inca religion for Catholicism."[45] His report of acceptance of Christianity is frankly a surprise; especially after the brutality of the Conquest and the looting of the treasures of a great empire. What explains the alleged ease of conversion among the Peruvians, when Indigenous peoples from Alaska on through Brazil often resisted conversion to Christianity?

Are there similarities between Christian beliefs and those of the Inca? A Jesuit priest named Blas Valera, who was born of an Inca mother and a Spanish father, has written that there are important similarities between Catholicism and Inca religious beliefs. Valera was the first mestizo Jesuit (person of mixed blood) to ever receive holy orders. [46]

Valera used his position as a Jesuit to explain similarities between Andean religious beliefs and Christianity. Foremost, he states that the Inca worshiped one God, named Pachacamac, described as "God, the creator of the universe."[47] This means that the Inca religion is not pagan. Pagan religious beliefs always have multiple gods. In addition, Valera wrote manuscripts stating that the Inca religion includes a Christ-like figure named Viracocha—a Christ like being who represents the incarnation of God as man.

Sabine Hyland in her book stresses the importance to which Valera interpreted Andean religious beliefs as similar to Christianity. She writes:

Valera's assertion that Viracocha was God incarnate is therefore equivalent to stating that Viracocha was Christ. In Sansevero's text, it is explained that the true God, Pachacamac, appeared in human form to a young Inca prince, the son of the emperor Yahuar Huacac. This apparition of God in human form—in other words, of Christ—told the prince a message that enabled the young man to lead the Incas to victory against one of their most important rival tribes. As emperor, this prince took the name Viracocha in honor of Christ's appearance to him. In fact, most other Spanish accounts claim that it was either the sun god or Viracocha who appeared to emperor Viracocha's son, Prince Yupanqui (who later would become emperor Pachacuti), to urge him to victory against the Chancas. Valera is telling us that this god was Christ and that the Incas, therefore, were very close to being Christians.[48]

Hubert Herring agrees with Valera that the Inca religion was monotheistic. He summarizes that concept as follows:

In exaltation of one chief creator-god, eternal and omnipotent, the maker of all other supernatural powers, of animals and of men, the Incas were in effect monotheists. The name assigned that creator, Hispanized by the sixteenth century scribes as Viracocha, carried titles "Ancient foundation, lord instructor of the world." All other gods and supernatural powers existed by the will and act of the creator Viracocha, and were subservient to him. The Sun, progenitor of the Inca dynasty, was the god assigned to the protection and the maturing of crops; despite his obvious importance, the sun-god was still overshadowed by Viracocha. Following these in order of importance came the thunder-god of weather; the moon-goddess, wife of the sun; the various gods of the stars; the goddesses of the earth and the sea. In addition, there were numerous local shrines and temples. Their theology included belief in a future life, with a comfortable heaven for the faithful—but members of the nobility were admitted without question as to their character. There was also a hell—very cold, and lacking in food.

Much of the literature of the peoples, preserved by oral tradition, was concerned with religion. [49]

In his work with Inca natives, Valera explained Andean religion in Christian terms. In 1582 Valera was brought to Lima and assigned the task of translating the Catholic catechism into Quechua. While in Lima he offered to teach Quechua to all priests and anyone else (Spanish colonists) free of charge. However, a high ranking Jesuit, Jose de Acosta, wanted to wean Andean peoples completely from their ancient religion, rather than build their Christian faiths on Andean religious beliefs. Similarities between Christianity and Andean religions, Acosta contended, were due simply to "demonic imitation of the true faith." [50]

Furthermore, the Jesuits considered the views of Valera as heretical. At the time of the Spanish Inquisition and coinciding with the "discovery," any religious belief outside of Christianity was forbidden. Syncretism, or the blending of non-Christian religious beliefs with Christianity was heresy. Valera was imprisoned by the Jesuit missionaries in Peru for heresy. He was later transferred to Spain, where he was killed in the city of Cadiz in 1597. The life and views of Valera greatly disturbed the Jesuits in Peru. Sabine Hyland, author of *The Jesuit & the Incas: The Extraordinary Life of Padre Blas Valera, S.J.* states:

The Jesuits in Peru voted unanimously in 1582 to never again allow mestizos into the Society, some claimed that this policy was necessary because of the dangerous example provided by the mestizo Valera. Valera's story provides a remarkable example of courage in the defense of the native Peruvians and sheds valuable insights into the controversies over religion, language, and Inca culture among sixteenth-century missionaries and native elites. [51]

If, as Hemming states, the Peruvians took to Christianity surprisingly well, that ease of converting natives did not last long. The popular mestizo Jesuit, Valera, was imprisoned and the Spanish continued to oppress the Inca population with brutality. Acosta, the high ranking Jesuit, wrote a manuscript, *De Procuranda,* in which he articulated reasons why Peruvians had difficulty accepting Christianity. One reason was the violence of the Spanish that accompanied evangelization. He specified numerous examples in his text. Hyland states:

> However, his discussion of Spanish atrocities was removed from his text by the order of the Jesuit general Aquaviva and has never been published. Apparently, the general felt that such criticisms of Spanish actions might threaten the reputation of the Society and incur the wrath of the Spanish Crown. In a letter to the Provincial of Toledo dated November 8, 1582, Aquaviva instructs the provincial to remove from **De Procuranda** the chapter that discusses the conquistadors' cruelty. [52]

Furthermore, Everardo Mercurian, the general of the Society at the time, ordered the Jesuits in Peru to refrain from criticizing the Spanish colonial policy for fear that the Crown might become angry with the Jesuit Society. [53]

The Expulsion of the Jesuits

Indeed the Crown was angry. In 1767 the Spanish King ordered the expulsion of the Society from all his dominions. Following the expulsion of the Society of Jesus from both the dominions of Spain and Portugal, Pope Clement XIV in 1773 declared the Society extinct.

The Incas of Peru were to face additional problems. The Christian missionary effort to convert the native peoples was hampered by the multitude of tiny hamlets of native peoples. To ease the work of converting the natives, a policy was implemented by the new viceroy, Francisco de Toledo, in 1570, to bring all native peoples from tiny and scattered hamlets into large towns. The town of El Crecado is one example of such an effort. The policy of forcing indigenous peoples to leave their settlements and move to larger towns was known as "reducing" the population. This occurred throughout the Andes. [54]

Life became very hard for the indigenous peoples of Peru, and that continues to this day. The Catholic Church is still the dominant religion in Peru, but it is strongly influenced by Liberation Theology.

Liberation Theology

One of the founders of Liberation Theology is the Peruvian Catholic priest Gustavo Gutierrez. He is also the founder of the Instituto Bartolome de Las Casas located in Lima, Peru. A main focus of liberation theology is the concern for human suffering and anguish of the innocent. In his book *On Job: God-Talk and the Suffering of the Innocent,* Gutierrez quotes from the writings of Bishop Desmond Tutu of Africa.

Liberation theology more than any other kind of theology issues out of the Crucible of human suffering and anguish. It happens because people cry out, "Oh God, how long?"

"Oh God, but Why?" All liberation theology stems from trying to make sense of human suffering when those who suffer are the victims of organized oppression and exploitation. When they are emasculated and treated as less than what they are: human persons created in the image of the Triune God, redeemed by the one Savior Jesus Christ and sanctified by the Holy Paraclete. This is the genesis of all liberation theology and so also of black theology, which is the theology of liberation in Africa. [55]

Gutierrez asserts that Christians must focus on the state of affairs caused by those who exploit and rob the poor. In many instances, the suffering of the innocent points clearly to guilty parties. He writes, "The daily life of the poor is a dying, says the Bible. The oppressors of the poor are therefore called murderers. The book of Ecclesiastics says it bluntly: 'The bread of the needy is the life of the poor; whoever deprives them of it is a man of blood. To take away a neighbor's living is to murder him; to deprive an employee of his wages is to shed blood.' Ecclesiastics 34: 21-22."[56]

Gutierrez provides a refreshing perspective on theology and religion. When we talk about God, he states, we must understand we know little:

But it is important to keep in mind from the very outset that theological thought about God is thought about a mystery. I mention this because it influences an attitude to be adopted in the effort to talk about God. I mean an attitude of respect that is incompatible with the kind of God-talk that is sure, that it knows everything there is to know about God. [57]

His work is focused on the suffering of the Amerindians of Peru and the injustices and oppression they experienced toward the end of the sixteenth century that continue today. Gutierrez remains focused on the suffering of the innocent and against a theology that justifies it, and against the depiction of God that such a theology conveys.

One of his concerns about current theology is the view that "God punishes the wicked and rewards the upright." [58] In his analysis and interpretation of the Book of Job, Gutierrez points out that friends of the suffering Job tell him that he must be guilty of a great sin and must confess his sins. Otherwise God will not restore him. His friends try to help him, but they can not do so except on their own rigid view of things, their own theology.

Gutierrez eloquently puts a perspective and focus on human suffering in today's world:

Human suffering, whatever its causes—social, personal, or other—is a major question for theological reflection. J.B. Metz has, with refined human and historical sensitivity, called the attention of contemporary theologians, those of Europe in particular, to what it means to talk about God after Auschwitz. For the terrible holocaust of millions of Jews is an inescapable challenge to the Christian conscience and an inexcusable reproach to the silence of many Christians in the face of that dreadful event. We must therefore ask: How can we talk about God without referring to our own age? More than that: How can we do it without taking into account situations like the Holocaust in which God seems to be absent from immense human suffering?

It needs to be realized, however, that for us Latin Americans the question is not precisely 'How are we to do theology after Auschwitz?' The reason is that in Latin America we are still experiencing every day the violations of human rights, murders, and the torture that we find so blameworthy in the Jewish Holocaust of World War II. Our task here is to find the words with which to talk about God in the midst of starvation of millions, the humiliation of races regarded as inferior, discrimination against women, especially women who are poor, systematic social injustice, a persistent high rate of infant mortality, those who simply "disappear" or are deprived of their freedom, the suffering of peoples who are struggling for their right to live, the exiles and the refugees, terrorism of every kind, and the corpse—filled common graves of Ayacucho. What we must deal with is not the past but, unfortunately, a cruel present and a dark tunnel with no apparent end. [60]

Endnotes Chapter 7 Peru

1. Frost, Peter. *Exploring Cusco.* 5th Edition. Nuevas Imagenes S.A. Av. S. Antunez de Mayolo 879, Lima 33, Peru. p. 61.
2. Ibid. p. 61.
3. Ibid. p. 62.
4. Ibid. p. 65.
5. Hemming, John. *The Conquest of the Incas,* London, 1970. p. 78
6. Frost. Op. cit. p. 80.
7. Ibid. p. 80
8. Ibid. p. 91.
9. Ibid. p. 90.
10. Ibid. p. 209.
11. Hemming, Op. cit. p. 118.
12. Herring, Hubert. *A History of Latin America,* New York, 1956. Alfred A. Knopf. p.138
13. Ibid. p. 138.
14. Hemming, Op. cit. p. 43.
15. Ibid. p. 78.
16. Ibid. p. 79.
17. Ibid. p. 79.
18. Ibid. p. 79.
19. Herring, Op. cit. p. 140.
20. Hemming, Op. cit. p. 88.
21. Ibid. p. 88.
22. Ibid. p. 90.
23. Ibid. p. 89.
24. Ibid. p. 98.
25. Ibid. p. 95.
26. Ibid. p. 96.
27. Ibid. p. 97.
28. Ibid. p. 106.
29. Ibid. p. 109.
30. Ibid. p. 109.

31. A French Ambassador's wife's view of the *auto de fe* of 1680. In *A Traveller's Companion to MADRID.* Introduced and edited by Hugh Thomas. 2005. p. 141-143.

32. Hemming, Op. cit. p. 102-105.

33. Ibid., p. 130.

34. Ibid., p. 132.

35. Gutierrez, Gustavo. *We Drink from our own Wells: The Spiritual Journey of a People.* Orbis Books, Maryknoll, New York. 1984. p. 98.

36. Ibid., p. 101.

37. Hemming, Op. cit. p. 135.

38. Ibid., p. 348.

39. Ibid., p. 348.

40. Ibid., p. 351

41. Ibid., p. 354.

42. Ibid., p. 355.

43. Ibid., p. 357.

44. Ibid., p. 361.

45. Ibid., p. 309.

46. Hyland, Sabine. *The Jesuit & the Incas: The Extraordinary Life of Padre Blas Valera, S.J.* The University of Michigan Press, Ann Arbor. 2003. p. 48

47. Ibid., p. 148.

48. Ibid., p. 145.

49. Herring, Op. cit. pp. 55-56.

50. Hyland, Op. cit. p. 171.

51. Ibid., p. 68.

52. Ibid., p. 176.

53. Ibid., p. 177.

54. Hemming, Op. cit. p. 49.

55. Gutierrez, Gustavo, *On Job: God Talk and the Suffering of the Innocent.* Orbis Books, Maryknoll, New York, 1987, p. 9.

56-60. Ibid, pp. 11-14

CHAPTER 8

The Tribes of Tierra del Fuego

January 2008 we travelled to the **Antarctic** aboard the Norwegian cruise ship the *NordNorge*. We travelled first to **Ushuaia, Argentina**, which is the capital of the Argentine province of Tierra del Fuego. Ushuaia is the southernmost city in the world and its port is the closest one to Antarctica. Tierra del Fuego, a large island, owes its name "Land of Fire" to discoverer Ferdinand Magellan. Tradition has it that when Magellan sighted the land in 1520 he spotted several fires on the coastline. The natives built fires for warmth and for cooking.

Before heading for the Antarctic we spent time in Ushuaia and travelled by ship into the **Tierra del Fuego National Park.** This park covers 300 square miles, with some on the Beagle Channel. It shares the same relative latitude, 55 degrees south, which is comparable to Ketchikan, Alaska, about 55 degrees latitude north. The park has snow capped mountains, glaciers, glacial lakes and waterfalls. As we went through the waterway of the park, I shared my interest in the missionary effort started by Captain Robert FitzRoy, with Jim Garlinghouse, the historian-lecturer aboard the NordNorge. From the deck of the ship, Jim pointed out the locations where four Fuegian natives were picked up by Captain FitzRoy in 1829 and brought to England to be taught the basics of Christianity. On the return trip starting in 1831, a young man named Charles Darwin was on board the *Beagle* as the Christian missionary effort unfolded.

Captain Robert FitzRoy Introduces Christianity to the Tribes of Tierra del Fuego

Captain FitzRoy was employed by the British navy to explore in detail a vast territory and prepare navigational charts. England had vast colonies throughout the world, all with major economic resources that provided great wealth to the British Empire. Consequently, the British captains and crew of both naval and commercial ships required precise navigational maps. A thousand times British naval ships, like the *Beagle,* were employed throughout the world recording latitude and longitude and plotting islands, headlands, shorelines, rocks, reefs, channels and river mouths to create effective navigational charts. For example, nearly simultaneously with the efforts of FitzRoy in Patagonia, Captain George Vancouver explored the Northwest Pacific coastline from what is now Oregon to Alaska. (Vancouver missed the Columbia River.) In arctic waters, the renowned Captain John Franklyn explored the North West Passage in an effort to find a short route to India.

In a sense the *Beagle* was a mother ship. The difficult, time-consuming work was done in rowboats. The *Beagle* carried six boats: a 28 foot yawl, three whaleboats of about 25 feet, a 23-foot rowing and sailing gig, and a 14-foot rowboat. The crews did their surveying work on these small crafts, as they recorded vast and detailed records hour by hour. During these efforts by crews in small boats, the *Beagle* was either in a safe harbor, or anchored off shore—oftentimes exposed to brutal weather. The small boats were necessary because the *Beagle,* a deep draft sailing ship, did not have the capability to maneuver close to shore in the uncharted waters that represented their task and challenge. Safety was another issue; if the ship hit a reef and foundered, the small boats were the only means of survival.

In 1826 Robert FitzRoy served as lieutenant aboard the *Beagle* under the command of Captain Pringle Stokes. Together with a larger ship, the HMS *Adventure,* under the overall command of captain Phillip King, the mission was dedicated to surveying the southern coast of South America on both the Atlantic, in Argentina waters, and the Pacific, in Chilean waters. During this protracted mission Captain Stokes became depressed. In addition, some crew aboard the *Beagle* suffered from scurvy with symptoms of bleeding gums, loose teeth, overall weakness and feelings of despair. Captain Stokes ordered a period of rest so he and his crew could recuperate. After a two-week rest, the *Beagle* continued on its mission and rejoined the *Adventure* under the temporary command of lieutenant William Skyring, who took over for the ailing captain Stokes. During the next four weeks, Captain Stokes remained in his cabin in deep despair; then, on August 12, 1828, he committed suicide. After the death of Stokes, the two ships sailed north in South America and sought refuge for the winter. The *Beagle* underwent repairs in Montevideo, Uruguay, from storm damage and then sailed on to Rio de Janeiro and rejoined the crew of the *Adventure*. In Rio, Skyring was relieved of command and resumed his former position as assistant surveyor. Robert FitzRoy was promoted from the rank of lieutenant to captain of the *Beagle* on December 15, 1828. He was then only twenty-two years old. FitzRoy had been trained at the Royal Naval College at Portsmouth. He entered the program at the young age of twelve, and completed the three-year course in the short span of twenty months. FitzRoy was hard working, and recognized as brilliant and proficient in matters of seamanship. His task was to continue the assignment of surveying the southern coasts of South America from Montevideo on the southern Atlantic to Chiloe Island in the Pacific. In January 1829 the three ships, HMS *Adventure*, HMS *Adelaide* and HMS *Beagle,* with FitzRoy as captain, set sail to restart their surveying mission. Two months later the ships entered the Strait of Magellan, and the crew of the *Beagle* noticed some natives on shore.

Captain FitzRoy Captures four Fuegian Natives

The focus in this chapter is the introduction of Christianity to the Indigenous peoples of Tierra del Fuego. Although FitzRoy's assignment was to complete navigational surveys, he shifted his focus and became the first person to introduce Christianity to the natives of Tierra del

Fuego. After a year of successful but dangerous surveying (he lost one of his crew in a savage storm.), some improbable events took place that profoundly impacted the lives of the natives of this remote land and forever changed concepts within the field of science and the Christian religion.

On January 30, 1830, Murray along with ten others departed from the *Beagle* and rowed a 26' whaleboat on a routine surveying mission with about a week's supply of food and equipment. They camped ashore that night. The next morning, to their shock and amazement, they discovered that their whaleboat was missing. It had been stolen by natives of Tierra del Fuego. Murray and his crew searched and searched for the whaleboat but without success. Murray was desperate, but he had resolve and determination. In a period of two days he and his crew built a large basket with materials at hand, essentially branches, which they intertwined, and pieces of canvas from their tent. This large wicker basket served as a boat.[1] Two of Murray's men then paddled this craft over a period of twenty hours in stormy and wet weather until they finally reached the *Beagle*.

Upon arriving aboard the *Beagle*, Murray informed Captain FitzRoy about the loss of the whaleboat. FitzRoy was astonished that native Fuegians would dare to steal such a boat. (Note: The Fuegians must have recognized that the British whaleboat was superior to their canoes. Similarly, Lewis and Clark stole an Indian canoe near present day Astoria in 1812. They noted in their journal that the Clatsop canoe was "better" than their own.)[2] At any rate, FitzRoy sent eleven men in another whaleboat to search for the missing boat. They returned days later without success. On February 17th, FitzRoy sent two teams, each with a week's provision, to search for the missing boat. The crew of one of the boats captured eleven Fuegian natives and hoped the natives could help them find the missing boat. They fed and clothed them and camped with them overnight. During the night all the Fuegians escaped, leaving behind a young girl who was brought on board the *Beagle*. FitzRoy decided to keep the girl and named her Fuegia Basket, after the wicker-like craft built by Murray. FitzRoy considered Fuegia Basket as "unclaimed property" because her mother did not come back to reclaim her. Fearing that the missing boat would not be located,

FitzRoy assigned carpenter Jonathan May to build a 26 foot whaleboat to replace the stolen one he had previously built in 1829—after another whaleboat had been destroyed in a storm. On board the *Beagle* were stores of wood and tools for the task. May went ashore and built a replacement boat in about three days. During this time some natives were seen nearby and FitzRoy enticed a young man to come aboard the *Beagle*. FitzRoy hoped to teach him English so that he might help locate the missing whaleboat. He named him York Minster, after a famous Cathedral in northern England. York Minster was captured near what is now called March Harbor.

   Note: *When Marge and I sailed through these waters in 2008, the historian aboard the NordNorge spoke informally to those of us who were observing the shorelines within Tierra del Fuego and pointed out the area where York Minster was "found" and brought aboard the Beagle. Then, in a more formal lecture aboard the NordNorge, he told us that the indigenous peoples probably go back more than 10,000 years and were represented as four main indigenous tribes: the Ona, Alcaluf, Yaganes, and Haush. In another lecture the instructor spoke of the Patagonian Missionary Society, their missionary effort, and the factors that led to the extinction of the tribes of Tierra del Fuego.*

   On May 1830, some crew came across a group of Fuegians who had with them some gear that had been on board the missing whale boat. After a struggle all the Fuegians escaped except for one young boy who was captured. He was brought on board the *Beagle* and FitzRoy named him Boat Memory. Then on May 11, 1830, the *Beagle* approached Murray Narrows (named after Murray who built the wicker boat) and gestured for a young man to board the ship. At the same time a crew member handed a large Mother-of-Pearl-Button to another native in the Fuegian canoe. FitzRoy noted that the young man seemed cheerful in the company of the other three Fuegians aboard and named him Jemmy Button. (The surname "Button" was in recognition of the Mother-of-Pearl-Button given to the unidentified native aboard the Fuegian canoe who accompanied the young boy.)

Captain FitzRoy Initiates a Missionary Plan

Captain FitzRoy then developed a plan. He would bring the four Fuegians to England for a period of about three years and teach them the English language and the basics of the Christian religion. His plans included the return of the four to Tierra del Fuego along with Christian missionaries to spread Christianity. The search for the missing whaleboat ended. The author Peter Nichols, who wrote *Evolution's Captain*, states that the missing boat, built by Jonathan May in 1829, is one of the most important lost artifacts in history.[3]

After returning to England aboard the *Beagle*, FitzRoy sought and received approval for his plans for the Fuegians from John Barrow, the Second Secretary of the Admiralty. The Admiralty agreed to provide berths on board a ship to return the Fuegians at some distant time to Tierra del Fuego. FitzRoy agreed to handle all expenses associated with educating and caring for them while in England. FitzRoy then made contact with Rev. J.L. Harris and asked him to bring the matter to the Anglican Church Mission Society to find a place for the Fuegians and to introduce them to the English language and the basics of Christianity. He preferred to find Christian homes where they might live rather than in an institutional setting. Unfortunately, FitzRoy mentioned in his request that Fuegian natives are cannibalistic but are "learning" to eat vegetables. On this, and many other points, FitzRoy was in error. The Fuegians did not practice cannibalism.[4] Nevertheless, the Society said "No." FitzRoy was now limited to finding institutional type arrangements for his Fuegian students. During this initial period the young boy, Boat Memory, became ill and died. FitzRoy was grief stricken but continued his plans for the other three.

Although the Church Mission Society declined to help, its secretary, Dandeson Coats contacted a Reverend Joseph Wigram and his associate William Wilson. They made arrangements with the director of the Walthamstow Infants School to provide the education of the remaining three Fuegians.[5] The program, according to FitzRoy, went well for the two younger of the three. Fuegia Basket was charming and learned English surprisingly quickly. She was a delight to many audiences as was Jemmy Button. However, York Minster, approximate age 26, did not respond well. The range of ages of his English classmates at the school was between the ages of two and four. This was tolerated by Fuegia Basket and Jemmy Button, but not by York Minster who became morose and disinterested. Furthermore, a child care worker at the Walthamstow Infant School reported that York Minster was having sexual relations with Fuegia Basket. FitzRoy was distraught about the accusation and felt his mission with the Fuegians was a failure. He began an intense effort to obtain a new commission to continue the surveying mission off the southern coasts of South America which would permit him to return the three Fuegians to their homeland in Tierra del Fuego. On July 4, 1831, he was given a commission to continue his surveying mission. Because of his authority and reputation, he was able to expand the scope of his mission to continue his voyage of discovery by sailing around the world before returning to England.

With approval and funding secured, FitzRoy pondered his innermost fears about this major upcoming mission. He knew that his mother's side of the family had problems with mental instability. A maternal uncle had committed suicide; and he remembered well the shocking suicide of Captain Stokes, who commanded the *Beagle* on the surveying mission in which FitzRoy had initially served as second lieutenant. He was also aware that he (FitzRoy) had personally experienced some serious depressive episodes. Furthermore, as captain, FitzRoy was responsible to maintain authority and discipline consistent with 19th Century British Naval traditions (very harsh). He could not have ongoing collegial relations with crew members who were beneath him in social standing and who must fear him and be absolutely obedient. He wanted a well educated person with a scientific mind to have on board as a companion. Upon his request a number of influential scholars and scientists searched for a candidate to accompany FitzRoy on a journey that would likely last four to five years. Sir Francis Beaufort, a British naval officer, recommended Charles Darwin.

Pursuing the recommendation given by Beaufort, FitzRoy contacted Darwin and they agreed to meet and discuss the mission. They met in August 1831. Charles Darwin was impressed with FitzRoy and wrote an account of his meeting with him to his sisters.

I have seen him; it is no use attempting to praise him as much as I feel inclined to do for you would not believe me. One thing I am certain, nothing could be more open and kind than he was to me . . . . He says nothing would be so miserable for him as having me with him if I was uncomfortable, as in a small vessel we must be thrown together, and thought it his duty to state everything in the worst point of view: I think I shall go on Sunday to Plymouth to see the vessel. There is something most extremely attractive in his manners and way of coming straight to the point. If I live with him, he says, I must live poorly—no wine, and the plainest of dinners . . . . I like his manner of proceeding. He asked me at once, "Shall you bear being told that I want the cabin to myself? when I want to be alone. If we treat each other this way, I hope we shall suit; if not probably we should wish each other the Devil." I am writing in a great hurry . . . . I shall dine with him today.[6]

FitzRoy instructed Darwin to prepare for the exploration and to report on board the *Beagle* at the end of October. Darwin's role aboard the ship was designated as *Naturalist*. The departure target date was set for November 4, 1831. However, the *Beagle* needed some repairs and an updating of equipment. The date of departure was reset to December 26, 1831. Unfortunately, four crewmen of the *Beagle* got seriously drunk over the Christmas holiday which made it necessary to postpone the trip one day to December 27.

As the ship left port the passengers included the three Fuegians: Fuegia Basket, Jemmy Button, and York Minster. Of critical importance to FitzRoy, was a Christian missionary on board, Richard Matthews, who would be the first ordained missionary to spread the gospel of Christ (as understood by missionaries at the time) to the tribes of Tierra del Fuego.

The first day of the trip was shocking to Charles Darwin. He could not get away from hearing the lash and the eerie and loud screaming of four seamen who were flogged for drunkenness and disobedience on Christmas day—and for causing a one day delay in the ship's departure. In his captain's log for the date, FitzRoy noted:

John Bruce: 25 lashes for drunkenness, quarrelling and insolence.

David Russel: Carpenter's crew, with 34 lashes for breaking his leave and disobedience of orders.
James Phipps: 44 lashes for breaking his leave, drunkenness and insolence.
Elias Davis: 31 lashes for reported neglect of duty.

FitzRoy wrote in his journal: *Hating, abhorring corporal punishment, I am nevertheless fully aware that there are too many course natures which cannot be restrained without it, (to the degree required on board a ship,) not to have a thorough conviction that it could only be dispensed with, by sacrificing a great deal of discipline and consequent efficiency.*[7]

Darwin had daily interactions with FitzRoy. He ate his meals with him and often accompanied him ashore. On one occasion while in Brazil, Captain Paget of the *Samarang*, came aboard the Beagle to dine with FitzRoy and Darwin. They discussed slavery, which was still legal in Brazil. FitzRoy expressed the view that slavery was not unlike the useful master-servant arrangement in England that had worked so well since feudal times.[8] FitzRoy also believed firmly that the Bible supported the institution of slavery, and later he put his thoughts about slavery in writing:

But, turning to the Bible, we find in the history of those by whom the earth was peopled, after the flood, a curse pronounced on Ham and his descendents; and it is curious that the name Ham should mean "Heat-brown-scorched," while that of Cush his son, means "Black;" that Japheth should imply "handsome," and that Shem, from whose line our Saviour was descended, should mean "name—renown—he who is put or placed."[9]

Nichols summarizes FitzRoy's views as follows, "The Bible made it clear, FitzRoy wrote, that the cursed Negro descendents of Cush ended up as the black, red, and brown "aborigines" of the southerly world of Africa, Australia, and the Pacific islands, while the handsome, renowned, and white descendents of Shem and Japheth made their way to northern Europe."[10]

While sharing the dinner discussion about slavery, with Captains Paget and FitzRoy, Darwin, who was a firm abolitionist, asked FitzRoy if he really believed the Biblical justification of slavery. Nichols writes, "He (FitzRoy) erupted furiously at Darwin, saying that as he doubted his word, they could no longer live together. The meal broke up instantly, and FitzRoy sent for Wickham to tell him that Darwin was no longer welcome at his table."[11] FitzRoy later welcomed Darwin back to the "dinner table" with him, but Darwin remembered the temper and the unnerving literalist views of FitzRoy.

As the *Beagle* entered the waters of Tierra del Fuego, Jemmy Button recognized his brother on shore. The *Beagle* anchored and members of the crew spent ten days establishing quarters for the three Fuegians, as well as a vegetable garden and a home for missionary Mathews. This was a major effort. FitzRoy allocated substantial resources to make the effort succeed. FitzRoy, Darwin, the missionary Matthews, the three Fuegians, the chief *Beagle's* surgeon Dr. Bynoe, and 27 seamen and officers filled three whaleboats and the ship's 26-foot yawl and made their way to shore to establish a community. The Church Missionary Society had donated substantial cargo to help the effort. Charles Darwin was not impressed with the donated cargo. He wrote:

The choice of articles showed the most culpable folly & negligence. Wine glasses, butter-bolts, tea-trays, soup turins, a mahogany dressing case, fine white linen, beaver hats & an endless variety of similar things shows how little was thought about the country where they were going to. The means absolutely wasted on such things would have purchased immense stock of really useful articles.[12]

In a place called Woollya—near present day Ushuaia, the flotilla came to shore and the crews built a missionary settlement. The sailors erected three homes, built of branches and thatched with grass and twigs and wrapped with sail cloth and rope for the Fuegians and their families.[13] For Mathews, the crew built a more substantial structure of wood brought from England aboard the *Beagle*. His house—and missionary headquarters—included an attic for the storage of abundant stores, as well as a cellar beneath the wooden floor of the house for additional storage. After developing the new settlement that included a substantial vegetable garden, FitzRoy, and all the crew, re-boarded the *Beagle* and left for one day and night before returning to check on progress. After returning, FitzRoy felt confident and told Matthews that he would return again in a week to evaluate the situation. One week later FitzRoy, and the crew of the *Beagle,* returned to the new settlement at Woollya. They found Matthews essentially scared witless, and FitzRoy agreed to bring him back to England. The three Fuegians would have no further contact with the British, until additional missionaries would return and take up the challenge. FitzRoy remained hopeful that his initial effort would succeed, because the three Fuegians represented a seed.[14] Darwin was not hopeful:

> It was quite melancholy leaving our Fuegians amongst their barbarous countrymen: there was one comfort; they appeared to have no personal fears.—But in contradiction to what has often been stated, 3 years has been sufficient to change savages, into as far as habits go, complete & voluntary Europeans.—But I am afraid whatever other ends their excursion to England produces, it will not be conducive to their happiness.—They have far too much sense not to see the vast superiority of civilized over uncivilized habits; & yet I am afraid to the latter they must return.[15]

The three Fuegians were left in Tierra del Fuego in February 1833. FitzRoy and Darwin would not see them again. However, FitzRoy was committed to have the missionary effort restarted at some later date.

Free to go about their business, without the day to day worry about the three Fuegians, the crew of the *Beagle* sailed on and focused on the tedious but important navigational surveying task. This gave Darwin uninterrupted time to study the plants, birds, snakes, turtles and other living things that he encountered. He took careful notes and collected a vast amount of species. When British ships came across the *Beagle*, Darwin sent many boxes of species back to England to scientists who carefully documented and preserved all the species. Darwin was intrigued by what he observed when the *Beagle* spent several months in the remote Galapagos Islands, off the coast of Ecuador. He wondered why the Creator would have placed a particular species of a finch on one island, and distinctly different variations of the bird on an island just

LEIF G. TERDAL

60 miles away. He pondered that. After Galapagos the *Beagle* turned to the west and to Australia and New Zealand and beyond before returning to England.[16]

The *Beagle* arrived in Falmouth, England on October 2, 1836, completing a journey lasting four years and ten months. Christians in England were eager to learn of the effort to introduce Christianity to the pagans of Tierra del Fuego. Religion was always an important aspect of Britain's colonizing efforts, and great efforts were expended by the government of England to support missionaries in British colonies in India, Africa, Australia, New Zealand and the Dominion of Canada.[17]

Rev. Allen Gardiner Succumbs to Patagonian Storms

Allen Gardiner, a naval officer, retired from the British navy at the young age of 32 to devote himself to missionary work. He and his wife went to Africa to preach the Christian message. While there he and his family (they had five children) became enmeshed in a great conflict and violence between the Zulu tribe and white traders and colonists. The war and fighting became known as the Boer war, between Dutch colonists, African tribes in South Africa, and British troops. Gardiner left Africa devastated by the conflict which made it impossible to remain and pursue missionary work.

Back in England he read of FitzRoy's attempt to establish a mission at Woollya in Tierra del Fuego with Matthews as the first missionary to the Fuegians.[18] After studying FitzRoy's book *Narrative of Surveying Voyages*, Gardiner made two initial efforts in 1845 and 1848 to establish a missionary effort in Tierra del Fuego. Both efforts were aborted, and Gardiner felt his initial efforts were exploratory and he resolved to try again with greater preparation. In 1850 he returned again, bringing with him six fellow Christians eager to do missionary work with the pagan Fuegians. The six included three fishermen, John Pierce, John Badcock, and John Bryan; a Sunday school teacher named John Maidment, a physician named Richard Williams, and a carpenter named Joseph Erwin. With money donated by a woman from Cheltenham, Gardiner purchased two 26-foot launches and two smaller dinghies and supplies, and headed back to Tierra del Fuego aboard a ship, the *Ocean Queen,* in December 1850.

They arrived within Tierra del Fuego, near Woollya, in hope of finding Jemmy Button. Instead they met with native tribesmen who forced them off the island. In bad weather they lost their two dinghies and later both launches were destroyed in a storm. By March 1851 they were hungry and sick. One by one they died, without being able to build an effective shelter, find food by hunting and gathering, or build a replacement boat out of their wrecked launches. They prayed and hoped for a rescue. None came. In October a merchant ship from Montevideo sailed into the Beagle Channel and saw wreckage visible on the beach. They stopped briefly, but had to leave because bad weather forced them back out to sea. They reached a British naval ship, HMS *Dido,* which investigated and found the bodies of all seven men as well as a diary written by Gardiner. His entries included the following:

The Lord in His providence has seen fit to bring us very low, but all is in (His) infinite wisdom, mercy, and love. The Lord is very pitiful and of tender compassion. He knows our frames. He appoints and measures all His afflictive dispensations, and when His set time is fully come, He will either remove us to His eternal and glorious kingdom, or supply our languishing bodies with food convenient for us.

After the tragic end of Gardiner's brief missionary effort, and the death of all seven missionaries, the *Times* in England called for an end of Patagonian missions:

Neither reverence for the cause in which they engaged nor admiration of the lofty qualities of the leader of the party, can blind our eyes to the unutterable folly of the enterprise as it was conducted, or smother the expression of natural indignation against those who could wantonly risk so many valuable lives on so hopeless an expedition. Let us hear no more of Patagonian missions![19]

In spite of the call to halt such ill conceived Christian missionary efforts in places like Tierra del Fuego, where essentially nothing was known about the natives, their language or their culture, interest and money poured in to the Patagonian Missionary Society. Reverend Despard, the society's secretary, responded to the *Times*: "With God's help the mission shall be maintained!" The Missionary Society received substantial funds sufficient to purchase a missionary ship, and to develop a missionary base in the Falkland Islands. Their thought was to follow the initial plan of Captain Robert FitzRoy. They would educate a core group of Fuegians at the Falkland base; these new converts would then be returned to Tierra del Fuego to spread the civilizing and Christian influence. Rev. Despard wrote to FitzRoy and asked for his assessment of the plan. FitzRoy was enthusiastic and wrote back.

I have given the subject of your letter my best consideration. It appears to me that your present plan is practicable and comparatively safe, that it offers a fairer prospect of success than most Missionary enterprises at their commencement, and that it would be difficult to suggest one less objectionable.[20]

The society purchased a ship of about 120 tons of displacement and outfitted it for the journey and with ample supplies including building materials. The society initiated a publication, *The Voice of Pity,* and predicted great and marvelous benefits for Tierra del Fuego.

A place of gardens, and farms and industrious villages . . . (where) *the church-going bell may awaken these silent forests; and round its cheerful hearth and kind teachers, the Sunday school may assemble the now joyless children of Navarin Island. The mariner may run his battered ship into Lennox Harbour, and leave her to the care of Fuegian caulkers and carpenters; and after rambling through the streets of a thriving sea port town, he may turn aside to read the papers in the Gardiner Institution, or may step into the week-evening service in the Richard Williams chapel.*[21]

In October 1854 the Society sent a new missionary team with Captain William Parker Snow as the leader. The ship was named *Allen Gardiner.* Captain Snow brought his ship and boat load of missionaries and support staff of carpenters and agriculturists through the very long and dangerous trip from England to the southern tip of South America.

They reached the Falkland Islands in January 1855, and the missionary team purchased land and began the process of building a missionary compound on Keppel Island within the Falklands. In November the *Allen Gardiner*, with Snow at the helm, passed the Murray Narrows making its way to Woolya. Two canoes, filled with Fuegian natives, approached with their arms waving. As they came close to the schooner, Snow stood at the stern and spoke in a loud and clear voice "Jemmy Button? Jemmy Button?" To his surprise and amazement an answer came back, "Yes, yes; Jam-mes Button, Jam-mes Button!" It had been 23 years earlier that Jemmy Button had last heard his name called by an Englishman!

Snow ordered the crew to anchor the schooner and lower the ladder. Jemmy Button, naked except for a coating of seal oil on his entire body, went aboard the *Allen Gardiner*. After Snow spoke with Jemmy Button about his family and his tribe, Snow made repeated efforts to convince Jemmy Button to join the new Christian missionary program. Jemmy was adamant in his refusal to participate in the new missionary venture. Then Snow heard Mrs. Jemmy Button calling loudly from one of the canoes for Jemmy to come back to her and their children.[22] The call from Jemmy's wife amazed Snow and he backed off and tried no further to persuade Jemmy to go to the new missionary compound at Keppel Island. Instead, he let Jemmy go back to his native lifestyle. Snow returned "empty handed" to the new base camp on the Falklands,

The Reverend George Packenham Despard learned through the Patagonia Missionary Society that the new missionary effort had stalled. He set sail for the Falklands, with sixteen Christian support staff, including Allen Gardiner Jr., the son of the deceased founder of the mission. They arrived in August 1856. When Rev. Despard met with William Parker Snow, he became ballistic in his outrage and fired Snow on the spot. Despard gave Snow and his wife three hours to get off the ship and made no provision for Snow to return to England—or receive financial compensation. Despard and his crew spent over a year enlarging the missionary compound and developing a significant live stock and agricultural program. The idea was to get the Fuegian natives away from a hunter-gatherer existence and to teach them to raise domestic animals and to farm. These steps to "civilize" the natives were preparatory to convert them to Christianity.

In June 1858, Rev. Despard and a team returned to the Murray Narrows and the Beagle Channel in search of Jemmy Button. They contacted Jemmy Button and coerced him to live on the missionary compound at Keppel Island to receive further instruction on the Christian faith. Despard did not give Jemmy Button the option of refusing. Jemmy Button, one of his two wives, and three of his children were taken to the mission station in the Falklands. There they lived in a ten foot square brick hut on the missionary compound.

At the mission Jemmy Button and his family lived a strict regimented life. It is reminiscent of the strict and harsh family life described by John Muir, as he was raised by his very earnest but also punitive Calvinist father. (see Chapter one). The natives were introduced to a schedule unfamiliar to their lifestyle. They were required to get up early, to attend church services every day and to follow strict adherence to many rules:

wiping their boots upon entering any house; table etiquette; floor sweeping. They were never accepted as equals. Jemmy was constantly admonished for what was seen as his chronic idleness. And there was always the suspicion of theft, thought to be endemic with Fuegians. Jemmy's wife was wrongly accused of stealing fence paling to use as firewood, and Jemmy was properly angry. They soon longed to return to their "countree."[23]

Jemmy Button and his family were taken back home in late November 1858. The *Allen Gardiner* remained at Woollya for a month while Rev. Despard and his crew searched for another group of Fuegian natives to go aboard ship to return to the Falklands with him. He promised clothing and other gifts. He recruited nine Fuegians who returned with him to Keppel Island. The duration of their stay lasted nine months. During this time the Fuegian men were put to physical labor, such as digging peat, making garden trenches, carrying stones away from plotted grounds. The women were taught to weave baskets from grasses and saplings. Author Peter Nichols summarizes the experience as follows:

They were homesick and unhappy. They were frequently accused of stealing, and though they were often guilty, the thefts were small: a comb, some turnips, items of no great value. The missionaries' scowling, Bible-thumping reprimands infuriated the Fuegians, to whom the accusation of theft—in their society made only in the most serious of cases, such as the theft of a canoe or a wife—was a particularly black slur. Relations between the missionaries and their guests worsened and continued to the very end of their stay. As they were boarding the Allen Gardiner to go home in late September 1859, they were subjected to a search as thorough as that now conducted at any airport. It revealed sundry small tools, rags, bits of animal carcasses, boxes of biscuits. Not much to show for nine months of hard labor, but it was too much for Despard; it was sin and he wouldn't over-look it. The Fuegians were outraged and ripped off their clothes and threw them into the water from the gangplank. Later, they retrieved their clothes and put them on again, their feelings still outraged, but they were headed for home.[24]

The Massacre at Woollya

The nine Fuegians were returned to their home in Woollya, on November 2, 1859, after a three week journey on board the *Allen Gardiner*. Four days later eight crew members of the ship participated in a church service in the small missionary church at Woollya. About three hundred Fuegians surrounded the church. During the service the Fuegians swarmed into the church with clubs and spears and killed all eight Englishmen. Coles watched and listened in horror as he heard the screams from the assault while he remained aboard the *Allen Gardiner*. Coles was not targeted for assault by the natives.

Concerned about the long delay without hearing from the *Allen Gardiner*, Rev. Despard chartered the American ship *Nancy*, with Captain William Smyley, to sail to Woollya cove and investigate. Four months after the massacre, the *Nancy* pulled alongside the now derelict *Allen Gardiner*. Native canoes pulled along side, including one with Jemmy Button aboard and another with Alfred Coles. Coles explained the terrible and tragic events to Captain Smyley. Coles then explained that he was personally treated well and cared for by women of the tribes who remained friendly to him. The natives even gave Coles a gun taken from one of the eight murdered men, so that Coles could hunt geese while waiting four long months to be rescued.

Darwin Publishes his *Origin of Species*

Darwin published his *Origin of Species* on November 24, 1859, and he sent a copy to FitzRoy. He could have been pleased that he provided the opportunity for Charles Darwin to develop his brilliant theory. However, FitzRoy was not pleased. Peter Nichols in his biography of Robert FitzRoy analyzes the beliefs of FitzRoy that were incompatible with Darwin's theory of evolution. FitzRoy had an, "an ardent faith in the literal word of the Bible, which he had begun to reread with the closest of attention."[25] FitzRoy concluded the following as certain truths from his Biblical studies:

1. God created Adam as an adult, not as an infant. "That man could have been first created as an infant, or a savage state, appears to my apprehension impossible; because—if an infant—who nursed, who fed, who protected him till able to subsist alone? And, if a savage, he would have been utterly helpless. The only idea I can reconcile to reason is that man was created perfect in body, perfect in mind, and knowing by inspiration enough for the part he had to perform; such a being it would be worse than folly to call savage. Have we a shadow of ground for thinking that wild animals or plants have improved since their creation? Can any reasonable man believe that the first of a race, species, or kind, was the most inferior?"[26]

2. Justification of slavery. Nichols summarizes the writing of FitzRoy that the cursed Negro descendents of Ham, the son of Noah who offended him, represent the black and red skilled natives of Africa, Australia, South America and the Pacific Islands, while the handsome, renowned, and white descendents of Shem and Japeth made their way to northern Europe. In FitzRoys words: *It is likely that some of Abraham's bond-women*

were either black or mulatto, being descendents of Ham; perhaps
of Cush: and it is hardly possible that Hagar should not have
been dark, even black, considering her parentage; in which case
Ishmael would have been copper-coloured, or mulatto, and some,
if not all of Abraham's sons by concubines, would have been of
those colours.[27] (Regarding the issue of slavery and the Bible,
see Chapter 9)

3. FitzRoy believed that the findings of seashells on land, and the
   findings of bones of extinct animals such as dinosaurs, giant
   rhinoceroses, and saber-tooth tigers were all proof of Noah's
   flood.[28]

4. FitzRoy believed that the earth has existed for a mere few
   thousands of years, and not long enough to account for the
   theory of evolution. The opinion of FitzRoy was widely shared
   in Europe and North America at the time. Nichols states that
   science and the Bible had become "comfortable bedfellows."
   For example, calculations from Biblical records described
   in the book of Genesis, indicated that the epic first week of
   creation, had begun on October 22, 4004 B.C. Six days later,
   by October 28, Earth and all its glories, including Man, were
   in place; and on October 29, God rested."[29]

A Major Conference in Oxford, England

On June 30 1860, Robert FitzRoy, and at least a thousand other
people attended a conference in Oxford. The University Museum of
Natural History sponsored a scientific meeting in which John William
Draper, a chemist and historian, was to give the lead lecture entitled:
On the Intellectual Development of Europe, Considered with Reference to
the Views of Mr. Darwin.

Included in his one hour and a half speech, was Draper's comment
that human progress was only possible when science pushed theology
aside. When Draper completed his presentation, John Henslow,
who chaired the lecture, asked if any members of the audience had
a comment. A number of people stood up and reacted to the lecture

including Bishop Samuel Wilberforce, Thomas Henry Huxley (a strong defender of Darwin) and Robert FitzRoy.

Bishop Wilberforce delivered a thirty-minute rebuttal to Darwin's book, *Origin of Species*. He asserted, the book was based on assumptions and not facts, and Charles Darwin had not supported his conclusions. Wilberforce then turned to Thomas Huxley and taunted him, "Was it on his grandfather's or his grandmother's side that he was descended from an ape?"[30]

Huxley rose and gave a thought out and measured response; then ended his rebuttal with the statement:

(As to whether) *I would rather have a miserable ape for a grandfather or a man highly endowed by nature and possessed of great means and influence, and yet who employs those faculties for the mere purpose of introducing ridicule into a grave scientific discussion—I unhesitatingly affirm my preference for the ape.*[31]

Robert FitzRoy then stood up and held a Bible over his head. He recounted discussions he had with Darwin, and affirmed his view that the ideas of Darwin were contradictory to the book of Genesis.[32] With the Bible still held over his head, he expressed his regret for taking Darwin on his long voyage. Nichols provides a summary statement of the brittle mindset of FitzRoy:

But he was stuck, deeply, by prejudice and the cleaving to an old order, to a mindset a thousand and more years old, when science was subservient to religion. That order was about to be toppled, and the constructs of the Bible smashed like an old wooden bridge, weakened by rot, before the torrents of a spring flood.[33]

FitzRoy's brief talk was met with silence by the thousand or so who were present at the conference; this was in contrast to the widespread interest aroused by the debate between Wilberforce and Huxley. Furthermore, the debate between Wilberforce and Huxley served to widen the scope and interest in Darwin's book, so that advances in science became of interest not only to philosophers, scientists, academics and clergy, but were passed on into the awareness and consciousness of the general public.[34] In particular, the Biblical accounts of creation had been challenged. Darwin's theory of evolution was one of an expanding number of examples in which the Bible was no longer accepted as authoritative in matters of science. FitzRoy, however, was unable to understand and adjust to the zeitgeist that was taking place.

1860 A Terrible Year for Robert FitzRoy

In May 1860, FitzRoy read in the press of the massacre of the missionaries at Woolly. He had feared the worst for his effort to introduce Christianity to the natives of Tierra del Fuego when it was alleged that York Minster, a grown young man, had sexual relations with the young Fuegia Basket. The massacre of the eight missionaries in 1859, following the death of seven others in a previous attempt to establish a viable missionary program was devastating to FitzRoy. Robert FitzRoy endured a number of health and family crises during the next several years and took his own life on April 30, 1865. He had accomplished a great deal in his life, and one might wonder how he failed to recognize his own part in contributing to the advancement of science and discovery. His tragic death brings to mind the early and tragic death of another adventurer and discoverer who accomplished a great deal and yet believed he had never accomplished anything of value. Meriwether Lewis killed himself just three years after leading the very successful Lewis and Clark expedition from St. Louis to the mouth of the Columbia River.

The Fuegian Natives face a Policy of Extermination

The British missionary effort did not end with the 1859 massacre. In 1863 Reverend Whait Stirling sailed the repaired *Allen Gardiner* to Tierra del Fuego and worked to reestablish a missionary connection. Thomas Bridges, the adoptive son of Reverend Despard, joined Stirling. Bridges created the Yamana-English dictionary which vastly facilitated communication with Fuegian natives. Together with Stirling, Bridges established a mission beachhead in Tierra del Fuego, at Ushuaia, on the north shore of the Beagle Channel. While there, in 1873, Bridges met

Fuegia Basket. She did not remember enough English for conversation, but Bridges was able to converse with her in her native language of Yamana. He learned from her that her first husband, York Minster, had been killed some years back in retaliation for murdering another man. By 1888 epidemics wiped out every native within thirty miles of the mission. Thomas Bridges then abandoned his long term commitment with the mission and took up sheep ranching. The Argentine government took over the abandoned missionary site and turned it into a prison.

There were rapid changes occurring within Argentina. Many people emigrated from Europe to settle in Argentina, and they brought their skills with them. Cattle ranching and sheep ranching became major industries. Sheep survived well in southern Argentina, and land was so plentiful, that sheep ranchers did not take the trouble of building fence enclosures. European settlers, primarily cattle ranchers and sheep herders, extended their ranches further south. Their sheep often wandered into the territory inhabited for centuries by indigenous natives. Many unarmed natives were shot and killed by the colonists.

Then, in the period of 1878-79, the remaining Indians were either killed or driven south into Patagonia by a military campaign commanded by General Julio Roca. General Roca was voted president of Argentina in 1880 on the strength of his Indian policy of extermination and/ or removal. His Indian policy of genocide opened up for European settlers huge areas of Argentina for cattle and sheep ranching and for wheat and corn production. Argentina leads all other South American countries in agriculture and cattle production. However, Argentina has the lowest indigenous Indian population of any country in Central or South America, with the exception of Cuba which has no remaining indigenous peoples.

End notes for Chp 8, Tierra del Fuego

My sources for this chapter are lecture notes from Jim Garlinghouse, the historian lecturer on board the *Nord Norge* as the ship travelled from Ushuaia, Argentina, to the Antarctic. He recommended the following book:

Nichols, Peter. EVOLUTION'S CAPTAIN: The Dark Fate of the Man who Sailed Charles Darwin Around the World. New York, Harper Collins, 2003.

1. Nichols, p. 43
2. Fort Clatsop, Astoria, Oregon, has a permanent display about the exhibit, stating that Lewis & Clark stole a native canoe because it was superior to their own.
3. Nichols, p. 121
4. Ibid, p. 121
5. Nichols, p. 75
6. Ibid, p. 121
7. p. 144
8. p. 150
9. p. 240
10. pp. 241-2
11. pp. 150-1
12. p. 169
13. p. 177
14. p. 186
15. p. 187
16. p. 234
17. p. 263
18. p. 264
19. p. 269
20. p. 270
21. p. 271
22. p. 273
23. p. 276

24. p. 277
25. p. 239
26. p. 243
27. p. 242
28. p. 245
29. p. 299
30. p. 317
31. p. 318
32. p. 319
33. pp. 246-7
34. p. 318

CHAPTER 9

'Tis a Pity

In the late 15th century both Jews and Muslims in Spain experienced a severe level of oppression and intolerance from the Catholic Church and its clergy. Members of both faiths were required to convert to Christianity or leave Spain. Those who professed to have converted to Christianity faced the grave risk of the inquisition and severe penalties if they continued to practice any aspect of their former religion. Was that policy of intolerance and exploitation by the Catholic Church carried forward to the New World, after the Discovery by Christopher Columbus in 1492?

In 1493 Pope Alexander VI gave advice to the explorers, adventurers and missionaries who planned to return to the New World.

He could have said the following:

"I will give you four rules to follow when you return to the New World and encounter their peoples:
1. Respect the spiritual traditions of the people you encounter.
2. Do not plunder or steal.
3. Do not enslave them.

4. Lastly, do not kill. You may not understand why I say this. But history will understand me, if you follow these directives."

Unfortunately, Pope Alexander VI did not give such instructions. Instead, and with his absolute authority, he instructed the adventurers and missionaries to convert the natives to Christianity. How that was to be done was fully established in the Spain of the fifteenth century, and that is a pity. All the tribes of indigenous peoples from Alaska to Tierra del Fuego had spiritual and religious practices and traditions. The conversion to Christianity for any of these persons, whether an Inca leader from Peru, or a Hopi from our Southwest, meant that all aspects of ancient religious practices and traditions were forbidden, never to be practiced again. Such restrictions were harshly and rigidly enforced, including the use of executions and absolute plunder of sacred sites.

This practice was essentially identical to how Jews and Muslims in Spain had been treated in the 15th and 16th centuries. Like them the indigenous peoples of the New World were forced to relinquish all aspects of their religious beliefs and practices. Plunder followed as their temples and places of worship were totally destroyed, then replaced with newly constructed Catholic churches to show the superiority of the Christian faith. All gold, silver and precious arts in temples and places of worship were taken out (confiscated as loot) and some were later installed in cathedrals and monasteries in Spain. Indigenous priests and rulers faced executions, often conducted in a grand public ceremony with Catholic priests participating.

Steve Newcomb, an American Indian of Shawnee and Lenape ancestry, has studied medieval documents related to the discovery and conquest of the New World, providing him with a background to understand the events leading up to 1492. Newcomb states: "In 1452, Pope Nicholas V issued to King Alfonso V of Portugal the bull Romanus Pontifex, declaring war against all non-Christians throughout the world, and specifically sanctioning and promoting the conquest, colonization and exploitation of non-Christian nations and their territories." [1] Newcomb states that the order specifically authorized King Alfonso "to capture, vanquish, and subdue the Saracens, pagans, and other enemies of Christ," and "to put them in perpetual slavery," and "to take all their possessions and property." [2] With such blanket authorization Portugal initiated its traffic in African slaves, expanded its claims of lands along the west coast of Africa, and took possession and control of Brazil in the year 1500.

Pope Alexander VI expanded the right of conquest by issuing a papal document, the bull *Inter Cetera* on May 3, 1493. This document granted Spain the right to conquer the lands which Columbus had already found as well as any lands which Spain might "discover" in the future. Newcomb asserts that the document further states that the people in the discovered lands be "subjugated and be brought to the faith itself." [3]

When Spain and Portugal argued about control of the new territories, the pope drew a line of demarcation between the two poles, giving Spain the rights of conquest and dominion over one side of the globe, and Portugal over the other—except that Portugal was given dominion over Brazil.

The official view of the Catholic Church in the 15th and 16th century was unequivocal; the church rejected religious freedom. Has the Catholic Church maintained its position against religious freedom, or has it been changed? In 1824, Pope Leo XII issued an encyclical condemning a variety of evils including religious tolerance. Furthermore, in 1832 an encyclical repeated the warning against religious tolerance, and stated people "will perish eternally if they do not hold the Catholic faith," and if freedom of conscience is allowed, "the pit of the abyss is open."[4] John Noonan summarizes the view of Pope Leo XII as follows: "What is incontestable is that in absolute terms, without qualification as to context, the pope pronounced freedom of conscience and freedom of religion to be pernicious errors." [5]

Other popes have continued to espouse a view opposed to religious freedom. In 1885 Pope Leo XIII denounced "that harmful and deplorable passion for innovation (in religion) which was aroused in the sixteenth century," from which came "all those later tenants of unbridled license" that included the principle "that each is free to think on every subject just as he may choose." He adds that instead, "no one is allowed to be remiss in the service due to God, and since the chief duty of all men is to cling to religion in both its teaching and practice—not such religion as they may have a preference for, but the religion which God enjoins."[6]

Author Mary Jo Bane states that in the course of his argument, Leo makes it clear that the "religion which God enjoins" is the religion of the Catholic Church.[7]

The Second Vatican Council Endorses Religious Liberty

In 1964 members of the Vatican Council II adopted a draft of a Declaration of Religious Liberty. A key paragraph of the declaration is the following:

The Vatican Council declares that the human person has a right to religious freedom. Freedom of this kind means that everyone should be immune from coercion by individuals, social groups and every human power so that, within due limits, no men or women are forced to act against their convictions nor are any persons to be restrained from acting in accordance with their convictions in religious matters in private or in public, alone or in associations with others.[8]

This important declaration is noteworthy, but it came about 500 years late. Millions of people throughout the world were deprived of religious freedom in the name of Christian missionary work. Those deprived of religious freedom were also often deprived of life, property and the liberty to live in their traditional settings.

The Second Vatican Council Condemns Slavery

In all the dominions in the New World discovered by Portugal (Brazil) and Spain (Mexico, Guatemala, Cuba, Peru and Argentina) brutal slavery was introduced and dominated the lives of the indigenous peoples. Bane writes:

The Vatican Council II Constitution on the Church in the Modern World contained a condemnation of slavery, which had been defended by

the church for many centuries, and was only officially denounced by this
1965 Constitution.[9]

Again, this is an important and remarkable document. But, it
is a pity! The church decides, after 500 years of contributing to the
practice of the enslavement of millions, to finally condemn the practice
of slavery.

The Catastrophic Period before Columbus

What events in Spain led to the militaristic conquest of the New
World and the subjugation of its peoples and the suppression of their
religious practices? Spain had been a Muslim country since the year
711 when the Moors, a Berber and Arab army, invaded and conquered
the Iberian Peninsula (today this includes Spain, Portugal, Gibraltar
and Andorra). For the next 750 years the entire area became known
as the Al-Andalus and remained under Muslim control. Religious
tolerance was the rule, allowing Jews and Christians complete freedom
of worship. Furthermore, Muslim control brought the end of Roman
rule in Spain and freedom for Iberian slaves.[10]

Although Christians were granted freedom of religion in Muslim-
controlled Spain, many Christians left for the northern part of the
Iberian Peninsula, where they prepared to drive out the Moors.
Christians soon afterwards began a long and slow recovery of the
peninsula, a process called the *Reconquista.*[11] Alfonso VI re-conquered
Toledo in 1065. In other areas of Spain, Muslim influence waned as the
Christian Reconquista continued with Christians conquering Cordoba
in 1237 and Sevilla in 1248. Unfortunately, the Christian re-conquest
brought with it intolerance and oppression towards Jews and Muslims.
The Christian control of Iberian territory from the Moors was achieved
with the conquest of Granada in 1492. Thus, in 1492, the Kingdom
of Spain was formed with the unification of the Kingdoms of Castile
and Aragon.[12] This provided the foundation for Spain's Golden Age.
However, it was the confiscation of vast wealth from Spain's colonies,
more so than cultural or scientific development, that brought on Spain's

golden age. The story started when, in Granada, Columbus pitched his idea to Isabella and Ferdinand to finance a sea voyage to the "Orient."

What is critical is that Columbus sailed for America at a time in which religious intolerance was re-emerging in Spain; in 1492, Jews lost the protection that had been given to them by the Moors. The defeated Moors could no longer protect members of their own religion nor the rights of Jews. As a background to the intolerance against other religious traditions of Spain in the Middle Ages, the following points of historical events are relevant. In areas of Spain controlled by Christians, anti-Semitism emerged. For example, in the 14th century there were widespread pogroms across many cities of Spain, including Seville, Cordoba, Valencia and Barcelona, in which many hundreds of Jews were killed and synagogues destroyed. This violence against Jews had followed centuries of religious tolerance when Spain was controlled by the Moors. The violence against Jews by Christians reached a peak in 1391 with large scale massacres in almost every major city in Spain that was controlled by Christians. In an effort to avoid persecution and violence many Jews converted to Catholicism.[13]

Isabella of Castile and Ferdinand of Aragon were granted the title of "Catholic Monarchs" by Pope Alexander VI. The pope honored them for their commitment and faithfulness to the Catholic faith. When they married in 1469, they combined their huge kingdoms of Castile and Aragon.

Under the new Kingdom of Spain, now Christian, Jews were required to convert to Christianity or be expelled from Spain. Thus the freedom for Jewish people to practice their religion while under Moorish control was abolished after the re-conquest. In 1492, Isabella and Ferdinand promised the Moors that they could remain in Spain and were free to worship. However, in 1499, that promise was withdrawn and Muslims in Spain were required to abandon their faith and convert to Christianity or be expelled. That unhappy event begs further explanation.[14]

During this chaotic period of cataclysmic religious turmoil with Christian intolerance expressed towards Jews and Muslims, the vast wealth brought back from the Americas made Spain's King Charles V the most powerful man in the world. He ruled a wealthy country that seethed in religious intolerance.

After Muslims lost control of territory in Spain in 1492, Muslim influence continued for a time because of their sophistication in engineering, culture, and architecture. Isabel and Ferdinand signed an agreement with the Moors that Muslims could remain in Spain and live in their own houses. Should they want to leave Spain, Isabella agreed to purchase their property at a fair price. If they chose to remain, the Moors were guaranteed freedom of religion. Archbishop Fray Hernando de Talavera supported Muslims. He learned Arabic and taught Muslims the basics of Christianity in their language and without coercion. That is, he placed no demands on the Muslims to convert.

Seven years later, in 1499, Archbishop Cisneros came to power and was furious at the toleration of Talavera toward Muslims. He ousted Archbishop Talavera and changed the rule for Muslims. Muslims must convert to Christianity or leave Spain, leaving their great wealth behind.[15] In 1609 King Phillip III decreed the expulsion of all Muslims, including those who had "converted" to Catholicism.[16] Archbishop Ribera quoted Old Testament texts ordering the enemies of God to be slain without mercy and setting forth the duties of the kings to carry out the slaughter. Intolerance surged, and is evident today throughout Spain in which mosques, created to worship Allah (the same God that Christians and Jews worship), have been taken over, rededicated, and now serve as Christian churches.

For example, in Granada we visited the Church of St Bartholomew which was built over a former mosque. In many areas of Spain this is still evident, as mosques are gone and replaced by Christian churches. The practice of replacing a Christian church over a mosque was a church policy to show the domination of Christianity over other religions. Spanish missionaries who came to the New World after Columbus carried forward the same pattern of intolerance towards religious and spiritual beliefs and practices of the peoples of the New World. The destruction of indigenous places of worship throughout the Americas, such as the Hopi kivas in New Mexico and the Sun Temple in Peru are examples of such religious intolerance. The Spanish ordered natives, under duress, to destroy their own places of worship and then build a Christian church to replace the destroyed "pagan" temple.

The Alhambra

The splendor of Moorish civilization remains evident in the Moorish palace of the Alhambra located in Granada. During the Middle Ages there was nothing in Christian Europe that was comparable to the artistry and beauty of the Alhambra. Fortunately, the beauty and integrity of the Alhambra remains preserved to this day.

Granada has a population of about 300,000 people, but about two million people visit the Alhambra each year. It is one of the most important archeological and historical sites in Europe. The Alhambra fortress was the last stronghold of the Muslim kingdom in Spain. In 1492 Christian forces took control of the Alhambra from the Moors. The Moors yielded the Alhambra without a fight to protect this splendid architectural splendor from utter destruction.

Rick Steves asserts that while Europe slumbered through the Dark Ages, civilization, the arts and exuberant gardens flourished under Moorish control.[17] The Alhambra's Palacios Nazaries (Nazrid Palace) was the Moorish royal palace, built in the 14th century. It stands in stark contrast to the comparatively more staid architecture that was the norm in Christian Europe during the Middle Ages. However, it is the dark side of Christian rule that engaged in religious intolerance and violence that all peoples should remember—especially those of us who call ourselves Christians. My extended focus on the extent of religious intolerance of 16th century Spain, rather than religious intolerance shown by other Christian European nations during that period, is because of the role that Spain played in introducing ruthless destruction of indigenous religious sites throughout the new world.

The Protestant Reformation in Europe also Embraced Intolerance and Violence

The 16th century in Europe was a period of extreme religious intolerance, turmoil and violence. The Protestant Reformation led by

Martin Luther, John Calvin and Ulrich Zwingli, while addressing important theological issues, contributed to the violence. Without focusing on theology or creed, a review of the Protestant Reformation and the ensuing violence will help understand the tragedy that unfolded in the New World after the Discovery and the subsequent oppression of every indigenous religion from Alaska to Tierra del Fuego.

Martin Luther was born on November 10, 1483. As a young man he planned to enter the field of law. In 1505 during his student days he was struck by lightning. He took that as a sign, resolved to serve God rather than law, and entered a monastery. The high level of intelligence of Luther was recognized by Johann Von Staupitz, his superior, who urged Luther to study for the Doctor's Degree.[18] After receiving his doctorate he became obsessed with what he viewed as grievous sins of the pope and the Roman Catholic Church (of which he was a part). On October 31, 1517, he posted his famous Ninety-Five Theses on the Castle Church Door at Wittenberg, Germany. That act of protest by Luther is said to be the beginning of the Protestant Reformation.

Martin Luther wanted Christianity to be open to the Jews of Europe, and he believed that the Roman Catholic Church had blocked that opportunity. Luther translated the New Testament from Greek to the vernacular German. During that period the Catholic Church was adamantly opposed to lay persons reading the Bible. Luther was angered when Jews did not convert. The explosive rage of Luther became directed at Jews.

Karen Armstrong writes: *He told the Jews of Germany that, because he had reformed Christianity and made the Scriptures central, they could now become Christians and they would find their own Scriptures venerated, free of Romish error. This monstrous piece of impertinence showed absolutely no appreciation of the strong objection Jews have to the main Christian message. It arrogantly continued the old tradition of seeing Judaism as a mere prelude to and subsection of the "higher" religion of Christianity. When the Jews replied that they found a closer approximation to their Scriptures in the Talmud, Luther became aggressive. In his pamphlet, **On the Jews and their Lies (1524)** he looked forward to Hitler: Jews should be absolutely segregated from Christians, their homes must be abolished and* *they must live under one roof and do forced labor. Synagogues and prayer books should be burned. In 1517 Luther had already had the Jews expelled from Lutheran cities.* [19]

(Note: The savage destruction of Jewish property including Synagogues on Nov. 9th and continuing on the 10th in 1938 in numerous German cities was scheduled to commemorate the birthday of Martin Luther and his virulent anti-Semitism. The assault, known as "Kristallnacht," was planned by the Nazis under the leadership of Goering.)[20]

Martin Luther and the Peasants' Revolt of 1525

As discussed in Chapter 5, the indigenous Cubans were enslaved by their Spanish masters who subjected them to life-endangering work and living conditions. The feudal system in Europe also placed great stress on peasants who were landless and long suffering. Recognizing that Martin Luther stood against the Roman Catholic Church, the peasants in Germany formed a league, the *Bundschuh,* and turned to Luther for support. The peasants had hoped that Luther would support their cause. He did not. When conflict arose the peasants ransacked castles and monasteries. Luther supported the feudal lords against the peasants. He wrote a pamphlet, *Against the Murderous and Thieving Hordes of Peasants* (1525), and urged violence against the peasants:

Therefore let everyone who can, smite, slay and stab, secretly or openly, remembering that nothing can be more poisonous, hurtful, or devilish than a rebel. It is just as when one must kill a mad dog; if you don't strike him he will strike you, and the whole land with you. [21]

In the violence and fighting that followed some five thousand peasants were slain. Some were captured, tortured and beheaded. In the 1930's and during WW II, German authorities used references to Martin Luther to support both anti-Semitism and the duty of Christians to be obedient to civil authority—and thus to Nazi Germany. Leaping back in time to the 16th century and the Discovery of the New World, the Spanish conquistadors, and the Catholic priests who accompanied them, shared the view of zero tolerance toward any indigenous religious beliefs and any resistance to Spanish rule.

John Calvin

John Calvin (1509-1564) was considered a brilliant student; he studied at the famous law school *Orleans* in Paris. At the age of 27 he published his *Institutes,* which made him famous. His writings came to the attention of Guillaume Farel (1489-1565), who was impressed with the theological views of John Calvin. He urged Calvin to move to Geneva, Switzerland, where the two theologians persuaded the government officials in Geneva, in 1535, to adopt Protestantism as the official religion of Geneva.[22] One immediate result was that the great Catholic Cathedral in Geneva, constructed between 1160 and 1220, became by order of the Geneva Council a Protestant center on May 21, 1536. This outrageous act is comparable to what occurred numerous times when missionaries, backed by military authority, tore down indigenous places of worship in the New World from New Mexico to Peru and replaced them with Christian churches. I want to stress the fact that these acts of religious intolerance, expressed by Protestants during the Reformation, occurred during the same time period that Jews and Muslims were ousted and brutalized in Spain, and the indigenous peoples in the New World were oppressed and subjected to loss of their religious freedom. John Calvin also played an important role in the tragic case of Michael Servetus.

Michael Servetus, a Spanish physician and philosopher, published *Christianissimi Restitutio* in which he denied the concept of the Holy Trinity consisting of God the father, Jesus the Son of God and the Holy Spirit as One.[23] In fact, the Bible is not clear about the relationship between Christ's human and divine natures. The Bible is also not the source of the concept of the Holy Trinity. The Roman Empire Constantine appointed a committee, the Council of Nicaea (in the year 325), to iron out conflicts in theology of the new state religion of his Empire. After the Creed was approved by the emperor, any dissenter was threatened with severe punishment. Karen Armstrong, in her book **A History of God, (1993),** provides ample coverage of the implausibility of the Doctrine of the Holy Trinity.[24] At any rate, John Calvin and Guillaume Farel charged Servetus with heresy. At the trial Servetus explained that the concept of the Holy Trinity was based not on the Bible but the Council of Nicaea. On that point Servetus was correct. Nevertheless, he was tried, convicted and burned at the stake in Geneva on October 27, 1553. Servetus is considered one of the co-founders of the Unitarian Church.

I visited the Institute for the study of the Protestant Reformation at the University of Geneva in 1999. While in Geneva, I took a walk and stood at the spot where Michael Servetus had been executed. After some time to reflect I then met and spoke with faculty at the Institute. I had assumed that the "Institute" was a public museum about the Protestant Reformation. I was mistaken; the Institute is a rigorous academic center within the University of Geneva that continues to study the Protestant Reformation. Nevertheless, members of the faculty were cordial and quite willing to talk with me. I discussed with them my concern about the level of intolerance, coercion and abusive methods used by Christian missionaries in Alaska and British Columbia in the nineteenth and twentieth centuries (my chapters one and two). Faculty members of the Institute, shared with me information about how the Protestant Reformation, initiated through the work of Martin Luther and John Calvin, did escalate the high level of intolerance which characterized Europe in the 16th century and contributed to the development of religious wars, massacres and pogroms.[25]

I met with Francis Higman who wrote a fascinating book, **WHY THE REFORMATION?**

Professor Higman made the following assertion:

I am making one stark point: that the Gospel message, seen as liberating, loving and joyful, turned with dreadful regularity into bloodshed and horror. Why should this be? How did the liberating joy of the Reformation turn into butchery?

At the time, and until much later, the idea that two religions could coexist in the same country was not thinkable: 'One king, one law, one faith' is the only arrangement perceived as possible. Even the Edict of Nantes, which ended the French religious wars in 1598 and granted limited rights to the Calvinists or Huguenots, sometimes seen as a first manifestation of religious toleration, was not actually intended as such. The 'toleration' of the Huguenots was conceived as a strictly temporary arrangement, pending the achievement of the 'real' solution, namely concord (which for some meant bringing the Huguenots back into the Roman Catholic Church, for others some form of 'French Reformed Catholic Church). The idea of 'toleration just wasn't on: there can't be more than one truth.[26]

The crimes committed in the name of Christianity thrust upon the indigenous peoples of the Americas were committed by both Protestants and Catholics. There were important theological differences introduced by the Protestant Reformation that set them apart from the Roman Catholic Church. Sadly, in the sixteenth century and until much later, both the Roman Catholic Church and the Protestant Reformers agreed unwittingly on several principles; they were anti-Semitic, intolerant of pagan religions, and ruthless against any deviation from official creed—either Catholic or Protestant. Religious liberty was non-existent. A faculty member of the Institute pointed out another example: Theodoros Beza (1519-1605), an associate of Calvin, justified the execution of Servetus and captured the zeitgeist of the day by his statement that religious freedom is ". . . a most diabolical dogma because it means that everyone should be left to go to hell in his own way."[27]

End Notes, chapter 9, 'Tis a Pity

1. Newcomb, Steve T. **Pagans in the Promised Land: Decoding the Doctrine of Christian Discovery.** Fulcrum Publishing Co., Golden, Co. p. 59

2. Ibid. p. 61

3. Ibid. p. 65

4. In 1824, Pope Leo XII issued an encyclical condemning a variety of evils of the time, among them religious toleration. An 1832 encyclical repeated the condemnation of "that absurd and erroneous teaching, or rather that folly, that it is necessary to assure and guarantee to whomever it may be the liberty of conscience." Because people "will perish eternally if they do not uphold the Catholic faith," If freedom of conscience is allowed, "the pit of the abyss is open."

   Many points concerning the Roman Catholic Church and Church Doctrine are on exhibit at the Jeronimos Monastery in Portugal. The exhibit is called "A Place in Time," and it documents changes in Roman Catholic Doctrine and interpretations over a five hundred year period from the 14th century through the year 1910. My wife and I visited the Monastery in 2011. The Jeronimos Monastery has recently celebrated its 500th anniversary. One current goal of this important monastery is to document the Monastery's five hundred years of existence and its context within Portuguese and world history.

5. Noonan, John T. (2005). **A Church That Can and Cannot Change: The Development of Catholic Moral Teaching.** Erasmus Institute Books.

6. Bane, Mary Jo. *"The Catholic Puzzle: Parishes and Civic Life."* In **Taking Faith Seriously,** Ed. Mary Jo Bane, Brent Coffin, and Richard Higgins. Harvard University Press, 2005, pp 63-93.

7. Ibid. p. 73

8. Vatican Council II.

9. Bane, Op. cit. p. 84

10. Rene Oliver was our guide and historian who lectured our group in Spain. The title of Road Scholar was "Christopher Columbus and Don Quixote."

   Note: the endnotes 11 through 16 represent notes I took from information shared by Rene Oliver.

17. Steves, Rick. **Spain, 2011.** Avalon Travel. Berkeley, CA. 2010.

18. Higman, Francis. **Why the Reformation? An Essay.** University De Geneve: Institute for the Study of the Reformation. 1996.

19. Armstrong, Karen. **Holy War: The Crusades and their Impact on Today's World.** Anchor Books, A division of Random House, Inc. N.Y. p. 469.

20. Terdal, Leif. **Our Escape from Nazi-Occupied Norway.** Trafford Publishing, 2008, p. 2

21. Luther, Martin. **On the Jews and their Lives (1524).**

22. Higman, Op. cit., p.85.

23. Firm, Vergilius. **A Pictorial History of Protestantism.** Philosophical Library. New York. p. 72.

24. Armstrong, Karen. **A History of God.** Anchor Books, New York. (1993).

25. Higman, Op. cit. The faculty at the Institute for the study of the Reformation discussed with me a number of points about how the Protestant Reformation contributed to religious intolerance. Many of the points are also discussed in chapter nine of his book, *Where do we go from Here?* In Higman, **Why the Reformation? An Essay,** cited above.

26. Ibid. p. 100.

27. Ibid. p. 97.